Advancing through Poland, Soviet infantrymen expand their bridgehead on the west bank of the Vistula in September 1944. With the crossing of the river, troops of the Red Army took a giant step in their relentless drive westward, which in two years brought them 1,400 miles from Stalingrad into Germany.

THE SOVIET JUGGERNAUT

WORLD WAR II · TIME-LIFE BOOKS · ALEXANDRIA, VIRGINIA

BY EARL F. ZIEMKE
AND THE EDITORS OF TIME-LIFE BOOKS

THE SOVIET JUGGERNAUT

Time-Life Books Inc.
is a wholly owned subsidiary of
TIME INCORPORATED

Founder: Henry R. Luce 1898-1967

Editor-in-Chief: Henry Anatole Grunwald
President: J. Richard Munro
Chairman of the Board: Ralph P. Davidson
Executive Vice President: Clifford J. Grum
Editorial Director: Ralph Graves
Vice Chairman: Arthur Temple

TIME-LIFE BOOKS INC.

Managing Editor: Jerry Korn
Executive Editor: David Maness
Assistant Managing Editors: Dale M. Brown
(planning), George Constable, Thomas H. Flaherty Jr.
(acting), Martin Mann, John Paul Porter
Art Director: Tom Suzuki
Chief of Research: David L. Harrison
Director of Photography: Robert G. Mason
Assistant Art Director: Arnold C. Holeywell
Assistant Chief of Research: Carolyn L. Sackett
Assistant Director of Photography: Dolores A. Littles

Chairman: Joan D. Manley
President: John D. McSweeney
Executive Vice Presidents: Carl G. Jaeger,
John Steven Maxwell, David J. Walsh
Vice Presidents: George Artandi (comptroller);
Stephen L. Bair (legal counsel); Peter G. Barnes;
Nicholas Benton (public relations); John L. Canova;
Beatrice T. Dobie (personnel); Carol Flaumenhaft
(consumer affairs); James L. Mercer (Europe/South
Pacific); Herbert Sorkin (production); Paul R. Stewart
(marketing)

WORLD WAR II

Editorial Staff for *The Soviet Juggernaut*
Editor: Gerald Simons
Designer/Picture Editor: Raymond Ripper
Chief Researcher: Charles S. Clark
Picture Editor: Josephine Burke
Text Editors: Brian McGinn, Robert Menaker,
Henry Woodhead
Staff Writers: Donald Davison Cantlay,
Peter Kaufman, John Newton
Researchers: LaVerle Berry, Loretta Y. Britten,
Mary G. Burns, Cronin Buck Sleeper, Jayne T. Wise,
Paula York
Art Assistants: Mikio Togashi, Susan White
Editorial Assistant: Connie Strawbridge

Special Contributors (text)
Champ Clark, David S. Thomson, Robert Wallace,
A. B. C. Whipple

Editorial Production
Production Editor: Douglas B. Graham
Operations Manager: Gennaro C. Esposito,
Gordon E. Buck (assistant)
Assistant Production Editor: Feliciano Madrid
Quality Control: Robert L. Young (director),
James J. Cox (assistant), Daniel J. McSweeney,
Michael G. Wight (associates)
Art Coordinator: Anne B. Landry
Copy Staff: Susan B. Galloway (chief), Allan Fallow,
Victoria Lee, Barbara F. Quarmby, Celia Beattie
Picture Department: Betty Hughes Weatherley
Traffic: Jeanne Potter

Correspondents: Elisabeth Kraemer (Bonn); Margot
Hapgood, Dorothy Bacon, Lesley Coleman (London);
Susan Jonas, Lucy T. Voulgaris (New York); Maria
Vincenza Aloisi, Josephine du Brusle (Paris); Ann
Natanson (Rome). Valuable assistance was also
provided by: Martha Mader (Bonn); Judy Aspinall,
Karin B. Pearce (London); Felix Rosenthal (Moscow);
Carolyn T. Chubet, Miriam Hsia, Christina Lieberman
(New York); M. T. Hirschkoff (Paris); Eva Stichova
(Prague); Mimi Murphy (Rome); Traudl Lessing
(Vienna); Bogdan Turek (Warsaw).

The Author: EARL F. ZIEMKE, a research professor of
history at the University of Georgia, specializes in
German history and World War II. After wartime service as a U.S. Marine in the Pacific, he received his
Ph.D. from the University of Wisconsin and worked
as a supervisory historian at the Department of the
Army in Washington, D.C. His books include *Stalingrad to Berlin: The German Defeat in the East, The
German Northern Theater of Operations* and *Battle
for Berlin.* He served as a consultant on the Time-Life
Books World War II volume *Red Army Resurgent.*

The Consultants: COLONEL JOHN R. ELTING, USA (Ret.),
is a military historian and author of *The Battle of
Bunker's Hill, The Battles of Saratoga* and *Military
History and Atlas of the Napoleonic Wars.* He edited
*Military Uniforms in America: The Era of the Ameri-
can Revolution, 1755-1795* and *Military Uniforms in
America: Years of Growth, 1796-1851,* and was asso-
ciate editor of *The West Point Atlas of American Wars.*

CHARLES V. P. VON LUTTICHAU served in the German
armed forces during World War II on the Eastern Front. After studies in Berlin and Munich and at The American University in Washington, D.C., he became a senior historian
at the U.S. Army Center of Military History, specializing in
Southeast Asian and European military and diplomatic history. He has contributed to numerous volumes of the official history series *The U.S. Army in World War II.*

Library of Congress Cataloguing in Publication Data

Ziemke, Earl Frederick, 1922-
The Soviet juggernaut.

(World War II; v. 25)
Bibliography: p.
Includes index.
1. World War, 1939-1945—Campaigns—Eastern.
2. Russia (1923-   U.S.S.R.). Armiia—History—
World War, 1939-1945.   3. World War, 1939-1945—
Diplomatic history.   I. Time-Life Books.   II. Title.
III. Series.
D764.Z4928   940.54'21   80-23634
ISBN 0-8094-3389-3
ISBN 0-8094-3388-5 (lib. bdg.)
ISBN 0-8094-3387-7 (retail ed.)

For information about any Time-Life book, please write:

Reader Information
Time-Life Books
541 North Fairbanks Court
Chicago, Illinois 60611

CHAPTERS

1: The Battle of 3,500 Tanks   20
2: Manstein's Flaming Retreat   54
3: The "Three Blows"   96
4: Clearing the Russian Land   126
5: The Doomed Uprising   154
6: Stalin Triumphant   178

PICTURE ESSAYS

The Last German Victory   6
A Clash of Titans   40
Operation "Scorched Earth"   72
A Raging Guerrilla War   84
The Red Air Force Reborn   112
Year of Victories   138
Revolt in Warsaw   164
Returning Home   190

Bibliography   202
Acknowledgments   203
Picture Credits   204
Index   205

CONTENTS

THE LAST GERMAN VICTORY

German infantrymen, one of them carrying an antitank weapon, take cover behind a building while a Mark IV tank blasts open a route into a suburb of Kharkov.

AN ELITE COMMAND, A MAVERICK GENERAL

On February 19, 1943, German armies on the south-central Russian front launched a bristling counterattack aimed at the industrial city of Kharkov, which Soviet forces had seized only three days before. The operation had been ordered by Adolf Hitler himself—for the best of reasons. Recapturing Kharkov might well stop the enemy's current winter offensive, the first strategic offensive mounted by the Russians in nearly a year and a half of warfare. Just as important, a great victory was urgently needed to assuage the grief of the German people: In early February, the Battle of Stalingrad had ended with more than 300,000 German soldiers dead or captured.

To spearhead the Kharkov assault, Hitler dipped into the ranks of the Waffen-SS—the combat arm of Reichsführer-SS Heinrich Himmler's police and intelligence empire—and chose the 2nd SS Panzer Corps. The three divisions that made up the corps—Das Reich, Leibstandarte (Bodyguard) Adolf Hitler and Totenkopf (Death's Head)—were among the finest German units. Their troops, carefully picked to embody the Nazi ideal of Aryan manhood, had sworn personal loyalty to Hitler and blind obedience to their commanders. Field Marshal Erich von Manstein, in overall command of the Kharkov operation, said that the Führer's faith in his SS troops was "practically unlimited."

The commander of the 2nd SS Panzer Corps was Lieut. General Paul Hausser, a distinguished soldier whose military career dated back to the turn of the century. But Hausser possessed a streak of independence that worried his superiors. In the previous battle for Kharkov, when two Soviet armies had trapped Hausser's divisions in the city, he had been ordered to fight in place to the last man, an assignment that seemed pointless to him. Instead, he and his troops cut their way out of Kharkov.

Hitler had been furious at Hausser's disobedience; the general knew his performance would be closely watched in the new attack on Kharkov. Once again, he would follow his own instincts, but this time his freewheeling ways would help win the last major German victory of the War.

General Hausser emerges from a tank turret displaying a battle-damaged face. In 1941, he lost an eye and part of his jaw to Soviet shrapnel.

Antitank gunners, poised for the German counterattack at Kharkov, exemplify the SS ideal of "the best physically, the most dependable and faithful Nazis."

General Hausser and his SS panzer corps were 60 miles southwest of Kharkov and still retreating when, on February 19, the order for a counterattack came through from Hausser's immediate superior, Colonel General Hermann Hoth, commanding officer of the Fourth Panzer Army. The corps reversed direction—and crashed into the Soviet Sixth Army, which had been in hot pursuit since Hausser escaped from Kharkov on February 15.

The three divisions of the 2nd SS Panzer Corps were joined in the battle by the 48th Panzer Corps, and they were supported by Luftwaffe bombers and strafing fighter planes. In heavy fighting, the Germans surrounded and pressed in on the Soviet army; at one point, a Soviet corps commander was killed just 100 yards from Hausser's command post.

Slowly the Germans ground down the Soviet army, and they would have obliterated it altogether if they had had more infantrymen to plug up gaps in their ring. By the time this phase of the fighting was over, they had killed 23,000 Russians, taken 9,000 prisoners and captured or destroyed 615 Soviet tanks.

Hausser's SS panzer corps, which had suffered only light casualties, resumed its drive toward Kharkov on February 28.

Crunching toward Kharkov over packed snow, self-propelled guns of the 2nd SS Panzer Corps pass a

Troopers of the SS Leibstandarte Adolf Hitler Division mark time while their comrades launch Nebelwerfer rockets (background) toward Kharkov.

trooper with a machine gun. The Germans gambled—successfully—that the usual February thaw would hold off.

Hausser's three SS panzer grenadier divisions rumbled northeastward for more than a week, fighting skirmishes in a number of lightly defended villages. But resistance stiffened as they drew near Kharkov. Men of the SS Leibstandarte Adolf Hitler sensed trouble when yet another nameless village loomed up on March 8.

"We close the hatches," a tanker wrote in his diary. "Another 600 meters and not a shot is heard. As the first panzers approach the silent houses, fire breaks out like a clap of thunder; the lead panzer is hit squarely in the turret. The Russians increase their fire and the light tanks of our company are struck."

The German losses prompted an order for the column to disengage and regroup. The tanker's diary went on: "Soon we roll out again, a mushy feeling inside us as we pass our own burning and exploding panzers. Suddenly three Russian T-34s break out between the houses and aim for our flank. Our turret swings to the left and a shell leaves the barrel. Hit and explosion almost simultaneous, and the next tank appears in the direction-finder's gun sight. Fire—and the enemy tank literally bursts asunder. The shell must have hit the gas tank. The third enemy tank turns away, shows us his stern—and he is hit too.

"The houses are smoked out with grenades and machine guns. Now we see where the defensive fire has come from: The Russians had moved their 47mm anti-tank guns right up into the houses and couldn't be spotted."

Peering cautiously around a log house, SS troopers reconnoiter a village on the road to Kharkov.

A German Mark IV panzer pounds a Soviet position. The commander of the 2nd SS Panzer Corps's reconnaissance unit looks on.

Leibstandarte Adolf Hitler Division officers watch the action. Second from right is Major General Theodor Wisch, who later commanded the division.

13

Raking a factory on the edge of Kharkov, machine gunners provide covering fire for infantrymen about to make a dash forward.

Wrestling their 75mm antitank gun into position in a street in Kharkov, SS artillerymen get ready to open fire on the diehard Soviet defenders.

SS tanks and infantrymen burst into Red Square, the foot soldiers scurrying for cover from snipers firing down at them from the surrounding buildings.

Hausser's SS panzer corps reached Kharkov on March 9. His orders from Hitler were to blockade the city from the west and north; his divisions were to help prevent any Soviet troops from escaping. He also had permission to reconnoiter the city and to capture it if the risk seemed small.

Small or not, the risk seemed eminently worth taking, so he sent in the Leibstandarte Adolf Hitler Division.

The Soviet defenders put up a hard fight in "street after street and house to house," one of the German attackers recalled later. "The rockets shriek through the town; ceaselessly our artillery hammers—an inferno. But we push our panzers forward, rolling over barricades and cannon, breaking through houses." In less than a day's time the division managed to open a corridor all the way to Red Square in the heart of the city.

A tank of the Totenkopf Division, carrying infantrymen with guns at the ready, stops near an intersection to cut off escaping Russians.

A sergeant of the Totenkopf, wearing an Iron Cross and other medals, directs a tank through Kharkov.

After his Leibstandarte Adolf Hitler Division plunged into Kharkov, General Hausser ordered a second division, the Das Reich, to attack the city from the west. But the next day, with victory almost in sight, his bold prosecution of the fighting was dampened by an order from General Hoth at Fourth Panzer Army headquarters.

"SS Panzer Corps," said Hoth, "will detach SS Das Reich and lead the division around north of Kharkov and prevent enemy from escaping to the southeast." Hoth was well aware of the panzers' vulnerability in city fighting and refused to allow Hausser's tanks to be trapped in rubble and then destroyed—the fate of many panzers in Stalingrad.

The ever-independent Hausser decided to take a shortcut, and sent the Das Reich straight through the city to the southeast. By noon, the division had reached Kharkov's central railroad station. Then Hoth radioed, reminding Hausser of his order. This time, Hausser obeyed. He withdrew the Das Reich from Kharkov and sent it circling to the north.

On the 15th of March, the Das Reich and Totenkopf Divisions closed the ring around Kharkov, sealing off the remaining Soviet defenders. And soon afterward, the Leibstandarte Adolf Hitler Division wiped out the Russians who were defending a tractor plant, the last pocket of resistance inside the city.

Battle-weary panzer grenadiers of the SS Leibstandarte Adolf Hitler Division walk away from Kharkov's tractor factory after crushing Soviet resistance there.

NEW LUSTER FOR "A DREAD REPUTATION"

Heinrich Himmler, attended by an SS officer, beams from a Tiger tank turret.

When the battle for Kharkov ended on March 15, the German counterattack had stopped the Soviet winter offensive and stabilized the front. Hausser's resourceful SS panzer corps got the lion's share of the credit, though its success was somewhat shadowed by annoyance from on high: The Führer was so incensed at Hausser's maverick actions that he delayed several weeks before including him among the recipients of medals for valorous deeds at Kharkov. But in almost every way that mattered, the 2nd SS Panzer Corps had lived up to Hitler's expectations.

His favorite fighting arm was now ordered to ready itself for a massive counteroffensive near Kursk, an action that would turn into the War's greatest tank battle. To urge the corps on, Reichsführer-SS Heinrich Himmler was dispatched to Kharkov. There, he addressed his troops in oratory brimming with new confidence: "We will never let that excellent weapon, the dread and terrible reputation that preceded us in the battles for Kharkov, fade, but will constantly add meaning to it."

With a sousaphone draped around its neck, a bust of Russian novelist Maxim Gorky stands marooned in the rubble of Kharkov as German vehicles pass by.

1

An attack that turned Hitler's stomach
The panzers' backhand swipe at Kharkov
Vital information from a spy called Lucy
Waiting for more Panthers
A hard-bitten general with metal teeth
"Who commands the Ninth Army, my Führer, you or I?"
Destructive preliminaries by the partisans
A second breakfast on the battlefield
Miniature tanks named Goliaths
"The earth was scorched with burning tanks"
A desperate attack with "sticky bombs"
Eisenhower changes Hitler's plans

"My Führer," asked Colonel General Heinz Guderian, the great German tank commander, "why do you want to attack in the East at all this year?"

"You are quite right," replied Adolf Hitler. "Whenever I think of this attack, my stomach turns over."

It was springtime 1943. A strange, foreboding lull had fallen upon the front that snaked for 1,750 miles from Leningrad in the north to Novorossiisk on the Black Sea in the south. Hitler was unwontedly hesitant, seeming to shrink from thoughts of the ordeal inexorably approaching—the time when the mighty armies, now confronting each other across oceans of ooze caused by the season's rains and thaws, would grapple again.

Yet no matter how sickening the prospect of once more feeding the flesh of his soldiery into the Soviet meat grinder, and no matter how much he might dawdle in issuing his fateful marching orders, Hitler's basic decision had already been made. He must give the German people at least the appearance of regaining the strategic initiative in Russia.

Hitler's European alliance had been built on military success. With the winter disaster at Stalingrad and with British and American troops already driving toward victory in North Africa, the coalition was threatening to crumble. Italy's Benito Mussolini was furtively casting about for a way out of the war in the East; Rumania's Marshal Ian Antonescu and Hungary's Admiral Miklos Horthy were angling for accommodations with the Western Allies that might later shield their countries from the bitter consequences of triumphant Russian wrath.

There were growing problems on the German home front as well. Since the War's beginning, the Nazi regime had tried to keep the *Herrenvolk* happy by maintaining creature comforts for consumers even while meeting military requirements. Stalingrad, however, clearly demonstrated that Germany could no longer afford a cosmetics-and-cannon economy. On February 18, just over a fortnight after Field Marshal Friedrich Paulus and the pitiful remnants of his Sixth Army had trudged into captivity, Minister of Propaganda Joseph Goebbels proclaimed a state of "Total War."

Consumer goods and services would now be curtailed. The number of jobs offering military exemption would be reduced. All civilian men between the ages of 16 and 65 and women between 17 and 50 would have to register for

THE BATTLE OF 3,500 TANKS

work in war plants. Hitler himself issued an astonishing decree that allowed any soldier in combat, from general to private, to punish disobedience and defeatism by shooting the transgressor on the spot.

At the top level of Nazi society, the new austerity was greeted with ill grace. When Hitler's mistress, Eva Braun, learned of a proposed ban on permanent waves and expressed her indignation, a beleaguered Führer told Minister of Armaments and War Production Albert Speer to amend the edict to call only for "a cessation of repairs upon apparatus for producing permanent waves."

Although Germany's conversion to Total War fell far short of its billing, it did achieve some substantive results. At considerable cost to the consumer economy (and with the immense help of slave labor from conquered territories), Speer worked wonders with war production: The output of military aircraft and tanks nearly doubled, and the production of heavy guns more than trebled. Partly by suspending the exemptions previously granted to youngest and sole-surviving sons, about 560,000 recruits were rounded up for military service; by the summer of 1943 the German armed forces would number some 10 million men—only 240,000 fewer than the pre-Stalingrad peak.

In sum, Total War—together with the terrible defeat at Stalingrad—gave to the German masses a sense that they were acting in a spirit of national self-sacrifice. For that, they were more than willing: Indeed, Goebbels confided to Speer that he could "sense a great readiness among the people to exert themselves to the utmost. In fact, significant restrictions were a real necessity if only to revive popular confidence in the leadership."

But in return, the people expected results—and they would hardly be satisfied by a spring and summer of static defense in the East.

Hitler's dilemma, then, was very real: His prestige with both his allies and his domestic constituents demanded a show of strength. Yet post-Stalingrad realities forced upon him the realization that his armies were no longer capable of carrying out the vast sweeps and deep stabs that had made them the masters of Europe and had taken them to the edge of Asia. Seeking a middle way, the Führer on March 13 told his military commanders: "It is important for us to take the initiative at certain sectors of the front if possible before the Russians do, so as to be able to dictate their actions in at least one sector."

Hitler was opting for a limited offensive whose main purpose would be to demonstrate that his legions still had the power to inflict punishment and inspire fear. As German planners pored over their maps in search of a place that might best fit their needs, one area stood out: a salient stretching some 70 miles from north to south at its base and thrusting about 90 miles westward between the fronts of Field Marshal Erich von Manstein's Army Group South and Field Marshal Hans Günther von Kluge's Army Group Center. Within that bulge lay a city of small renown and slight significance that would give its name to one of the decisive conflicts of world history—the Battle of Kursk.

Code-named *Zitadelle (Citadel)* and planned as a short, sharp surgical operation to snip off the bulge at its base, the Battle of Kursk took on a life of its own and became a colossal clash of steel and explosive power. Around the salient's 250-mile front the Germans assembled immense and massive forces—570,000 men, nearly 2,500 tanks and self-propelled guns and about 10,000 field guns and mortars, supported by almost 2,000 aircraft. Opposing the Wehrmacht were 977,000 Russians with more than 3,300 tanks and assault guns, 20,000 guns and mortars and nearly 3,000 aircraft. The Soviets were, moreover, protected by six concentric defensive belts, totaling more than 6,000 miles of trenchworks and sown with an average of 2,400 antitank and 2,700 antipersonnel mines for each mile of front.

At its roaring crescendo, Kursk would see nearly 3,000 armored behemoths locked in the mortal struggle of the greatest tank battle ever fought. Within the salient there was little room for maneuver, and the tanks stood hull-down amid charred fields of wheat and rye and sunflowers, blasting away at point-blank range in a brutal slugging match. And when the last wisps of smoke finally cleared from the battlefield, the course of World War II was irrevocably changed and the Nazi cause had been lost beyond redemption.

The surge of the German armies had been stopped first outside Moscow in the winter of 1941-1942 and again on the banks of the Volga at Stalingrad in the winter of 1942-1943. After the Battle of Kursk, despite desperate fighting by an enemy that would remain dangerous until its dying moments, the Soviet juggernaut would roll invincibly west-

In the spring of 1943, five million Soviet
troops and four million German troops
faced each other across a 1,750-mile-long
battlefront (red line) that extended from
Leningrad in the north to the Black Sea in the
south. The Germans still held about 400,000
square miles of Soviet territory, but the
Soviet winter offensive, which began with the
victory at Stalingrad, had dramatically
altered the strategic picture. Henceforth, the
Red Army would hold the initiative.

ward. The Red Army would reconquer about 360,000 square miles of Soviet territory and 40,000 square miles of formerly Polish territory. Kharkov and Kiev, Smolensk and Sevastopol would be reclaimed, and the long siege of Leningrad would be lifted. The Donets and the Dnieper, the Bug and the Vistula Rivers would be crossed, and the tragedy of Warsaw would be played out. By February of 1945, when the Western Allies were girding themselves for their assault on Germany's West Wall and the Rhine, the Soviet forces would stand a mere 40 miles from Berlin. And, from the position of raw power provided him by the performance of his armies, Josef Stalin would to a devastating degree impose his will upon an Allied summit conference held in a Black Sea resort town named Yalta.

Planning for the 1943 German offensive fell to the Army High Command (OKH) under General Kurt Zeitzler—who was just the one to get things rolling. A bouncy little man, Zeitzler was known because of his kinetic and rotund qualities as "General Lightning Ball"; shortly after the assaults on Stalingrad were launched, Hitler had plucked Zeitzler from an army group in Holland, named him to succeed General Franz Halder as the OKH chief of staff, and noted that "he buzzes back and forth like a bumblebee and so prevents the troops from falling asleep."

The operation Zeitzler now contemplated was shaped by the post-Stalingrad fighting under the consummate generalship of Field Marshal von Manstein. Shocked and even subdued by the debacle on the Volga, Hitler for once had agreed to give ground deliberately. He allowed Manstein to employ what the field marshal called the "backhand" strategy of a mobile defensive in which, after retreating to the Mius River, 40 miles west of Rostov, and to the upper Dnie-

per, he would wait for the Russians to reach the end of their offensive tether, then lash back at their extended flanks.

The Red Army came on with a rush—and Manstein lashed it viciously. Rostov fell on the 14th of February, but only after Field Marshal Ewald von Kleist's Army Group A had been extricated from the Caucasus trap into which it had marched in the summer of 1942. By February 17, a day on which Hitler, in his closest approach of the War to the Eastern fighting front, was at Manstein's Zaporozhye headquarters on the Dnieper, Russian tanks of General Nikolai F. Vatutin's Southwest Front (front being the Soviet term for an army group) were probing only 40 miles to the northeast.

Farther north, Lieut. General F. I. Golikov's Voronezh Front on February 8 had captured Kursk. On February 16, Golikov had taken Kharkov, onetime capital of the Ukraine, the Soviet Union's fourth largest city and a prestigious objective for both Stalin and Hitler.

But the Soviet surge was already beginning to falter: The Red Army, after all, had been on the defensive throughout most of the War and was hardly accustomed to sustaining an offensive, much less a far-sweeping, deep-reaching offensive. Toward the end of February, for example, one of Vatutin's tank corps, running 60 miles in advance of his main forces, came to a standstill—out of gas.

Poised to strike at the floundering Soviets was Colonel General Hermann Hoth's Fourth Panzer Army, which had been heavily reinforced and masterfully reorganized in the very face of Vatutin's offensive. Hoth, a stumpy man whose fierce fighting qualities belied his avuncular appearance, had been one of the few German generals to emerge with distinction from the debris of Stalingrad. Now, on February 18, he sent the SS panzer division known as Das Reich slashing down from the north against the spearheads of Va-

Troops of the Leningrad and Volkhov Fronts embrace after breaking the German blockade of Leningrad in January 1943. The Soviet push cleared the rail line from Moscow, which, in spite of repeated German counterattacks, transported 4.5 million tons of freight to the city of Leningrad over the following 11 months.

tutin's First Guards and Sixth Armies, which had reached the Dnieper between Dnepropetrovsk and Zaporozhye. Several days later two SS panzer divisions attacked from the west—and within a week Vatutin had been hurled back 95 miles to the Donets in disarray.

Hoth now swung north, taking dead aim on Kharkov and covering 50 miles in the next five days. Ordinarily, that would have been nothing to brag about, but the spring thaw was starting and the ground was already dissolving into a morass in which even tracked vehicles could not navigate, or was opening up into huge potholes that could engulf trucks and tanks. Just as it seemed that Hoth might have to stop, a mere 10 miles short of Kharkov, a hard freeze set in and the Fourth Panzer Army continued its drive.

On March 9, the 2nd SS Panzer Corps was west of Kharkov, its right flank brushing the city's outskirts. To retake as much territory as was possible before the full thaw began, Hoth wanted to head farther north, then double back and isolate Kharkov from the east. The panzer corps's commander, SS Lieut. General Paul Hausser, sent two divisions into the city from the east, while units of the 48th Panzer Corps attacked from the south. To the mortification of the

Soviet commanders, the Germans on March 15 captured Kharkov for the third time in the War. General Golikov could only say lamely, "I had a mistaken estimate of the enemy's intentions and capabilities."

On March 18, the 2nd SS Panzer Corps captured Belgorod, 30 miles north of Kharkov—and then the mud took over. Although no one could have guessed it, Adolf Hitler's armies had just concluded their last successful major offensive action of the war in Russia.

That, then, was the situation confronting General Zeitzler and his OKH planners as they used the period of the thaw to formulate their next move. Manstein's "backhand" blows had left the Russians in possession of Kursk and the big bubble of territory around it. The salient was, however, sandwiched between two German-occupied bulges pushing eastward into the Russian line: One was bordered by Belgorod, 75 miles south of Kursk; the other centered on Orel, 80 miles north of Kursk. These could obviously be used for converging assaults to lop off the Kursk salient. But even a quick glance at a map also showed that the Germans assailing Kursk from the north and south within the Orel and Belgorod-Kharkov areas would have Russians at their own backs and would be vulnerable to attacks from the rear.

To Zeitzler, the possible results seemed worth the risk. The scores of thousands of Soviet troops already massed in the Kursk salient might be cut off and encircled in a manner reminiscent of the War's earlier days. Kursk could be denied to the Red Army as a springboard for new offensives—which were, in fact, being planned by Stavka, General Headquarters of the Soviet High Command. Eliminating the Kursk bulge would shorten the serpentine Eastern Front by 150 miles, thereby freeing German troops for transfer to Western Europe—probably Italy—which the Allies seemed certain to invade in the near future. Finally, there was the glittering if improbable chance that victory at Kursk might so shake the Soviets as to open the way for a German offensive in the old style.

On April 11, Zeitzler submitted a memorandum urging that the Kursk salient be simultaneously attacked from the north by General Walter Model's Ninth Army, which belonged to Kluge's Army Group Center, and from the south by Hoth's Fourth Panzer Army of Manstein's Army Group South. In his perky optimism, Zeitzler argued that no more

This diagram, taken from a Wehrmacht training manual, compares the effective ranges of the Tiger tank's 88mm gun and the Soviet T-34's 76mm gun. The Tiger (center of the cloverleaf) could destroy the 32-ton T-34 with a side or rear hit at 2,000 meters or a frontal hit at 950 meters. The Tiger itself—weighing 56 tons and more heavily armored—was threatened only at much shorter ranges: 1,500 meters from the side or rear, and 500 from the front. The sentence slanting toward the lower left says facetiously, "I can get you but you can't get me!"

than a dozen panzer divisions, with supporting infantry, should be needed to do the job.

Hitler had his doubts—and from them sprang a series of delays that eventually doomed Operation Citadel.

Germany's leader had at last come to recognize the sorry condition into which his armored forces had fallen. In January of 1943, only 495 tanks remained fit for fighting on the entire Eastern Front. Although the panzer force had been reinforced from other theaters, many units were still made up almost entirely of outmoded Mark III and Mark IV tanks, which were badly outmatched by the agile and power-packed Soviet T-34. A new generation of German tanks was, however, beginning to come off the production line, and Hitler wanted to delay Operation Citadel until the heavy Tiger, the medium Panther and an odd contraption known as the Ferdinand could be thrown into the offensive in large numbers.

The Tiger would eventually prove to be superior to its heavy Soviet equivalent, the KV1; it was bigger (56 versus 52 tons), had heavier armor and, with its 88mm converted antiaircraft gun, could easily outslug the KV1 with its 76.2mm gun. But although Tigers had been tested near Leningrad in the autumn of 1942, they had been beset by production problems and even now were coming from the Henschel plant at a rate of only 25 a month.

Hitler had equally high hopes for the Panther as Germany's answer to the already famed T-34. Somewhat faster (34 versus 32 miles per hour), it was 30 per cent larger than the T-34 (49 versus 32 tons), and its long-barreled high-velocity 75mm gun packed a more lethal punch than the shorter-barreled 76mm gun of the Soviet tank. By April of 1943, Panther production stood at a disappointing 50 a month (Soviet factories at that time were churning out about 1,000 T-34s every month).

As for the Ferdinand, it was from beginning to end a fiasco, sharing not only its name but also its eccentricity with its designer, Dr. Ferdinand Porsche, whose genius Hitler greatly admired. In the early 1930s, Porsche had designed the single-seat, six-liter Auto-Union, a racing car so hot that only three men had been deemed capable of handling it—and two of them had died at its wheel. Later, Porsche had come up with the idea for the Volkswagen, which, despite its phenomenal postwar success, had engineering problems

so severe that it took 10 years to get the automobile from the drawing board into production.

In his wartime work for the Krupp arms works, Porsche turned his erratic hand to weapons design—with woeful results. His version of a Tiger tank was rejected by the Army's ordnance department. Undaunted, Porsche came up with the Ferdinand, an elephantine tank-destroyer that was helpless in anything but head-on combat (pages 26-27).

In all, 90-odd Ferdinands would be produced. All would be sent into battle on the same day. Few would survive.

To Adolf Hitler, the Tiger, the Panther and the Ferdinand promised victory in the approaching offensive, and he was determined to have them at hand. On April 15, four days

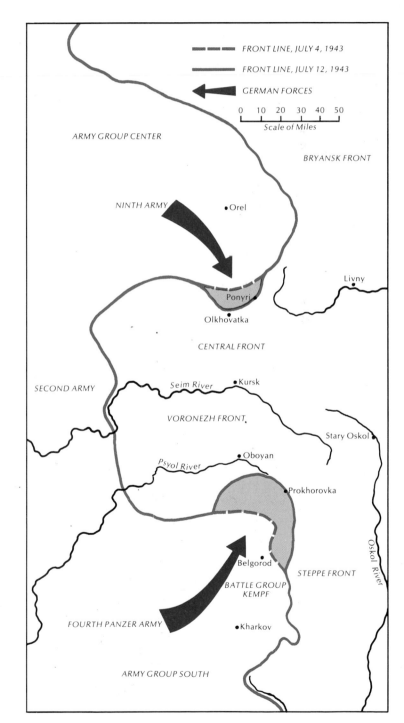

Operation Citadel, the German plan to destroy the Soviet forces in the Kursk salient, called for a gigantic pincers movement: The German Ninth Army was to attack southward from Orel while the Fourth Panzer Army and Battle Group Kempf drove northward from Belgorod. The jaws of the pincers were to snap shut at the town of Kursk. Defending the salient against the Germans were three Soviet army groups, the Central Front in the north, the Voronezh Front in the south and the Steppe Front, which was being held in reserve in the east.

after receiving Zeitzler's memorandum, Hitler issued Operations Order No. 6, setting forth in meticulous detail the plans for attacking the Kursk salient—but leaving the date of the assault open so as to allow time for the arrival of the new armor. The order specified merely that commanders must be ready, "so that from April 28 on, an offensive can be taken within six days of receipt of an order from OKH. The earliest date for the offensive will be May 3."

Operations Order No. 6 ranks among the most consequential documents of World War II. Behind the bravado of its preamble could be detected a shrill note of desperation. "This offensive," wrote Hitler, "is of decisive importance. It must be carried out quickly and shatteringly. It *must* give us the initiative for the spring and summer of this year. The best formations, the best armies, the best leaders, great stocks of ammunition are to be placed at the decisive points. Every officer and every man must be indoctrinated with the decisive significance of this offensive. The victory of Kursk must be a torch to the world."

The aim of the onslaught was simply stated. It was "to encircle the enemy forces deployed in the Kursk area by one attacking army each from the areas of Belgorod and south of Orel, and annihilating them through a concentric attack."

Surprise and secrecy were especially stressed. "Surprise must be maintained as far as possible," the order said, "and above all the enemy must be kept in doubt as to the time of the offensive. To preserve secrecy only essential personalities are to be identified, so that enemy espionage can be fought constantly."

Yet in those vital elements the German failure would, as things turned out, be total—and fatal. From the very inception of the operation, German plans for *Citadel* came with speed and unerring accuracy into the hands of Stavka—thanks to an extraordinary espionage apparatus led by a spy called Lucy.

Much about the Lucy ring remains unknown. What is known is that Lucy was the code name for Rudolf Rössler, a German veteran of the First World War, who went on to manage a Berlin publishing house. An anti-Nazi, he moved to Switzerland in 1934, and by 1942 was well established in the espionage community there, which included Swiss, British, American, Soviet, Nazi and anti-Nazi German agents.

The 72-ton Ferdinand looked exactly like what it had been designed to be, a deadly tank-destroyer that would help revive the Wehrmacht's fortunes on the Eastern Front. Built on the chassis of the powerful Tiger tank, the Ferdinand was armed with a hard-hitting gun and girded with steel plate up to 200mm thick, nearly twice the gauge of the Tiger's armor. But as the behemoth's dismal showing at Kursk proved, it was deadlier to its own six-man crew than it was to enemy tanks.

In almost every respect, the Ferdinand was abysmally designed. It had two engines that together produced 640 horsepower, but was so ponderous that it could

THE FERDINAND: GERMANY'S HAPLESS GIANT

manage only 12.5 miles per hour on hard-surfaced roads and 11 mph cross-country. To save the added weight needed for the machinery to turn a turret, the Ferdinand's superstructure was a rigid steel box, and its cannon could be traversed only 14 degrees—by slow hand cranking.

Worst of all, the Ferdinand was terribly vulnerable to infantry attack. It carried not a single machine gun, and depended for protection on German riflemen to either side. Once a Ferdinand lost its defenders, Soviet infantrymen could safely approach from almost any direction, disable the Ferdinand's tracks with explosive charges and destroy the tank-destroyer at their leisure.

Judging by the accuracy of his information, Lucy appeared to have access to the topmost levels of the German High Command; his reports to the Soviets included detailed descriptions of troop movements, invasion timetables, production statistics and casualty figures. So amazingly precise was Lucy's information that his means of acquiring it would long remain a tantalizing mystery: Indeed, it would later be theorized that Lucy was even fed information from top-level British intelligence, with the express purpose of passing it on to the Soviet Union. Presumably, the British used Rössler to conceal from the Russians the fact that their most secret intelligence group, known as Ultra, had broken the most secret German codes.

Lucy was passing along plans for Operation *Citadel* to Stavka even as they were being formulated by Zeitzler, a full fortnight before Hitler issued Operations Order No. 6.

Armed with foreknowledge and dispatched with all possible haste to the Kursk area, the Soviet deputy supreme commander, Marshal Georgy K. Zhukov, on the 8th of April sent to Stalin a recommendation that would shape the Battle of Kursk: "I consider that it would be pointless for our forces to go over to the offensive in the near future. It would be better for us to wear out the enemy on our defense, to smash his tanks and then by introducing fresh reserves and going over to a general offensive to beat the main enemy force once and for all."

Summoned back to Moscow by a telephone call from Stalin, Zhukov arrived on the evening of April 11, only to be informed at Stavka headquarters that the dictator was demanding that situation maps, detailed estimates and proposals for Kursk be ready for his inspection by the following night. It was a measure of the hugely increased professionalism of the Soviet General Staff that the job was done in a manner that would later withstand the cruel test of fire and steel. It was also a gauge of Stalin's enhanced confidence in his generals, whose advice he had earlier in the War scorned with instinctive contempt, that he accepted the plan without a quibble.

Quite simply, the Soviets meant to turn the Kursk salient into a gigantic fortress, cramming as many men and as much matériel as they could gather into the bulge and deploying them in defensive formations of great depth.

On the northern face of the salient, confronting Model's Ninth Army, would be the Central Front—five field armies, one tank army, two independent tank corps, and an air army, one cavalry corps and several tank-destroyer units. The array would be commanded by General Konstantin K. Rokossovsky, the onetime construction worker who had somehow survived Stalin's military purges of the 1930s, emerging from the torture chambers with a mouthful of metal teeth and a steel will to prove his worth as a fighter.

Cool, courageous and possessed of a personal charm rare among the scowling Soviet military elite, Rokossovsky had an upsetting habit of making independent decisions and carrying them out without a by-your-leave from above. Now, almost alone among the top Soviet commanders, he was arguing for a preemptive attack that would catch the Germans off-balance before they could properly organize for *Citadel*. To make sure that Rokossovsky worked in concert with commanders on either flank, Stalin sent none other than Zhukov himself to the Central Front.

Facing Hermann Hoth's Fourth Panzer Army from within the salient to the south would be the Voronezh Front, equal in size to Rokossovsky's force, now under Nikolai Vatutin, who had been transferred from the Southwest Front to relieve General Golikov, the man who had captured Kursk the previous February. A staff officer throughout his career, Vatutin had risen to the position of deputy chief of the Army General Staff. Yet as one of his juniors noted, he had "a strong dash of romanticism in his make-up," and although he had never commanded so much as a division in the field, in July 1942 he asked Stalin to give him a combat front. During the abortive post-Stalingrad offensive, Vatutin's performance had been shaky at best. It remained to be seen how he would do on the defensive—and to serve as his on-the-scene overseer Stavka sent its own chief, Marshal Aleksandr M. Vasilevsky.

As if 10 ground armies, two air armies and assorted small but deadly units within the bulge were not enough, a massive reserve was assembled about 100 miles southeast of Kursk on a north-south line across the open end of the salient, from where it could either be fed piecemeal into the battle to meet emergencies or flung in force against the German flanks. Designated by the deceptively static name of the Steppe Military District, it included five field armies, a tank army, an air army, a rifle corps, and three tank, three mechanized and three cavalry corps. Its commander was General Ivan S. Konev, once a political commissar—a ferocious fighting leader whose ambitions Stalin periodically played off against Zhukov's.

Even as the armies of the Central Front, the Voronezh Front and the Steppe Military District were moving hurriedly toward history's greatest military concentration, they were granted time to prepare and perfect their defenses. On April 20, a signal came through from Lucy: "Date of offensive against Kursk, originally envisaged for first week of May, has been postponed."

Lucy was right. May 3—the date specified by Operations Order No. 6 as the earliest time for an assault on the Kursk salient—passed quietly. On May 3, Hitler summoned his senior commanders to a series of conferences in Munich. He still seemed to have qualms about *Citadel.*

On May 4, the Führer opened the discussion with a 45-minute discourse about the situation on the Russian front, appearing to be especially impressed with the opinions of

the Ninth Army's Walter Model, who had submitted distressing reports.

Model stood high in Hitler's esteem. Although he affected the trappings of the typical Junker general, right down to his ever-present monocle, he was a faithful pro-Nazi—the sort of man with whom Hitler could feel comfortable. He was also a towering egoist in a profession notable for inflated egos. He had taken over command of the Ninth Army in the winter of 1941-1942 at a time when it was isolated and in desperate straits north of Vyazma, 150 miles southwest of Moscow. "And what, sir, have you brought us to restore the situation?" asked a division officer. Answered Model: "Myself."

A difference of opinion soon developed between Model and Hitler regarding the disposition of a panzer corps, and in a heated exchange the general faced down the dictator: "Who commands the Ninth Army, my Führer, you or I?" Remarkably, Hitler let Model have his way—although he made it ominously clear that the general would be held fully accountable for any failures. As it turned out, the Russians attacked at precisely the spot where Model had deployed

A RISING COMMISSAR UNDER ENEMY FIRE

A future head of the Soviet state, Lieut. Colonel Leonid I. Brezhnev, rose to prominence in 1943 during 225 days of bloody siege on Malaya Zemlya, a tiny peninsula near the German-held Black Sea port of Novorossiisk. As political commissar of the Eighteenth Shock Army, Brezhnev accompanied boatloads of reinforcements to a fortified beachhead and did whatever he could to bolster morale. "We put out a newspaper," Brezhnev recalled, "held party meetings and attended lectures. We even organized a chess tournament."

On one voyage to the beachhead with a boatload of soldiers, Brezhnev nearly lost his life. He was standing beside the pilot when their small ship hit a mine and, he later wrote, "the explosion shot us both into the air." Fortunately the two men landed a safe distance from the sinking ship and were found by a Soviet motorboat. Brezhnev boosted several heavily armed soldiers aboard, noting proudly that "not a single one of them had abandoned his weapons." Finally, with German shells exploding nearby, Brezhnev himself was hauled into the boat. "Only then," he said, "did I sense my trembling."

Commissar Brezhnev (third from right) consults with Soviet officers on the Black Sea beachhead.

his tanks, and thus the German line was soon restored.

Model's reports to Hitler were anything but optimistic: Aerial photographs showed a Soviet build-up of staggering proportions in and around the Kursk salient. Hitler seemed swayed, and concluded: "Model drew the correct deduction, namely that the enemy was counting on our launching this attack."

For the rest of that day, the conference was thrown open to discussion—and the German generals chose sides.

Manstein and Kluge, the army-group commanders who would conduct the offensive, expressed conditional approval of *Citadel*. Manstein thought the plan's chances "would have been excellent in April," but that delay had already been costly. The offensive, he said, could succeed only if undertaken immediately—and then only if he were given two additional infantry divisions. Hitler, who personally disliked the aristocratic Manstein, dismissed out of hand the request for more troops. General Alfred Jodl, chief of the operations staff of the Armed Forces High Command (OKW), suggested that the plan would expend too much of the Reich's armored reserve.

But Kluge, whose Army Group Center had been largely idle for more than a year, was thirsting for a prestige-building victory. He favored the offensive but, like Manstein, argued that there must be no further delay. OKH's Kurt Zeitzler, bursting with the pride of authorship, stood in unqualified support of the plan. In a marvel of topsy-turvy reasoning, Zeitzler advanced the proposition that Model's aerial photographs were proof of the importance that the Soviets attached to Kursk—and were therefore cause enough for the Germans to attack.

Heinz Guderian was foursquare against *Citadel*. Made a scapegoat and relieved of his command outside Moscow in December 1941, Guderian had recently been called back to duty as inspector general of the armored forces. He urgently wished to spend 1943 on the defensive in order to allow time for rebuilding his panzer armies. If the attack on Kursk were to be undertaken, he insisted, Germany was "certain to suffer heavy tank casualties, that we would not be able to replace."

At a special tank-production conference held in Berlin a week later, Guderian found himself at loggerheads with the head of OKW, Field Marshal Wilhelm Keitel. "We must attack for political reasons," said Keitel. Retorted Guderian: "How many people do you think know where Kursk is? It's a matter of profound indifference to the world whether we hold Kursk or not."

Hitler kept steering the discussions back to the Panther tank. At least 250 had been promised by the end of May, but only 130 had been produced so far and fewer than 100 of these had been delivered to the Army. These were discouraging statistics, but Armaments Minister Speer had good news: Production difficulties had been ironed out, he said, and not only would the goal be met but no fewer than 324 Panthers could be expected by the end of May. Guderian was unimpressed. The Panther, he argued, was "still suffering from the many teething problems inherent in all new equipment." Model, too, had concerns about the German tanks. The Mark IVs would still make up the bulk of his armor, and he doubted that they could withstand the new Soviet antitank weapons.

As always, the final decision fell to Hitler, and again he waffled: *Citadel* would go on—at some indefinite time.

During the rest of May and most of June, Hitler seemed to lose interest in *Citadel*. At his Bavarian retreat, the Berghof, and in the Reich Chancellery in Berlin, he preoccupied himself with routine affairs; even within his closest circle of companions, he talked lovingly about "wonder weapons" but little about the grim test that lay on the horizon.

Meanwhile, commanders and troops on both sides prepared for battle as never before. In arduous field exercises, the Germans worked against the sort of defenses upon which they would be hurling themselves: They burrowed and blasted their way through cordons of barbed wire; they destroyed concrete bunkers with demolition charges; they cleared fields of mines; and they improved their skills at avoiding tank traps. The commanders, using aerial photographs and sand tables, studied every inch of the terrain into which they would be venturing.

Kursk itself, a city on the central Russian plateau with a prewar population of 120,000, was of little consequence except as a reference point. It was the land around Kursk that counted, and it was with a keen military eye that Colonel Friedrich von Mellenthin, chief of staff of the 48th Panzer Corps, described the area: "The terrain over which the advance was to take place was a far-flung plain, broken by numerous valleys, small copses, irregularly laid-out villages and some rivers and brooks; of those, the Pena ran with a swift current between steep banks. The ground rose slightly to the north, thus favoring the defender. Roads consisted of tracks through the sand and became impassable for all motor transport during rain. Large cornfields covered the landscape and made visibility difficult. All in all, it was not good 'tank country,' but it was by no means 'tankproof.' ''

For their part, the Russians took superlative advantage of the time allowed them by Hitler. Into the salient and its eastern environs poured 200,000 civilian workers, who built a new 50-mile railway supply line from Stary Oskol to Rzhava and repaired more than 250 bridges and 1,800 miles of roads. Fighting units meticulously prepared and familiarized themselves with the defensive areas to which they had been assigned. A Soviet captain told how his brigade had spotted five places where the Germans might strike, ''and at each of them we know alongside whom we shall be fighting, our replacements and command posts. The brigade is stationed in the rear, but our trenches and shelters are ready up in front, and the routes by which we are to get there are marked out. The ground, of which we have made a topographical survey, has been provided with guide marks. The depths of fords, the maximum loads of bridges are known to us. Liaisons with division have been doubled, codes and signals are arranged.''

Of invaluable aid to the Red Army were the tens of thousands of Russian partisans who infested the enemy's rear areas and worked havoc with German supply lines (pages 84-95). In January, the Germans had reported 397 guerrilla attacks against their railways; by June the number had soared to 1,092. During that month, in the rear of Army Group Center alone 44 bridges were blown up and 298 locomotives and 1,223 railroad cars were either destroyed or damaged. Wrote a German corporal to his wife: ''With us trains move for one day and three days have to be spent repairing the tracks since the partisans blow everything up. The night before last they arranged a collision between an express train and a leave train so that the trains aren't running. That's how we live in Russia.''

But the period of preparation and preliminary action was almost over. On July 1, just as he was leaving to fly to Bucharest, where he was scheduled to adorn Marshal Antonescu with a German medal, Manstein received a signal from Hitler's Rastenburg headquarters in the forests of East Prussia: ''The Führer expects you for a top-secret conference at Wolf's Lair. Bucharest is being informed that your takeoff has been delayed by bad weather.''

Arriving at Rastenburg, Manstein found a considerable number of senior generals already in attendance. Hitler greeted them with rare warmth and invited them into the tearoom, in one of the rustic, one-story wooden buildings. Once they were seated, the Führer wasted no time in disclosing his purpose: ''I have decided to fix the starting date of Citadel for July 5.''

Hitler added a special caution: ''This time we must make absolutely sure that nothing of our intention is betrayed either through carelessness or neglect.''

By that evening, Stavka knew of the impending attack.

On the afternoon of July 2, Lieut. General Mikhail Y. Katukov, commander of the Soviet First Tank Army, was informed that two important visitors were about to call upon

Inspector General of Armored Forces Heinz Guderian (upper right) questions a Tiger crewman during an inspection of the SS Leibstandarte Adolf Hitler Division near Kharkov in April 1943. Guderian, who was a leading architect of blitzkrieg tactics, won the nickname ''Heinz the Hustler'' for his bold dashes through Poland and France early in the War.

his command post, set in a clump of oaks near a village about 25 miles behind the line in the salient's southern sector. Soon the Voronezh Front commander, General Vatutin, and his bouncy political commissar, Lieut. General Nikita S. Khrushchev, arrived. Khrushchev got right down to business. "The fascists are attacking between July 3 and 5," he announced. "This isn't a guess but a fact. We know it."

The daylight hours of July 3 passed without major incident, but that night both sides of the salient's southern line were alive with activity. "The night streets were loud with the noise of engines," recalled a general attached to the First Tank Army. "Convoys of tanks and guns, covered with dust, were rumbling into the sector where we expected the German onslaught."

The Germans had more stealthy affairs in progress. Before the Fourth Panzer Army's Hoth could launch his main attack, he had some yard work to do: To his immediate front, Soviet troops with artillery observers held a low line of hills, which Hoth meant to seize with a preliminary assault on the afternoon of July 4. To clear the minefields that lay in his way, he sent German sappers creeping forth in a darkness eerily illuminated by lightning from passing thunderstorms and by Soviet flares arcing above. Before the night was done, one 10-man team removed no fewer than 2,700 mines from the area fronting the little town of Butovo alone.

A brief thunderstorm on the afternoon of July 4 ended at 2:45 p.m. and at almost that instant Stuka squadrons swooped screaming onto the hills that were Hoth's objective; within 15 minutes they plastered an area no more than two miles wide and 500 yards deep with 2,500 bombs.

At 3 o'clock, tanks of the 48th Panzer Corps and the 2nd SS Panzer Corps on its right emerged from their hiding places in sunken lanes and gullies. Recalled a Tiger radio operator: "The Russian artillery plowed the earth around us. Ivan, with his usual cunning, had held his fire in the weeks before. But now the whole front was a girdle of flashes. It seemed as if we were driving into a ring of flame. Four times our valiant 'Rosinante' shuddered under a direct hit, and we thanked the fates for the strength of our good Krupp steel."

Within the narrow area of the operation, the German armor was overpowering. By nightfall, the hills were in German hands—and Hermann Hoth had his starting line for the great offensive that was soon to get under way.

For his lunge in the south, Hoth had been given the most powerful force ever entrusted to the commander of a single German army. Concentrated along a front of only 30 miles were 11 infantry divisions, six of Hitler's finest armored divisions and five panzer grenadier divisions. In the past, panzer divisions had gobbled up hundreds of miles at a time in their headlong rushes. For *Citadel,* if all went well, they would need to advance only about 35 miles before linking up with Model's Ninth Army from the north.

With his ponderous weight of armor, Army Group South's Manstein, now installed in a railway-car headquarters close behind the German lines, had decided to adopt what the Germans called armored wedge tactics. Successive wedge formations would be spearheaded by the fearsome new Tigers; fanning out behind them would be hundreds of Panthers and Mark IVs, followed by infantry with automatic weapons and grenades and, finally, at the base of each wedge, soldiers with mortars in armored carriers.

Against Manstein's awesome array, Vatutin had assigned the Thirty-eighth and Fortieth Armies to his far right as a hedge against the improbable event that the enemy, rather than attempting a pincers movement, would be foolish enough to attack frontally against the western end of the salient. By far the bulk of Vatutin's strength, however, faced south along a line where the Stalingrad-seasoned Sixth Guards and Seventh Guards Armies manned the outer defensive belts between Soldatskoye and Volchansk. Behind the hinge of the Guards armies, a potentially vulnerable point, the Sixty-ninth Army was deployed. In perhaps the most critical sector of all, Katukov's First Tank Army stood in the second Soviet echelon astride the road and rail routes leading north to Kursk.

The Russians had prepared a most unpleasant tactical reception for their enemy. The myriad minefields had been laid in patterns calculated to channel German tanks toward strong points bristling with as many as 10 antitank guns, each group under fire-control orders from a single commander. According to a recent order, all the guns in each unit would deliver a broadside at a single tank at a time—with each salvo presumably delivering enough firepower to destroy the target.

Perhaps because of information received from Lucy, per-

German tank crewmen, concealing telltale evidence from Soviet spotter planes, spade up soil to cover the tread marks of their Tiger tank, hidden in a wood outside Kursk before the start of the battle in July 1943.

haps simply because their maps showed that it was the straightest, fastest route across the salient, the Russians fully expected Hoth to direct his main thrust through Oboyan toward Kursk. But at least one senior Soviet officer was not so sure: General S. Krivoshein, commanding the First Tank Army's III Mechanized Corps, had observed the panzers operating in Poland during the days of the German-Soviet alliance, and he knew his German tankman. "Hoth is a cunning fox," Krivoshein told his chief of staff. "Will he really do the obvious?"

Hoth would not. Orders from Hitler's headquarters specified unmistakably that he must strike through Oboyan, but he had other ideas. Painfully aware that the First Tank Army stood massively in his way, he also knew that the movement straight north through Oboyan would open his right flank to attack from Soviet tank reserves coming from the east. Those tanks, he thought, would have to pass through the town of Prokhorovka, 24 miles southeast of Oboyan on a narrow neck of land between the Psyol and Seim Rivers. Hoth therefore told his staff: "It would be better to deal with the enemy to be expected via Prokhorovka before continuing our northward thrust in the direction of Kursk."

Under Hoth's amended plan, the 48th Panzer Corps would, as expected, head full tilt toward Oboyan—but it would pull up short and, after securing a bridgehead across the Psyol River, turn east toward Prokhorovka. Meanwhile, the 2nd SS Panzer Corps would drive directly toward Prokhorovka, its right flank covered by Battle Group Kempf—three panzer and three infantry divisions under the command of Lieut. General Werner Kempf.

The sullen, sultry dawn of July 5 was shattered by the thunder of German guns and the shriek of Stukas overhead as Hoth's tanks rumbled into the maelstrom of Kursk. Soviet 76mm guns answered instantly, their roar in satanic symphony with the wail of "Katyusha" rockets and the crackle of small-arms fire.

The Tigers, all but impervious even to direct hits from the Soviet 76s, crashed through the first defense line. But behind them the lighter Mark IVs and the sleek new Panthers were in deep trouble. Said a general of the Panthers' performance: "They were easily set ablaze, the oil and fuel systems were inadequately protected and the crews were insufficiently trained."

On the left of the 48th Panzer Corps's Grossdeutschland Division, one Panther brigade had 200 tanks. Just after starting, the tanks plunged blindly into a minefield; within mo-

ments 36 Panthers lay crippled and helpless. The others withdrew in disorder, returning to their starting point while smoke from their comrades still plumed into the sky.

Opposite the 2nd SS Panzer Corps on the German right, the troops of the Soviet Sixth Guards Army had been warned by their commander, General I. M. Chistyakov: "In front of you stand Hitler's guards formations. We must expect the main effort of the German offensive on this sector."

But Chistyakov himself was evidently unprepared either for the violence of the German assault or for its drive in the direction of Prokhorovka rather than Oboyan. Three hours after the attack had begun, the general, a noted trencherman, sat down beneath an apple tree outside his headquarters and ate a second breakfast. Before long, the First Tank Army's Katukov and his political adviser, Major General Nikolai K. Popel, arrived on the scene for consultation. Wrote Popel in his memoirs: "On the table were cold mutton, scrambled eggs, a carafe with chilled vodka and finely sliced white bread—Chistyakov was doing himself well."

But not for long. Shells suddenly began crashing about, and an aide breathlessly reported to Chistyakov that the 2nd SS Panzer Corps, its way cleared by devastating fire from Stukas armed with antitank cannon, had broken through the front of the 52nd Guards Rifle Division and was even now pounding toward Chistyakov's headquarters. Katukov and Popel, departing a good deal more hastily than they had come, returned to their own headquarters and threw in heavy reinforcements to strengthen Chistyakov's line.

In Hoth's deepest penetration of the day, the 2nd SS Panzer Corps had fought 11 miles into the salient. But by nightfall, the attack had been brought to a halt.

Massed in the Orel salient to the north, the German Ninth Army was made up of 14 infantry divisions, six panzer divisions and one panzer grenadier division. Walter Model opted for tactics suiting the balance of his forces: Instead of leading with his main tank units, he would push his infantry forward to probe weaknesses in the Soviet lines, then exploit the soft spots with armor. Perhaps to confound the enemy with sheer size, perhaps because he could not figure out what else to do with the things, Model decided to send his 90 giant Ferdinands along with the infantry.

Rokossovsky's dispositions were simple and straightforward: With the Sixtieth and Sixty-fifth Armies guarding the western end of the Kursk salient, he deployed—facing north from his left to his right—the Seventieth, Thirteenth and Forty-eighth Armies. Backing them up and ready to roll to threatened areas were several tank and infantry corps.

Shortly before 10 o'clock on the night of July 4, the eve of battle, Rokossovsky got a bonus. A Soviet patrol spotted German mine-clearing sappers, killed several and took prisoner a Corporal Bruno Fermello—who convincingly informed his captors that the Ninth Army offensive would start at 3:30 a.m., only a few hours away.

By the time Fermello's news filtered to the top, little more than an hour remained before the Germans were scheduled to get under way. Zhukov and Rokossovsky were in a quandary. Though their doctrine called for "counterpreparation" fire—a tremendous artillery barrage designed to smash the Germans as they were forming—it was always dangerous to undertake major initiatives without Stalin's go-ahead.

"What shall we do?" asked Rokossovsky.

"Let's lose no time," replied Zhukov. "Issue the order. Meanwhile I will telephone Stalin and tell him about this information and the decision taken."

Zhukov located Stalin at Stavka headquarters—the usually icy dictator, Zhukov would later recall, was in a highly excited condition—and got his permission for the bombardment. At 2:20 a.m., Rokossovsky opened fire with fully half of all his artillery (the Soviet antitank guns had been ordered to remain silent lest they give away their positions). At Rokossovsky's headquarters, 12 miles behind the front, Zhukov "could hear and sense the hurricane of fire and could well picture the terrible plight of the enemy suddenly struck down by violent fire."

The reality was something less than the vision. Probably because it had been laid down on predetermined areas rather than on known targets, the Soviet bombardment caused more noise than damage. Still, it did cause confusion in the German ranks, and it was a good two hours before they got straightened out.

Then they came.

After feinting east and northeast, Model aimed his main thrust at two rifle divisions on the left flank of the Thirteenth Army. Into a curtain of Soviet fire the German infantry swarmed in tens of thousands. Even as they scurried across

Stuka pilot Hans-Ulrich Rudel, renowned as the ''Panzerknacker,'' or ''Tank Cracker,'' waves from the cockpit of his modified Junkers-87, which was armed with a deadly 37mm antitank cannon under each wing (far right). Rudel destroyed no fewer than 519 Soviet tanks while flying more missions—2,530 in six years—than any other pilot in the War.

the blazing landscape, Soviet sappers laid new antipersonnel mines in their path—6,000 in the Thirteenth Army area during the day. From above came merciless attacks by planes of the Soviet Sixteenth Air Army. Said the commander of a German infantry division: "The Russians used aircraft in numbers such as we had never yet seen in the East."

By noon, the report made by a German aide to the commander of an infantry regiment was typical: "3rd Battalion is unable to get beyond the second enemy trench on the right-hand slope. 1st Battalion is stuck in a minefield in the ravine. It has another 500 yards to go to the enemy positions on the left flank of the ravine in 'Squirrel Wood.' Some companies have lost nearly all their officers and about half their men. The Russian defensive fire is indescribable."

Porsche's Ferdinands were worse than useless. As they waddled sluggishly into battle, some were halted by mechanical failure; others plowed on but were victimized when they lost their infantry support. Soviet infantrymen picked off the riflemen who rode the Ferdinands, then leaped aboard the slowly moving vehicles and squirted flamethrowers through the engine ventilation slats. The Ferdinands died ponderously.

Another of Hitler's gadgets was of little more value. It was a midget tank, two feet high and four feet long, almost inevitably named Goliath. It carried a 200-pound explosive charge that could be detonated by radio when it reached its target—which it rarely did, since the charge could also be set off by enemy gunfire.

Nevertheless, the Soviet 15th Rifle Division grudgingly gave ground before the sheer weight of Model's concentration on its narrow front, and by nightfall the Germans held the towns of Bobrik and Butyrki, a bare six miles within the Soviet defenses on the Thirteenth Army's left. To the east,

German forces took the railroad station at Maloarkhangelsk, three miles from their starting point.

Toward midnight, Model assessed his situation. So far, he had used only one of his six panzer divisions, the 20th. Model decided to throw three more into the next day's fighting in an attempt to enlarge on his meager success around Bobrik and Gnilets. The remaining two panzer divisions would continue to be held in reserve until Model needed them—which might well be sooner than he liked. For he had just been informed by his intelligence officer of a new Soviet threat: "Major formations, including armor, are moving up from the east, from the Livny area, against Maloarkhangelsk, Ponyri and Olkhovatka." Rokossovsky had called up his operational reserve.

Model's undisguised intention on July 6 was to seize a line of hills stretching about 15 miles from Ponyri in the east to Molotychi in the west and passing just north of Olkhovatka, 13 miles within the Soviet defenses. From the 400-foot-high ridge he would be able to see Kursk 40 miles to the south—and his troops would have a downhill run all the way.

Just as clearly, Rokossovsky meant to use everything he had—including the Second Tank Army and his operational reserves—to deny to the Ninth Army the ridge, which was the last major natural obstacle in Model's path to Kursk. Rokossovsky had transformed the hills and the tiny towns on their slopes into a warren of underground bunkers and connecting trenches, antitank strongholds, rocket-launcher emplacements, machine-gun nests. Every copse of woodland, every farmhouse and field, every gully and bump in the land bristled with arms and men. Rokossovsky even ordered his tanks to dig in and meet the attack hull-down.

Model gave it his best. He attacked with wave after wave,

first at the western end of the narrow front, then at the eastern. In a single hour, one company of the 112th Panzer Grenadier Regiment lost all its officers. By night, the Ninth Army had advanced six more miles, but at a fearful cost: 25,000 casualties and about 200 tanks and self-propelled guns. And Model was still on the wrong side of the ridge, a mile short of Olkhovatka.

For four more days and nights the battle for the hills raged hand to hand and steel against steel in unrelenting ferocity. At its peak, as many as 1,200 tanks and self-propelled guns and 3,000 artillery pieces were engaged.

On July 8, midway through the cataclysmic struggle, Model summoned the 4th Panzer Division, the last of the armored reserve he had so carefully husbanded. He ordered it, together with two motorized infantry divisions, to strike at the hillside hamlet of Tyoploye, near the western end of the line. The 4th Panzer ran into two Soviet rifle divisions, an artillery division, two tank brigades and a brigade of assault guns. With a superb effort, the panzers blasted their way to the top of the ridge; they were driven back down by a savage Soviet counterattack. Back and forth surged the gasping, bleeding antagonists. Twice more the Germans ascended the heights, twice more they wrested the crest from their enemy, twice more the Russians clawed back and sent the Germans reeling away. The Germans did not return. The 4th Panzer Division had done its utmost, and failed.

At the eastern end of the ridge reposed the dreary little town of Ponyri—a railway station, a water tower, a tractor depot, a schoolhouse and a few other ramshackle buildings scattered along the tracks of the Orel-Kursk railroad. If the Germans took Ponyri they might use it as a hinge to swing westward behind Olkhovatka, ripping open the entire front and clearing the Ninth Army's way to Kursk. Early in the struggle for Ponyri, the Germans captured the northern end of the village, including the railroad station; the Soviets clung grimly to the section south of Ponyri's crossroads, using the schoolhouse as their strong point.

On the night of July 10, Model sent his last mechanized infantry reserve, the 10th Panzer Grenadier Division, into the step-by-step, building-by-building brawl. A grenadier regiment gained 500 yards, only to be counterattacked by a rifle regiment. A Soviet officer drove to the front of his battalion and jumped out of his jeep to lead his men into the fight. He was seen by a German battalion commander, who also raced to the front and leaped from his vehicle, spraying about with a submachine gun. Both men fell dead at almost the same instant.

To all intents and purposes, Model's offensive was done. He had gained six miles on the first day of fighting—and only six in the seven days that followed. Both sides lay exhausted, unable to advance and unwilling to retreat. And far behind Model's right shoulder the risk inherent in *Citadel* from its inception was becoming an awful reality: The Soviet West and Bryansk Fronts were launching an offensive against the Orel salient that could bring them onto the Ninth Army's rear.

If a decisive German breakthrough was to be achieved, it must clearly come from the south. In the first two days of fighting, Hoth's 48th Panzer Corps had made modest progress in its feint toward Oboyan, and his 2nd SS Panzer Corps in its thrust toward Prokhorovka had given General Chistyakov's Sixth Guards Army a good shaking. Only General Kempf's powerful force, whose three panzer divisions were to cover Hoth's right wing and to block enemy reinforcements coming in from the east, had lagged behind; it had contributed little to the advance. In the days to follow, both the 48th Panzer Corps and the 2nd SS Panzer Corps would do everything Hoth might reasonably expect of them. Battle Group Kempf, having failed in its primary mission, would be within sound and sight of the transcending tank battle at Prokhorovka—but still too far removed to add its armored weight to the precarious balance.

At dawn on July 7, the Grossdeutschland Division took Dubrovka, on the road to Oboyan, even though its Panther brigade again strayed into a minefield and suffered heavy casualties. Elements of the Soviet Sixth Guards Army and First Tank Army, both by now badly mauled, fell back to the Pena River. From there, General Krivoshein's III Mechanized Corps, its back to the stream, counterattacked with 40 T-34s. Tigers of the Grossdeutschland made short work of them, destroying 10 T-34s and putting the rest to flight across the Pena. Around dusk, Nikita Khrushchev appeared at First Tank Army headquarters and exhorted Katukov. "The next two or three days will be terrible," he said. "Either we hold out or the Germans take Kursk. They are staking everything on this one card. For them it is a matter of life or death. We must see to it that they break their necks!"

Two days later the 48th Panzer Corps stood on the high ground overlooking the Psyol River, the last natural barrier before Oboyan, only 12 miles beyond. Around Oboyan waited not only the weary units of the Soviet Sixth Guards and First Tank Armies but also two armies that had come by forced marches from the east; these units were part of the Steppe Military District, now designated the Steppe Front. But the 48th Panzer Corps had no intention of storming Oboyan. Instead, while leaving a holding force, it wheeled southeast and, in accordance with Hoth's plan, followed the Psyol toward Prokhorovka and an anticipated linkup with General Hausser's 2nd SS Panzer Corps.

Since surprising General Chistyakov at his breakfast, the 2nd SS Panzer Corps had more than justified its special place in Hitler's affections. At about noon on July 6 it took Luchki I (so named to distinguish it from a town farther north called Luchki II), 20 miles inside the salient, slashing a wide gap in the Sixth Guards Army defenses. Hausser drove through the breach and by the next day his tanks were astride the Luchki II-Tetervino road. From there, the SS Totenkopf and SS Leibstandarte Adolf Hitler Divisions peeled off toward the northwest and the Psyol to break into the last Soviet defense lines in front of the river at Greznoye. Meanwhile, the SS Das Reich Division arched northeast toward Prokhorovka, where—or so Hoth supposed—the battered Soviet First Tank Army would make its last stand.

Hoth meant to annihilate Katukov's army, and in pursuit of that purpose he ordered an all-out attack in the Prokhorovka area for July 12. By momentous coincidence, the Red Army was planning its own massive attack at the same time in the same place.

Even as the First Tank Army had tumbled back toward Prokhorovka, Khrushchev had remained at Katukov's side, endlessly admonishing: "Hold out, hold out, hold out!" The Voronezh Front's Nikolai Vatutin needed time, and only Katukov could provide it. In his frequent telephone calls to Vatutin, Khrushchev's questions were always the same: "When are the reserves of the Steppe Front arriving? Where are the armored corps of the Fifth Guards Tank Army?" Vatutin's reply was invariable: "They are on their way."

And so they were. A few days earlier, the Fifth Guards Tank Army of the Steppe Front had been ordered to Prokhorovka. It had hastily marched 225 miles, arriving at its assembly area northeast of Prokhorovka in dire need of a brief respite before it could fight. Not until the evening of July 11 did the Fifth Guards Tank Army arrive at the northeastern entrance to the Prokhorovka corridor, ready to assault the SS panzer corps on the morrow.

The armored army's commander, Lieut. General Pavel A. Rotmistrov, already well on his way toward a marshal's rank as one of the Soviet Army's most talented tank handlers, had met Hermann Hoth before—at Stalingrad, where their armies fought to a savage standoff. Now, in the early morning of July 12, 1943, Rotmistrov stationed himself on a hillock from which he could watch while his tanks delivered the blow that—he hoped and expected—would write finish to an old and formidable foe.

Beneath Rotmistrov lay the Prokhorovka passageway, only a few miles wide, constricted on the Soviet Army's right by the Psyol River and on its left by a steep railway embankment. Into that alley barreled Rotmistrov's tanks, 850 strong, almost all of them T-34s. At almost the same instant, before Rotmistrov's astonished gaze, into the opposite end of the corridor roared Hausser's SS panzer corps, some 600 tanks, including about 100 Tigers, at their best speed on a headlong collision course.

From his vantage point on the knoll, Rotmistrov had a panoramic, expert's-eye view of the explosive clash:

"Our tanks advanced across the steppe in small groups, using copses and hedges as cover. Initial staccato gunfire soon merged in a great sustained roar. The Russian tanks met the German advanced formation flat out.

"Both sides' tanks were mixed up together, and there was no opportunity, either in time or space, to disengage and reform in battle order, or to fight in battle formation."

The range was so short that the Soviet shells pierced not only the sides but the frontal armor of the German tanks. At such ranges, Rotmistrov said, armor offered no protection whatsoever. "When a tank was hit, frequently its turret was blown off and tossed through the air for dozens of yards.

"At the same time, over the battlefield furious air fighting built up, with both Russian and German airmen trying to help their own sides. Prokhorovka seemed to be permanently in the shadow of bomber, ground-attack and fighter aircraft, and one dogfight seemed to follow another without respite.

"In no time at all, the sky seemed to be palled by the smoke of the various wrecks. The earth was black and scorched, with tanks burning like torches."

Although they could not match Hoth's Tigers and firepower, the Russian T-34s used their greater agility with telling effect, wheeling to dash into the German columns from oblique angles, thereby isolating the leading Tigers from the Panthers and Mark IVs that swarmed behind them. Recalled a German tank commander: "Soon many of the T-34s had broken past our screen and were streaming like rats all over the battlefield." Amid the blinding, stifling clouds of dust flung up by churning tank tracks the struggle raged until, imperceptibly and with their guns still spewing ruin the Germans grudgingly began to give ground.

But by afternoon, although forced onto the defensive, Hausser and his SS panzer corps were holding their own. Time and again, Soviet brigades hurtled into Hausser's formations; time and again, the panzers repulsed them. From a forward position with the Das Reich Division, General Hoth peered through a telescope, then placed a call to his chief of staff back at Fourth Panzer Army headquarters: "Have you any news of Kempf? Where is his 3rd Panzer Corps?"

The answer came instantly: Word had moments before arrived that Kempf's force, with nearly 300 tanks of its 6th, 7th and 19th Panzer Divisions, was at Rzhavets, a mere 12 miles from Prokhorovka—but on the far side of the Donets.

From the moment it left its starting point below Belgorod to begin the long northeasterly swing toward its presumptive blocking position above Prokhorovka, the 3rd Panzer Corps had had to fight every inch of the way. Late on July 11, long after the time when Battle Group Kempf might possibly have prevented Rotmistrov from reinforcing Vatutin,

the corps's lead element, the 6th Panzer Division, pulled up eight miles short of the heavily defended town of Rzhavets on the Donets. Strung out in line far behind the 6th Panzer Division were the 7th and 19th Panzer Divisions.

When his divisional commander hesitated as to his next move, Major Franz Bäke, leader of a tank battalion, urged that Rzhavets be taken by ruse under cover of darkness. His commander agreed. Thus began one of World War II's weirder episodes.

Beneath a pallid moon, Bäke's battalion and another set out in a column led by a captured Soviet T-34 whose silhouette, Bäke devoutly hoped, would deceive the enemy. Past gun emplacements, past sleepy Soviet sentinels, between lines of marching men, the little column threaded its way.

"After about six miles," Bäke later recalled, "our T-34 went on strike. Moved no doubt by national sentiment, it stopped and blocked the road. So our men had to climb out of their tanks and in spite of the Russians standing all round them, watching curiously, they had to haul the T-34 off the road and push it into the ditch in order to clear the way for the rest of the formation.

"In spite of the order that not a word of German was to be spoken, a few German curses were heard. But the Russians still did not notice anything. The crew of our T-34 was picked up, and on we moved."

Nearing Rzhavets, Bäke in the command tank received a radiotelephone report from the lieutenant in charge of the lead tank: "Russian tanks coming up to meet us. What am I to do?" Answered Bäke: "Take a deep breath so I can hear it in my earphones, and start counting them."

The slow, agonizing count began: "One, two, three . . . ten . . . fifteen . . . twenty, twenty-one, twenty-two."

Almost track-to-track, the columns passed in opposite directions. Then, for no obvious reason, seven T-34s suddenly spun out of the Soviet formation and headed back toward

Lieut. General Pavel A. Rotmistrov (center), commanding officer of the Soviet Fifth Guards Tank Army, confers with subordinates at his hilltop command post during the Battle of Kursk in July of 1943. Rotmistrov's success in one of history's biggest tank-versus-tank brawls broke the German attack on the southern flank and assured the Soviet victory.

Bäke's tanks at high speed. Bäke ordered his lead tanks to head on toward Rzhavets, then turned his own vehicle to block the road. The T-34s gathered about him in a semicircle, their guns menacing at no more than 20 yards' range.

To make matters worse—much worse—Bäke's tank had only a dummy wooden gun. Like many other German command tanks, its real armament had been removed to make room in its innards for radio and other control equipment.

There was nothing for it. Bäke and his adjutant, a Lieutenant Zumpel, leaped from the tank carrying adhesive explosive charges—"sticky bombs"—which each man plastered onto a T-34. Then they both dived for the roadside ditch. *Whooomp! Whoomp!* Back out of the ditch. Two more charges were stuck on two more tanks—but this time only one *Whooomp.* A charge had failed to detonate.

Bäke and Zumpel leaped onto a German tank in the line behind theirs. "Open fire!" shouted Bäke. A T-34 burst into flames from a point-blank hit, machine guns stuttered from all sides and amid the wild confusion, Bäke and his tanks made a dash for Rzhavets. During the rest of the night they somehow managed not only to control the town but even to establish a small bridgehead across the Donets.

The rest of the 6th Panzer Division came up early the next morning. But not until late afternoon—just when Hoth needed them most—did the 7th and 19th Panzers assemble in Rzhavets.

On July 13, the 3rd Panzer Corps arrived in full force on the smoking battlefield of Prokhorovka. It found Hausser's 2nd SS Panzer Corps in possession of the ground; Rotmistrov's tanks had retired to regroup. Each side had lost at least 300 tanks. But both were still full of fight and ready to renew the battle; if they had, the accretion of 3rd Panzer Corps tanks might well have turned the conflict in Hoth's favor.

But it was all academic. Astonishingly, Adolf Hitler had on that very day ordered an end to Operation *Citadel.*

Hitler's commanders learned the reason for his order on July 13. Summoned to Rastenburg, Army Group South's Erich von Manstein and Army Group Center's Günther von Kluge found OKH and OKW staff officers moping about with dolorous faces and the Führer in foul humor.

Three days before, Allied troops had landed on Sicily and Italian resistance had folded forthwith.

"Thanks to the miserable generalship of the Italians," Hitler raged, "it is as good as certain that Sicily will be lost. Maybe Eisenhower will land tomorrow on the Italian mainland or in the Balkans; when that happens our entire European south flank will be directly threatened.

"I must prevent that. And so I need divisions for Italy from the Balkans. And since they can't be taken from any other place, they will have to be released from the Kursk front.

"Therefore I am forced to stop *Citadel.*"

Kluge was only too happy to agree. Model was bogged down, and the Soviet offensive by the West and Bryansk Fronts was already beginning to bite sharply into Army Group Center. But Manstein was aghast; he believed that a suspension of the offensive would free Soviet tank forces to attack his army group to the south. Hitler permitted Manstein's army group to continue the fight alone.

The battle dragged on for six more days, most of it in pelting rain. Major German units were transferred to Italy, arriving in plenty of time to contest the Allied campaign there.

In the battle for Kursk, German casualties included nearly 30,000 dead and more than 60,000 wounded. Russian losses were presumably at least comparable, although they have never been disclosed. But the German panzer force never recovered, and Soviet General Ivan Konev was probably right enough when he described Kursk as "the swan song of the German armor."

Even more momentous, Kursk had dislodged and set into irresistible motion the Red Army avalanche.

A CLASH OF TITANS

Advancing behind T-34 tanks, Soviet soldiers on the Kursk steppe charge toward German positions amid a hail of dirt clods kicked up by exploding shells.

TOTAL WAR ON THE STEPPE

"Until late in the evening, the unending roar of engines and the clatter of treads hung over the battlefield. Shells were bursting all around. Hundreds of tanks and self-propelled guns were in flames. Clouds of dust and smoke rose in the sky." This enormous clash, described by a Red Army general, was but one small fragment of the titanic battle for the Kursk salient, a 6,300-square-mile bulge in the German lines on the central Russian plateau.

The battle began July 5, 1943, when the Wehrmacht launched an all-out offensive against Soviet forces defending the salient between Orel in the north and Belgorod in the south. On each mile of front in the main attack areas, the Germans deployed between 5,000 and 8,000 troops, 130 artillery pieces, 30 to 40 tanks and assault guns and more than 140 squadrons of aircraft. The Germans hoped that the sheer weight of their assault force would bring them a swift victory. Instead, they found themselves locked in a nightmare struggle with even more powerful Soviet armies.

Soviet minefields channeled the advancing German formations into the Red Army artillery's fields of fire. When the panzers penetrated one line of defense, they were immediately pinned down in another. Low-flying Il-2 Stormoviks bombed them. Antitank guns and dynamite charges blew them up. Hundreds of T-34 tanks met them head on. "It was hard to tell who was attacking and who was defending," said a Soviet commander. "There was no place to maneuver. When their tanks got tangled up in our defenses, their strategy crumbled."

Both sides poured in increasing numbers of men and machines: altogether 2.2 million men, 5,000 airplanes, 6,000 armored vehicles—more than fought on the entire Western Front. For eight days the pounding continued, but the Germans could only dent the rugged Soviet defenses. Then the offensive collapsed. Wrote a retreating Wehrmacht soldier, "Now we know what total war means."

Launching the powerful German offensive near the city of Belgorod, the commander of a Waffen-SS tank unit equipped with new Panther tanks waves his troops forward. The Panthers' fuel systems were poorly protected and caught fire easily; after a few days of combat, one panzer division had only a handful of its 80 Panthers left in operation.

Red Army soldiers outside the town of Kursk dig trenches and disguise a communications center (left) with sod. Anticipating the battle, Soviet troops, assisted by 300,000 civilians, hacked out 6,000 miles of trenches.

Soviet antitank teams with their long-barreled weapons move into position south of Kursk. Their mission was to destroy German armor at close range.

Camouflaged with netting and straw, Soviet guns fire at advancing
German armor. Well-hidden artillery accounted for more than 60 per cent
of the German armor damaged or destroyed during the Kursk battle.

German 150mm field howitzers soften up the Soviet defenses to prepare
for a panzer assault. During their offensive, the Germans deployed 10,000
artillery pieces—barely one half of what the Red Army possessed.

DOGFIGHTS AND AIR-TO-GROUND ATTACKS

DOGFIGHTS AND AIR-TO-GROUND ATTACKS

A German supply column goes up in smoke after strafing attacks by
Soviet planes. During the Battle of Kursk, the Red Air Force flew 28,000
sorties and, admitted a German officer, "displayed remarkable dash."

A Soviet plane, shot down by the Luftwaffe, burns at the side of the
road as a column of German armor and trucks advances. Aerial combat
went on almost nonstop; there were as many as 200 dogfights a day.

Two panzer grenadiers watch a long line of German armor advance into
battle. To split the Soviet defenses, the Germans attacked in wedges;
Tiger tanks formed the spearheads, followed by lighter tanks and infantry.

Two Red Army infantrymen, one of them armed with an antitank rifle
and the other carrying a submachine gun, sprint past a knocked-out
German Mark III tank during a small-scale attack in the battle for Kursk.

A lucky German leaps clear of his Mark IV tank, set aflame by a Soviet shell. "When they hit one of our panzers," a crewman wrote, "there is an explosion, too loud, thank God, to let us hear the cries of the crew."

Oily black smoke pours from a burning Soviet T-34 tank. In eight days of fighting, Soviet tank strength dropped from 3,800 to 1,500. But only two weeks later, most of the disabled tanks had been repaired or replaced.

After the German retreat, Soviet officers examine an empty Ferdinand tracked vehicle, its hatch blown off by the shell that pierced its side. "Gun cartridges, rusty

weapons, torn uniforms, bloody bandages and smashed guns are scattered everywhere,'' wrote a Red Army commissar. ''The wind carries the stench of death.''

2

Slugfest for a ruined city
"Kharkov must be held at all costs"
A clash of armor in a sea of sunflowers
An urgent visit to the "Werewolf" headquarters
The race for the Dnieper
Tanks that turned into submarines
The raucous charge to Kiev
An epidemic of self-inflicted wounds
The birth of the United Nations

In one of his many moments of exasperation with Hitler's insistence on defending every acre of conquered Russian territory, Field Marshal von Manstein asked OKH a loaded question: Which was preferable—to cling precariously to the Donets region at the risk of a dangerous Soviet breakthrough or, after withdrawing in orderly fashion to prepared positions along the western bank of the Dnieper River, to bleed the Red Army as it attempted to cross that forbidding waterway?

The OKH reply was prompt, unequivocal and impossible to fulfill: "The Führer wants both"—to keep the Donets Basin and to bleed the Russians there.

Hitler got neither. In hopes of holding the rich Donets Basin despite the Wehrmacht's tremendous losses at Kursk, he would thrice turn down Manstein's pleas to withdraw Army Group South to the defense of the Dnieper River, and when he finally consented to the move, it would be too late. By the end of 1943, when the Allied Big Three met in the Iranian capital of Teheran to discuss the War and its aftermath, the line of the Dnieper—the Germans' last major defensive barrier on Russian territory—would lie in the Red Army's rear area.

The offensive that would take the Soviet armies across the Dnieper began as early as July 12—the very day that General Model's Ninth Army bogged down in its effort to burst through the hills north of Kursk. The first step was to drive the Germans from their two salients sandwiching the Kursk bulge (map, page 56).

The northern salient, centered on the city of Orel, would be attacked from the north by Lieut. General Vasily D. Sokolovsky's West Front, from Kursk in the south by Konstantin Rokossovsky's Central Front, and from the east by Lieut. General Markian M. Popov's Bryansk Front. The salient south of the Kursk bulge was to be attacked simultaneously: Nikolai Vatutin's Voronezh Front would strike south, take Belgorod and then join with Ivan Konev's Steppe Front, pouring in from the east, to recapture Kharkov. With both the Orel and the Belgorod-Kharkov salients cleared, the Red Army would erupt along a 600-mile front in its massive move toward the Dnieper.

These heady plans developed with only one brief hitch. At Stalin's office in the Kremlin, a tabletop had been littered with maps and other documents while Stalin and his top

MANSTEIN'S FLAMING RETREAT

staff officers reviewed the Orel assaults, code-named Operation *Kutuzov*. When the session ended, Lieut. General Sergei M. Shtemenko, Stavka's chief of operations, returned to his office and discovered to his horror that two key maps were missing. After searching and interrogating his fellow officers throughout the next day, Shtemenko decided there could be only one culprit. And so, screwing up his courage, he went to Stalin in quest of the maps.

"Please return them to me," said Shtemenko.

Stalin was all innocence. "What makes you think I have them?" he asked. "I have nothing here."

Shtemenko insisted, "The maps could not be anywhere else. You must have them."

Stalin, having played out one of his cruel games to test his generals, went into another room and reappeared carrying the maps.

For Operation *Kutuzov,* the Red Army amassed overwhelming superiority: 1,286,000 troops against fewer than 600,000 Germans within the Orel salient, 2,400 Russian tanks and self-propelled guns against about 1,000 for the enemy, 21,000 guns against 7,000, and more than 2,000 aircraft against 1,100.

At first light on July 12, the Soviet forces exploded from their starting lines and plunged headlong into immense thickets of man-high thistles, which had grown up everywhere on lands devastated during the German invasion in 1941. At first, the Russians made steady progress. By the night of July 13, the West Front's Eleventh Guards Army had thrust 16 miles and Bryansk Front troops had advanced about 10 miles.

But that day Hitler had placed the Second Panzer Army, protecting the northern and eastern sectors of the salient, under General Model's direct command, and though Model had not succeeded in his offensive against Kursk, he was as tenacious a defensive fighter as the War produced. Moreover, the Germans had used their long tenancy within the Orel area to good advantage, and the salient bristled with field fortifications. Despite these defenses, Orel would have to be taken by foot soldiers. Stalin, having learned from the disastrous German example at Stalingrad, laid down a general order: "A tank army shouldn't get involved in street fighting in such a large city."

For three weeks more, the opposing armies traded thud-

ding blows in a bloody slugfest, and not until the night of August 3 did the troops of three Soviet rifle divisions arrive at Orel's outskirts. The sky was glowing with the light of countless fires. The Military Council of the Bryansk Front issued an appeal to the troops to step up their already desperate efforts to "prevent the Nazi bandits from destroying our dear city entirely."

It was no use. When, after another day and night of fighting, the Russians finally fought their way into the heart of Orel, they found the city in ruins—and the Germans gone. General Model and his armies were skillfully fighting their way toward a prepared defensive line running straight south from Kirov across the western end of the Orel salient. Although the quarry had escaped, the victory was a big one for the Russians.

Meanwhile, 150 miles to the south, the offensive against Belgorod-Kharkov was delayed by Field Marshal von Manstein's continued tank offensive in the Kursk salient. His attack was not stopped until July 23, and then the Soviet forces paused to refit, regroup and refine their tactical plans.

The Soviet plan for the Belgorod-Kharkov operation was simply, in Shtemenko's words, "to smash the enemy in the Belgorod-Kharkov area, after which the way would lie open for Soviet troops to reach the Dnieper." From their concentration point northwest of Belgorod, the rifle divisions of the Soviet Fifth and Sixth Guards Armies would make the initial assaults. Once they had broken into the German lines, the crack armored corps of the First Tank and the Fifth Guards Tank Armies would rumble into the breach, fanning out south and west toward Akhtyrka, thereby outflanking Kharkov from the west. Meanwhile Konev, with three infantry armies and a mechanized corps, would drive west to seize Belgorod, then swing south and head directly for Kharkov. Just as at Orel, the Russians had a marked advantage in manpower and weaponry: nearly one million troops against 300,000; 2,400 tanks against 600; 12,000 guns against 3,500; and 1,275 aircraft against 900.

On August 2, after the lull in the heavy fighting, the Fourth Panzer Army reported to Manstein that Soviet radio traffic was extremely heavy—so heavy that a new enemy offensive was "inevitable within two or three days."

That estimate was overoptimistic: Vatutin's attack began

at dawn the next day. After only three hours, the Soviet infantry had pushed deep into the German positions. At noon, Vatutin sent his tanks surging forward, ripping a wide gap between the Fourth Panzer Army and Battle Group Kempf. The Germans tumbled back to form a new defensive line north of Kharkov. And at 6 a.m. on August 5, the same day that Orel fell, the Soviet troops broke into Belgorod.

Later that day, Stalin had a celebration in mind. He summoned two Stavka officers and asked them if they read military history. Without awaiting an answer, Stalin went on to say: "If you did read any, you would know that in ancient times, when the troops won victories, all the bells would ring in honor of the generals and their troops. And it would not be a bad idea for us to mark our victories more impressively than by merely issuing congratulatory orders."

That night, Moscow shook to the thunder of 12 salvos fired from 124 guns in celebration of the victories at Orel and Belgorod. Many citizens, awakened from their slumber and believing that an air raid was in progress, hastily took to their cellars.

Stalin promulgated an order of the day, exulting that "the German myth that Soviet troops are unable to wage a successful offensive in the summer has been dispelled." The order ended: "Eternal glory to the heroes who fell in the struggle for the freedom of our country. Death to the German invaders!" Stalin liked the ring of the words. Henceforth he would use them to conclude every announcement of a Soviet victory—more than 300 times before the end of the War.

The Red Army's successful assault on Belgorod had covered 15 miles in two days. Kharkov lay another 45 miles to the south; to reach there would take 17 days of vicious fighting.

Ironically, the Russians' drive on Kharkov almost got an assist from Hitler. After the Allied landings on Sicily on July 10 and the July 25 ouster and arrest of Benito Mussolini, the Führer issued an inexplicable if not irrational order sending the SS Das Reich and Totenkopf Divisions to Italy. But as the two powerful units began pulling out, the threat to Manstein's line and to Kharkov prompted Hitler to change his mind and cancel the order. The SS divisions returned to the front in time to help turn an impending rout into a protracted battle of attrition.

Sprawling Kharkov was about the same size as Kiev, and the two were the largest Soviet cities to be captured by the Germans during the War. In fact, the Germans had captured Kharkov, lost it, then taken it again; now Stalin wanted it back for good. "The city must fall quickly," he instructed his commanders. But Hitler meant to keep it, ordering, "Kharkov must be held at all costs."

The Russians exploited the breakthrough in the Belgorod area with bewildering speed. By August 6—the day after the capture of Belgorod—Vatutin was well on his way toward Akhtyrka, 60 miles northwest of Kharkov, in a sweeping movement to outflank the city. From the headquarters of the 48th Panzer Corps, Lieut. General Gustav Schmidt, commander of the 19th Panzer Division, was ordered to

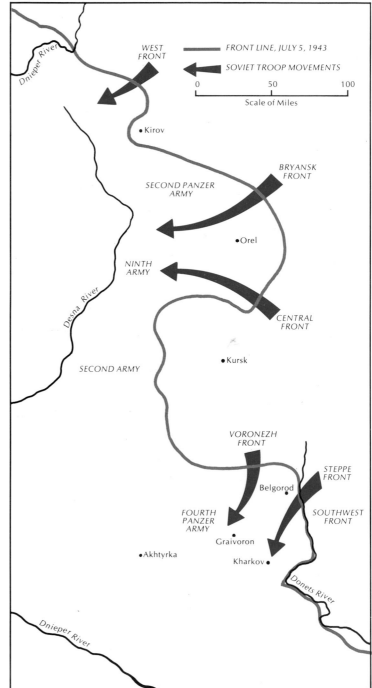

To clear the way for the drive to the Dnieper, the Soviet commanders in July 1943 planned simultaneous operations against the two German-held salients protruding on either side of the recent battleground in the Kursk area. The Orel salient to the north was to be attacked from three directions (arrows) by as many Soviet army groups. To the south, the Belgorod-Kharkov salient was to be eliminated in a pincers attack.

speed his tanks to aid the Grossdeutschland Division in setting up a blocking line between Akhtyrka and Graivoron. Unknown either to Schmidt or to corps headquarters, Soviet troops were already swarming through the area.

On the morning of August 7, Schmidt was at the head of his column when a storm of antitank fire came from the woods on both sides of the road, isolating his tank from those behind. Schmidt, his aides and the tank's crew dived for a ditch and then, when Soviet T-34s approached, made a dash for the woods. The division's chief of operations was killed on the way by machine-gun fire, but Schmidt, his aide-de-camp, a Lieutenant Köhne, and two enlisted men managed to reach the forest. They thought they were safe until they spotted a number of Soviet infantrymen deploying to search for them.

"We haven't a hope," General Schmidt told the enlisted men. "You two try to get through. Lieutenant Köhne and I will try to divert the Russians and give you fire cover."

When the enlisted men left, Schmidt and Köhne each had only four rounds remaining in their pistols. Later, after being taken prisoner by the Soviets, the enlisted men were escorted back to the scene where Schmidt and Köhne now lay twisted in death. With their captors looking on, the two Germans buried their officers.

Surrounded by Soviet tanks and infantry, many men of the 19th Panzer Division were killed or wounded manning a circular defense line. But the survivors concentrated their strength in the west and finally broke out. They drove through a narrow corridor and joined the Grossdeutschland Division at Akhtyrka.

With their help, the 48th Panzer Corps blocked Vatutin between Akhtyrka and Sumy. But on August 10 a major threat against Kharkov came from the east. In the Soviet path, at the juncture of the German 11th and 42nd Corps, stood the raw 282nd Infantry Division, which had been organized in 1942 for police duty in France and was ignorant of the cruelties of fighting in the East. Assaulted by powerful Soviet armor of Konev's Steppe Front, the 282nd broke. The division's chief of operations tried to stem the tide of T-34s with his pistol and was casually crushed by a tank. The Russians crashed into Kharkov's eastern outskirts, where they captured a tractor factory.

At Manstein's headquarters, officers discussed reviving the ancient Romans' grim custom of discipline by decimation—executing every 10th survivor of the 282nd Division as an example to the rest of the Army. The idea was dropped when the 6th Panzer Division drove the Russians out of the tractor factory and repaired the ruptured German line.

Thwarted in the east and stalled at Akhtyrka, General Vatutin now wheeled around General Rotmistrov's renowned Fifth Guards Tank Army to try its luck at Kharkov from the northwest. Awaiting the Guardsmen on Kharkov's outer defense belt was General Erhard Raus, a tough Austrian whose 11th Corps had the main burden of carrying out Hitler's obstinate order to hold Kharkov to the last.

For that thankless job, Raus had the 6th Panzer Division, five infantry divisions and, just coming up, the SS Das Reich Division with its Tiger and Panther tanks. Raus stationed his forces in depth behind a yellow sea of giant sunflowers. On the morning of August 19, Rotmistrov attacked head on and throttles out.

The Soviet tanks came in three wedge formations, slashing broad swaths through the sunflowers. The German guns blazed and the Russians reeled back, leaving behind them no fewer than 184 wrecked T-34s. Next day Rotmistrov struck again, this time with 200 T-34s in a single, massive wedge. Through the field of sunflowers they roared—and again they fell back before a solid sheet of German fire. About 150 blazing Soviet tanks dotted the battlefield.

Rotmistrov dug deeper into his seemingly inexhaustible resources, and at midnight on August 20 he returned with 160 tanks. In a wild melee Soviet and German tanks fired at murderously close range, sometimes colliding with a screech of metal as they surged and swirled in the darkness. After three hours, with both sides exhausted, an eerie quiet descended upon the field.

When the sun rose next morning, at least 80 more Soviet tanks lay smoking amid the carnage. The rest of Rotmistrov's force had retired—all but three T-34s. These tanks had somehow blasted their way into Kharkov, where they were soon put out of action by an antitank unit guarding a division headquarters.

The victors were hardly better off than the vanquished: The 6th Panzer Division had only 15 tanks still operational, a reconnaissance battalion was down to 80 men and a gren-

Workers line up for a construction detail outside one of Stalingrad's tent dormitories. More than 200,000 people took part in rebuilding the city.

Metalworkers use an American-made I-beam as a workbench in the tractor factory. Workers hauled away 5,000 carloads of debris from this site.

Women salvage bricks from the ruins of a Stalingrad water tower.

A lineman tests a connection. By March 15, phones were in operation.

STALINGRAD REBUILT

"Stalingrad has been laid bare," wrote a visitor in February 1943, shortly after the Red Army had wrested it from the Germans in an epic five-month struggle. "In every direction, the ruins of walls rear up, the sinister architecture of a ruined city." Stalingrad was 99 per cent destroyed.

But a city so important to the Russians —emotionally as well as economically— could not be left in ruins. On February 4, just two days after the bombing and shelling ceased, the rebuilding effort got under way. From all over the Soviet Union came thousands of volunteer workers, many of them women. With them came a steady stream of supplies: building materials from Kazan, thousands of head of cattle from Azerbaijan and 50 combine harvester motors from Gorky to help revive the produc-

tivity of once-rich collective farms nearby. Before the reconstruction work could begin, however, everyone had to pitch in to find and bury the bodies of those who had died with the city.

Until better facilities could be devised, workers lived in tents, wattle huts, dugouts and cellars, hauling water from the Volga and cooking over campfires. They rejoiced in the first semblances of normal life. A *Pravda* reporter wrote, "Even the opening of a newspaper stand is an event."

But the restoration of factories, hospitals and clinics took priority, and the job was done at a prodigious pace. On the 12th of June, workers at the reopened Stalingrad tractor factory finished their first job—repairing some battle-damaged tanks. Stalingrad was back in the War.

adier regiment had only 200 survivors. Obviously, Raus could not withstand another such blow. Field Marshal von Manstein now determined to abandon Kharkov. Unless he withdrew, Raus's 11th Corps would surely be trapped and the Soviets would be able to roll almost unimpeded to the southwest, circling behind and cutting off the German Eighth Army—formerly Battle Group Kempf. It would be another Stalingrad, and Manstein had no intention of risking such a catastrophe. "I'd rather lose a city than an army," he told his chief of staff.

Informed of Manstein's decision, Hitler all but begged him to change his mind. "The fall of the city could have serious political repercussions," he told Manstein. "The attitude of the Turks depends on it. And Bulgaria's attitude. If we abandon Kharkov we'll lose face in Ankara and Sofia."

Erich von Manstein was unimpressed by such esoteric considerations. On August 22, with Hitler's resentful permission, he ordered Raus out of Kharkov—and the ruined city changed hands for the last time.

Manstein's problems were far from over, however. Even as Kharkov was being evacuated, a new crisis arose far to the south. There, Lieut. General F. I. Tolbukhin's Southern Front mounted a furious attack on the German Sixth Army, a replacement force that was supposed to extirpate the humiliation of the original Sixth Army's surrender at Stalingrad. When Manstein withdrew essential reserves to the north for the Kharkov battle, the Sixth Army was left hanging by its fingernails to the line of the Mius River. If Tolbukhin could break through, he not only would have a clear run to the Dnieper but could seal off both the Crimea and the German Seventeenth Army in the Taman Peninsula bridgehead.

Manstein therefore gave Hitler an ultimatum: Either send half a dozen panzer divisions or authorize the Sixth Army to withdraw westward. "I request freedom of movement," he said. To Adolf Hitler, such words were anathema, and from the Führer's East Prussian headquarters came a quick reply: "Don't do anything. I am coming myself."

They met on August 27 at Vinnitsa, the southwest Ukrainian headquarters, code-named Werewolf, where Hitler had presided over his 1942 summer offensive. Closed in by a dense pine forest, the blockhouses were stifling in summertime—and heat had always made Hitler peevish. Today, however, the Führer kept his temper in check and seemed perplexed by the plight of his armies.

Hitler had brought only a few staffers in his four-engined Condor. With Manstein had come his army commanders, including Colonel General Kar Hollidt of the afflicted Sixth Army. Manstein began by reciting his manpower shortages: The First Panzer Army between July 17 and August 21 had lost 27,291 men and had received only 6,174 replacements; during that same period, the Sixth Army had suffered losses of 23,830 and had been given only 3,312 in return; in all, Army Group South over the last few months had suffered a net loss of 100,000 men.

Finishing his gloomy litany, Manstein turned to the Sixth Army commander and said: "General Hollidt, will you please give the Führer a comparative picture of the enemy's and our own strength?"

Hollidt knew the sorry statistics by heart: "My 29th Corps has 8,706 men left. Facing it are 69,000 Russians. My 17th Corps has 9,284 men; facing it are 49,500 Russians. My 4th Corps is relatively best off—it has 13,143 men faced by 18,000 Russians. Altogether 31,133 Germans against 136,500 Russians. The relative strength in tanks is similar: Tolbukhin yesterday had 165 tanks in operation; we had seven tanks and 38 assault guns."

Manstein summed up his case for Hitler: "Either you let us have fresh forces, and that means 12 divisions, or the Donets region must be abandoned. I see no other solution."

"Where am I to find reinforcements?" Hitler asked.

Said Manstein, "Get Army Groups Center and North to make available any formations they can possibly spare, my Führer, so that we may employ them here, at the focal point of the Soviet offensive."

Hitler hemmed and hawed. "I need to think about it," he said. But Manstein insisted that the time for meditation had run out, and Hitler finally agreed to order the transfer of several divisions to Manstein's Army Group South from Field Marshal Kluge's Army Group Center.

But the next day, Soviet forces attacked Army Group Center, mauling the Second and Fourth Armies. Hitler's promise was a dead letter; Manstein would get no reinforcements from Kluge, whose troubles were nearly as bad as his own.

At the same time, two Soviet mechanized corps sliced through Hollidt's line on the Mius and swung south, isolating the German 29th Corps and pinning it to the Sea of Azov. As the situation worsened, Manstein called Kluge by telephone and the two agreed to fly to see Hitler on September 3 at the Wolf's Lair headquarters in East Prussia.

The field marshals had high aspirations—and made modest gains. Fed up with the schizophrenic bickerings of the German High Command as represented by the rival OKH and OKW, Manstein and Kluge urged that an integrated grand general staff be established to direct the entire German war effort. It would come under a single, militarily professional supreme commander—a function now fulfilled by Hitler himself. They also asked that a military man be given responsibilty for all operations in the East—another job that Hitler had delegated to himself.

To both requests, Hitler's answer was entirely predictable: No. The Führer did agree, however, to let Kluge pull back the southern wing of Army Group Center, now under heavy Soviet pressure, across the Desna River, a tributary of the Dnieper. He also consented to move the Seventeenth Army to the Crimea, relinquishing the Taman Peninsula bridgehead that he had previously insisted on holding in hopes that it might one day be used as a launching point for a return to the Caucasus. And, if it became absolutely necessary, Manstein would at least be permitted to withdraw the Sixth Army from the Mius to a prepared defensive line 40 miles to the west.

Later that same day came word that Allied armies had landed on the toe of Italy. As if in exultant celebration, the Red Army soon renewed its offensive. Lieut. General Rodion Y. Malinovsky's Southwest Front cracked the joint between the First Panzer and Sixth Armies and raced beyond Hollidt's sketchy new defensive line. To the north, Rokossovsky's Central Front knifed through the Second Army at the junction of Army Group Center and Army Group South.

Manstein, his northern flank now exposed, signaled Hitler, "I need reinforcements or a free hand for a further withdrawal to shortened, more favorable sectors." The response was a flying visit by Hitler to Manstein's headquarters at Zaporozhye on September 8—the third confrontation between the two in less than two weeks.

This time, Manstein, after reviewing the situation on a map, said without qualification: "Whether we like it or not, we've got to move back."

Asked Hitler, "What do you propose?"

Said Manstein: "I propose to pull Army Group Center back to the Dnieper at once. With the forces thus saved, the Dnieper line, including the approaches to the Crimea on the lower Dnieper, can be strengthened and held."

Hitler replied, "No! I will not withdraw Army Group Center behind the Dnieper."

As a sop, Hitler promised to give Manstein two panzer divisions and two infantry divisions from Army Group Center. But Kluge, still cruelly pressed, simply could not detach the units, and the next day Manstein, in despair, telephoned OKH Chief of Staff Zeitzler, "Kindly inform the Führer that he may expect the beginning of a disastrous Soviet breakthrough to the Dnieper at any moment."

The disaster came on September 14; divisions of Vatutin's Voronezh Front shattered Manstein's northern wing, swept southwest and soon reached Okop, 75 miles from Cherkassy on the Dnieper River's great bend. Farther to the north, troops of Rokossovsky's Central Front probed within 46 miles of Kiev.

"Tomorrow morning," Manstein informed Hitler's headquarters, "I shall order Fourth Panzer Army to withdraw to the Dnieper on both sides of Kiev in order to prevent the

The commanding officer of Army Group South, Field Marshal Erich von Manstein, greets Adolf Hitler on an airfield in the Ukraine on the 8th of September, 1943. In talks later that day, Manstein pleaded desperately for either reinforcements or permission to retreat, but the Führer refused both of his requests.

army from being encircled in small groups and smashed in front of the river."

At a Wolf's Lair conference with Manstein the following day, the Führer had no real alternative but to give his consent to the retreat. And the race for the Dnieper River bridges began.

In its advance to the Dnieper, the Red Army juggernaut was far from fancy. Unlike the Germans, who were partial to sophisticated maneuvers aimed at encircling large numbers of Russians, the Soviet forces simply tried to shoulder the enemy aside by sheer weight of men and metal. They had plenty of both.

By the summer of 1943 the Russians had perhaps six million men in the line of battle stretching from northern Finland to the Caucasus; Stavka reserves amounted to approximately one million more, grouped in at least 11 armies. The Germans had only about 3.5 million troops assigned to the Eastern Front.

The Red Army's greatest strength lay in some 400 infantry divisions. This enormous reservoir of manpower gave the Red Army the ability to muster crushing numerical superiority at key points. To win a victory, Soviet generals expended their manpower freely, and the infantrymen went out to die without protest, charging into machine-gun fire or through known minefields. To the Germans, there was something terrible about the stoicism of the Soviet soldier. Wrote Colonel von Mellenthin: "To step on walls of dead, composed of the bodies of his former friends and companions, makes not the slightest impression on him and does not upset his equanimity at all; without so much as blinking an eyelid he stolidly continues the attack."

Yet the Soviet infantryman was a limiting factor. After the other branches of the Army had taken the better-educated, more capable men, the infantry got what was left over: many illiterate peasants, the underage, the overage and, by reason of the polyglot nature of the Soviet Union, large numbers of men who neither spoke nor understood Russian. The quality of the infantry was further diluted by the Army's policy of impressing men found in newly liberated areas. Hundreds of thousands of such recruits were sent into action with only the sketchiest training. "These men," said a German corps commander, "were not 100 per cent sol-

diers, but they ran along with the rest, they burst into the gaps in the line and flooded us."

Sensibly enough, Stalin and Stavka were reluctant to undertake operations that required difficult infantry maneuvers. Even simple infantry tactics might fail, but with the Soviets' overwhelming manpower edge, attrition alone could defeat the Germans.

The Russians also had a wide and increasing edge in matériel. By the summer of 1943 they possessed more than 10,000 tanks, whereas the German armies fighting in the East had scarcely more than 3,000 tanks. The annual rate of Soviet production was fast approaching 24,000 tanks and self-propelled guns and 35,000 aircraft, compared with the Germans' 19,800 tanks and self-propelled guns and 25,000 planes. And in addition to the production of its own factories, the Soviet Union during the last year had received shipments totaling 7,500 tanks and 2,500 aircraft from the United States and Great Britain under the terms of the Lend-Lease program.

By mid-1943, the Red Army possessed probably the world's largest artillery arm. It had 105,000 field guns and heavy mortars against an estimated 54,000 for the Germans. It had enough 76mm and 45mm guns to equip 20 antitank artillery brigades and 164 separate antitank artillery regiments. The standard issue of big guns and heavy mortars was increasing, and Soviet ordnance was just completing the development of two heavy antitank guns, a 122mm and a long-barreled 100mm.

During the first two years of the War, the Red Army had been much less mobile than the Germans. But the Russians were now receiving large numbers of American-made vehicles, by far the most valuable commodity provided by Lend-Lease. In the year ending in July 1943, the Russians received 120,000 trucks plus 24,000 scout cars and jeeps. The next year they would get 122,000 more trucks.

The bulk of the manpower and matériel was brought to bear during the great Soviet offensive to the Dnieper. Involved were 50 armies, which were divided into eight fronts; in linear terms, each front had an army for every 12 miles of the original 600-mile line of battle. The mission of the armies was to push almost due west on 14 parallel lines of advance. They were unable to kick off simultaneously, and for several weeks the fighting front was rocked continually with explosions that came like a string of giant fire-crackers as one army after another roared into the attack behind a storm of shellfire.

Hitler bowed to urgent necessity, permitting Manstein and Kluge to set their forces in motion toward the Dnieper. Kluge's Army Group Center gave ground slowly and stubbornly, retreating an average of about two and a half miles a day. But Manstein's Army Group South was under much greater pressure.

Standing square in the path of the onrushing mastodon, Manstein faced an appalling combination of difficulties: He had to synchronize his withdrawal on a broad front, over a woefully inadequate road system, amid a large and hostile population and under steady harassment from an enemy superior in all arms. His problems were compounded by Hitler's refusal to consider the idea of retreat until the last minute. Had the withdrawal been planned in advance, roads and river crossings could have been improved, transportation and traffic control arrangements developed, defensive positions prepared, demolitions and minefields emplaced—all this done systematically rather than piecemeal and in great haste.

In the absence of such preparations, Army Group South was in great peril. Colonel von Mellenthin of the 48th Panzer Corps remembered, ''There was no longer a coherent front and Russian mobile units were already operating far in our rear. We had to get back to the Dnieper as quickly as possible, and grave risks and heavy sacrifices had to be readily accepted.''

The average distance between Manstein's positions on September 15 and the far side of the Dnieper was about 100 miles. On Manstein's southern flank, the Sixth Army would remain east of the Dnieper as a rear guard. But the Eighth Army, the First Panzer and the Fourth Panzer Armies, with a total of about 750,000 soldiers and civilian employees, would be crowded across only six bridges on a 280-mile stretch of the river. Once across, they would have to redeploy at top speed to defend 400 miles of the Dnieper against Soviet attempts to force crossings.

Burdened by some 200,000 wounded, impeded by the hordes of refugees fleeing the oncoming tide of destruction, plagued by partisans and Soviet vanguards, the troops of Army Group South plodded westward in painful fits and starts. A German lieutenant wrote, ''Everyone is making for the great river, which we hope''—and here he expressed the thought foremost in every mind—''will give us a safe defensive line again.''

Although the river itself was a formidable defensive asset, it by no means assured safety. There had been talk of an East Wall—a mighty Dnieper rampart similar to the West Wall (Siegfried Line), which had been in place since the 1930s, and the Atlantic Wall, then being built along the English Channel and France's Atlantic coast. Indeed, even as Army Group South retreated, Luftwaffe planes showered the advancing Russians with propaganda leaflets claiming that ''Germany has clad the west bank of the Dnieper in concrete and shod it with iron. We have created an eastern rampart there, as impregnable as our West Wall. You are being sent to your deaths.''

In fact, Hitler had put off building the East Wall. He said, ''The knowledge that there is a well-established fortified line behind them merely induces my generals and troops to take to their heels.'' Discouraged by the Führer's opposition, OKH had delayed completing a study of possible Dnieper fortifications until August 1943, and construction had barely begun when Manstein's beleaguered soldiers neared their presumed west-bank haven.

More to Hitler's taste than defensive works was his Operation *Scorched Earth (pages 72-83)*. German Army commanders were ordered to carry off all foodstuffs, livestock, raw materials, agricultural machinery, arms-manufacturing tools—and Russians fit for military duty or war work. That done, a broad belt of land along the east bank of the Dnieper was declared a waste zone where everything that could not be removed was to be destroyed—or, by German euphemism, ''sterilized.''

Since it took time to spread ruin and the Germans had no time to spare, Manstein ordered that the edict cover only resources of military value. German military analysts estimated that the retreating armies gathered up more than 350,000 cattle and horses and 268,000 tons of grain, and destroyed 13,000 cattle and 941,000 tons of grain. Many factories, power plants, railroads and bridges were demolished. Some 280,000 people were transported by the Germans.

All the while that Manstein was struggling to reach the

Dnieper, Stalin was flogging his armies to greater efforts in their race to beat the Germans to the river. Once, when Vatutin seemed to be lagging, Stalin sent him a menacing memo: "I am once again compelled to point out to you inadmissible mistakes, which you have more than once perpetrated in carrying out operations."

Just in case the stick failed to produce the desired results, Stalin also offered quantities of carrots. Officers and men who were instrumental in achieving crossings of the Desna and the Dnieper would receive medals. The awards were generally unegalitarian: for army commanders, the Order of Suvorov, First Class; for division and brigade commanders, the Order of Suvorov, Second Class; for regimental and battalion officers, the Order of Suvorov, Third Class. But even men of lower ranks who distinguished themselves in the passage of the Dnieper would be proclaimed Heroes of the Soviet Union—the highest decoration, and an honor earned by more than 2,000 soldiers.

Much of the race was run on a muddy track, with unseasonable rains miring machines and men. The results were a photo finish. On September 21, the Fourth Panzer Army's 24th Corps, with the Soviet Third Guards Tank Army hard at its heels, began to cross the Dnieper at Kanev, 65 miles south of Kiev. Shortly before 4 o'clock that afternoon, German monitors intercepted an uncoded radio message from a partisan band, reporting that there were no Germans in the so-called Bukrin Bend of the Dnieper, 10 miles north of Kanev. German troops were swiftly sent off in that direction.

Of course the Russians had also heeded the partisans' message. Around midnight, the call of a bittern sounded three times on the Soviet side of the river. The calls were a signal from Guards Private I. D. Semyonov, crouched amid the reeds on the marshy ground. Three other soldiers crept up to join Semyonov and an unknown partisan. Silently, with sacks wrapped around their oars and their submachine guns swaddled in cloth, the group crossed the Dnieper in a skiff that had been hidden among the reeds. About 120 partisans and the bulk of a submachine-gun company followed soon after, and next morning most of a battalion came across. The Russians had their bridgehead on the far side of the Dnieper—and they were already prepared to try to expand it by dramatic means.

To exploit a bridgehead when and if Soviet ground forces seized one, Stavka had readied three paratroop brigades. The Red Army had experimented with airborne operations as early as 1932, but this would be the first large-scale Soviet drop under combat conditions. It would also be the last.

By September 24, the Russians had expanded the Bukrin bridgehead to a depth of three miles and a width of four miles, and they were more than holding their own against the Germans sent to dislodge them. Late that afternoon, Soviet transport planes in large numbers flew over the Bukrin Bend at 2,000 feet or a little higher. Parachutes bloomed. Disaster followed.

"The Soviet formation," recalled the 19th Panzer Division's chief of operations, "was very open—the big machines arrived singly, or two at a time at the most, at intervals of half a minute, and so dropped their parachutists. Our devastating defensive fire and the brilliant white flares that were zooming up everywhere clearly unnerved the Soviets. They were now dropping their men haphazardly, all over the place. Split up into small and very small groups, they were doomed."

The operation was botched from beginning to end. Many of the paratroopers were poorly trained, and half had never jumped before. Many of the troopers had been dropped di-

Riding a jury-rigged raft, Soviet soldiers cross the Dnieper under German fire. At the Lyutezh crossing, according to a Soviet account, the Red Army troops were ferried by a wizened peasant woman who said to them: "Even though I am old, I still have enough strength left to help you, my sons."

rectly over the 10th Panzer Grenadier Division as it moved toward the bridgehead; most of these men were shot before they hit the ground. Others came down among elements of the 19th Panzer Division and were also quickly exterminated. Of the 7,000 who had embarked on the mission, only 2,300 survived to join partisan groups in the forests.

While Stalin raged at the fiasco, Red Army pressure against the river barrier continued to build. One way or another, riding on skiffs or crude rafts, clinging to empty metal drums and doorframes and garden benches, Soviet troops crossed the Dnieper and established 23 bridgeheads before the end of September. But all were relatively small, and try as they might, the Soviet troops were unable to break out through the intense German resistance. The shortage of bridges slowed down Soviet efforts to bring across tanks and mechanized infantry.

Despite the airdrop calamity, the Bukrin bridgehead still struck Stalin as the most promising one. When Marshal Zhukov and Stavka warned him that the terrain there was too rough for tanks or any other kind of mobile operations, Stalin scoffed at them: "You're giving up before you have even tried to launch a proper attack." The Twenty-seventh and Fortieth Armies, together with all the infantry of the Third Guards Tank Army, were herded into the bridgehead, which measured 6.5 miles wide and 3.5 miles deep by the end of a week. And there they stayed in spite of their repeated attempts to burst through the crack German 24th and 48th Panzer Corps.

All but ignored in the Russians' preoccupation with the Bukrin Bend was a Dnieper River crossing pioneered by a tiny advance unit of the Soviet Thirty-eighth Army. Yet that inconspicuous bridgehead would eventually provide the key to Kiev, the capital of the Ukraine.

On the night of September 26, three small units from the Soviet 240th Rifle Division tried to cross the Dnieper at Lyutezh, a village 12 miles north of Kiev and about 10 miles above the confluence of the Dnieper and the Desna. All three groups were spotted in midstream by German machine gunners and were forced to row for their lives back to their own bank.

But at about 4 a.m., 22 men of a platoon led by Sergeant P. P. Nefedov succeeded in bringing four fishing boats to the west bank. With a modest arsenal of five carbines, eight submachine guns, a light and a heavy machine gun, they took up a strong position on a steep slope about 200 yards from the river. Throughout that day the Germans tried to pry the lonely group from its little foothold. They attacked at platoon strength and at company strength. At the coming of dark, Nefedov had only 10 men alive. That night, however, the 240th Rifle Division pushed 75 more men across, and by September 30 two infantry regiments and part of a heavy mortar regiment were lodged in the Lyutezh bridgehead. They were unable to enlarge their position in the face of burgeoning enemy strength until October 3, when their small success finally caught the eye of Voronezh Front commander Vatutin.

The general was unenthusiastic about the prospects for Lyutezh. To develop the bridgehead he would require a massive infusion of armor, and so far he had been unsuccessful at getting large numbers of tanks across the Dnieper. Nonetheless, he decided to give it a good try.

Vatutin summoned Lieut. General A. G. Kravchenko, commander of the Fifth Guards's tank corps, to his headquarters and explained the situation. He noted that Kravchenko's tanks—presently located in a forest a few miles south of the Desna—would have to cross that river, which was more than 300 yards wide at that point, before advancing to the Dnieper. "We've no other choice," said Vatutin. "You've got to find a ford."

With the aid of some Desna fishermen, Kravchenko located a place where the river was only seven feet deep. But that was considerably more than the wading depth of the T-34s. "We therefore had to turn our tanks into makeshift submarines," Kravchenko later wrote. "All slits, hatches and covers on the tank hulls and the turrets were made watertight with putty or pitch, and moreover covered with oiled canvas. The air entered the engine by way of the hatch covers and the exhaust gases were let out through a vertical extension to the exhaust tube. The ford was marked out by two rows of posts.

"The tanks then drove off in low gear through the strange corridor, the drivers steering blind to the orders of their commanders, who sat in the turrets."

Ninety T-34s safely splashed across the Desna—only to face the far wider, deeper Dnieper a few miles beyond. The

Dnieper crossing was accomplished more easily than anyone had a right to expect. Soviet troops found two large barges that the Germans had left behind; both were damaged but still able to carry three tanks each. On the night of October 5, ten crossings were made, ferrying 60 tanks. During the next day, with the remainder of the tanks following, the Lyutezh bridgehead was expanded to a width of six miles and a depth of four. There it was contained by the Germans. To go farther, Kravchenko would require more armor—much more.

Stalin and Stavka, however, were still intent on Bukrin, and they kept hammering away at the encircling Germans all through the first half of October. On the 18th, Vatutin's political commissar, Lieut. General Nikita Khrushchev, reported to Stavka that Lyutezh offered hope for a breakout. Stavka ignored the message. A few days later Khrushchev wrote again, arguing more strongly that a decisive success might be achieved if a tank army could be transferred to the Lyutezh sector.

By then, Stavka had decided that the Bukrin bridgehead was a hopeless case. It now agreed to switch the focus of the Dnieper offensive from Bukrin to Lyutezh—with the splendid Third Guards Tank Army, which had been stalled for a month in the Bukrin area, assigned to the new job.

The task of disengaging and moving the huge army was dangerous and delicate, but the Soviet commanders handled it like masters—aided by the weather. "Pouring rain reduced visibility and muffled the noise," wrote Vatutin's deputy commander, Lieut. General Andrei A. Grechko. "The troops rested during the day and marched at night. There were four march routes, all of them parallel to the front line. They made it in seven nights. Elaborate security measures were taken. There was a complete ban on radio traffic for the formations on the march. On the other hand, all communications of the Third Guards Tank Army were left behind in the Bukrin bridgehead and they kept up a busy radio traffic. In the old positions the withdrawn tanks and vehicles were replaced by dummies."

Into the Lyutezh bridgehead Vatutin crammed an awesome mass of firepower, including 2,000 cannon and mor-

tars and 500 rocket launchers—which averaged out at one cannon or mortar for every 10 feet of the bridgehead's perimeter. At dawn on November 3, after an earth-shaking 40-minute bombardment, Vatutin attacked with six rifle divisions of the Thirty-eighth Army, which had seized the bridgehead in the first place, and a tank corps of the Fifth Guards Tank Army.

There was no pretense at finesse. After his first waves punched a six-mile hole in the reeling ranks of three German infantry divisions, Vatutin poured in his reserves. On the night of November 4, the armor of the Third Guards Tank Army, which had crossed the Dnieper on pontoon bridges, staged one of the War's wildest charges: With the soldiers of two rifle divisions riding on their hulls, the tanks smashed into the remnants of the German line with headlights on, sirens howling and guns blazing. Roaring into the open, they swung south—toward Kiev.

The attack never stopped. After nightfall on November 5 the Third Guards Tank Army was passing west of Kiev, cutting roads and railroads, and the Thirty-eighth Army was at the city's northern outskirts. Shortly after midnight, a submachine-gun detachment raised the Red Flag over the building that had once been the headquarters of the Ukrainian Communist Party.

On November 7, 1943, the Red Army was in complete control of Kiev and the Third Guards Tank Army was already speeding toward Fastov, an important rail junction 40 miles to the southwest.

Reflecting their changed geographic situations, the Soviet army groups had by now been renamed: Rokossovsky's Central Front was designated the Belorussian Front; the four great forces to Rokossovsky's south—Vatutin's Voronezh Front, Konev's Steppe Front, Malinovsky's Southwest Front and Tolbukhin's South Front—became respectively the First, Second, Third and Fourth Ukrainian Fronts.

On the German side, the weeks of defeat and retreat had caused a noticeable decline in morale. One sure sign was an increase in incidents of self-inflicted wounds; men desperate to escape further service in the East were shooting themselves, mostly in the hand. "In such cases of point-blank injury," a German medical officer wrote, "the edges of the wound are usually serrated in a characteristic manner: There are traces of blackened powder all around the wound and the fine hairs of the skin have been singed. All such cases had to be reported and they usually ended with a court-martial and a firing squad."

Yet when opportunity arose, the Germans could still deliver a sting. Vatutin repeated the mistake he had made in his abortive offensive the previous winter and split his forces west of the Dnieper. While the Third Guards Tank Army was securing Fastov, the First Guards Tank Army captured Zhitomir, 45 miles away, and its isolated position attracted the attention of Colonel General Hermann Hoth's Fourth Panzer Army. Hoth attacked on November 14, and five days later knocked the First Guards Tank Army out of the city it had just captured. For all his pains, Hoth was later fired by Hitler for failing to recapture Kiev. The Führer called the canny veteran "a bird of ill omen."

Meanwhile the loss of Zhitomir very nearly cost Vatutin his command. Stalin ordered Konstantin Rokossovsky to the First Ukrainian Front headquarters with instructions to relieve Vatutin if it seemed advisable. It was an awkward meeting. Recalled Rokossovsky: "Vatutin, forewarned of my arrival, met me with a group of staff officers. He looked worried. At first he refused to be drawn into a friendly discussion, though I kept stressing that I regarded our meeting as no more than that of two comrades, the commanders of neighboring fronts."

Discovering that Rokossovsky was not bearing a hatchet, Vatutin warmed up. The two finally decided that no great harm had been done: The two Soviet tank armies could handle the Fourth Panzer Army. And anyhow, there would be few major military movements for a while. The Russian mud was beginning to freeze.

As the year neared its end, the German defense line on the Dnieper was a thing of the past; it had begun to crumble with the fall of Kiev, and Manstein held only a 50-mile stretch upstream from Cherkassy.

For a time, the fighting was overshadowed by top-level Allied diplomacy.

On November 28, 1943, Franklin D. Roosevelt, Josef Stalin and Winston Churchill met in Teheran to settle matters vital to the future. The groundwork for their visit had been laid the previous month at a Moscow conference in which Soviet Foreign Minister Vyacheslav M. Molotov was host to U.S.

Fireworks light up the night as Moscow stages a double celebration on November 7, 1943, in honor of the 26th anniversary of the Bolshevik Revolution—and the Red Army's liberation of Kiev the day before.

A CASE OF MASS MURDER

On April 13, 1943, Radio Berlin broadcast news of "a most horrific discovery": In the Katyn Forest outside the city of Smolensk, authorities of the German Occupation uncovered "a great pit filled with layers of bodies of Polish officers." The Germans said that the Poles had been shot by the Russians. Moscow quickly retorted that Germans had perpetrated the massacre late in June of 1941, in the course of their invasion of the Soviet Union.

The Germans went to great lengths to prove their charge. They chose a mixed panel to investigate the killings, including an anti-Nazi pathologist from Switzerland and even some Allied prisoners of war. At the site of the massacre, the Germans showed many documents taken from 4,143 bodies, none dated later than May 6, 1941, when the Russians were still in control of Smolensk. The Germans produced witnesses who had seen Soviet troops trucking Polish prisoners toward the forest. The doctors agreed that the bodies had been in the ground for at least three years.

When the Russians recaptured the area in September of 1943, they conducted their own investigation. They showed a few Polish letters dated about the time the Germans took Smolensk.

The same witnesses who had testified against the Russians now declared that the troops they had seen taking prisoners to the Katyn Forest were actually not Red Army soldiers, but Germans.

The Americans and British avoided questioning the Soviet account of the massacre closely; they wanted no dissension among the Allies. But one of the American prisoners of war who had attended the German probe later wrote: "We pursued every line of attack to weaken the German story and avoid the conclusion that the Russians had done the killing. I decided finally that for once the Germans weren't lying."

A pathologist dissects a body exhumed at Katyn during the German investigation. All of the victims had been shot in the back of the head.

Secretary of State Cordell Hull and British Foreign Secretary Anthony Eden.

For the Moscow sessions, the Soviet leaders had prepared an agenda with only one topic for discussion: "Ways and Means of Hastening the Conclusion of the War." In plain language, the Russians wished to talk about nothing but the Western Allies' plans to open a second front in Western Europe in 1944. The Americans and the British, who had been promising a second front since 1942, pledged that a cross-Channel invasion of France would be launched in the spring. Molotov was satisfied.

Cordell Hull and Roosevelt attached the highest priority to a Four-Power Declaration—to be signed by the United States, Great Britain, the Soviet Union and China—on the necessity of establishing a postwar international peace-keeping oranizaton. After muttering about the inclusion of China among the major powers and aspersing the efficacy of peace-keeping efforts, Molotov agreed to the declaration—and the United Nations took form as a healthy embryo. "It was," wrote a member of the American delegation, "the crowning achievement of Secretary Hull's career." Like Molotov, Cordell Hull was pleased.

Not so Anthony Eden. He had set out for Moscow deeply concerned about the postwar status of the nations of Eastern Europe. He desired especially to work out agreements concerning the future independence of Poland, that horribly abused nation on whose behalf Great Britain had gone to war. Exacerbating Eden's anxieties was the fact that relations between the Soviet Union and the Polish government-in-exile in London had recently taken an ugly turn.

The trouble arose from one of the War's most gruesome discoveries and dated back to 1939, when Hitler and Stalin joined as allies in the dismemberment of Poland. Some 250,000 Poles, including about 10,000 military officers, had been transported as prisoners of war to the Soviet Union. But in 1941, after Hitler invaded the Soviet Union, the Russians signed an agreement with the London Poles granting "amnesty to all Polish citizens who are at present deprived of their freedom on the territory of the U.S.S.R."

That was fine—except that about 8,400 of the captured Polish officers were not returned. In an effort to locate the missing officers, the London Poles managed to follow their trail to the Smolensk area where, for all the Poles were able to find out, the officers might just as well have been swallowed by the earth.

In fact, they had. Early in 1943, in the gloomy Katyn Forest 10 miles west of Smolensk, the Germans who then occupied the area uncovered mass graves containing the bodies of several thousand men who were identified by what was left of their clothing as the missing Polish officers. Each corpse had a bullet hole in its skull.

German propagandists made the most of their opportunity and promptly accused the Soviet Union of having committed the hideous atrocity. In fact, later evidence left little doubt that Soviet troops were indeed responsible. But when the Red Army captured Smolensk in the autumn of 1943, Soviet authorities took over the cadavers, conducted their own investigation and declared that the Germans had perpetrated the Katyn Massacre.

By then the London Poles had requested that the International Red Cross initiate an impartial investigation, a move that Stalin immediately denounced as a "treacherous blow at the Soviet Union." Breaking off Soviet recognition of the London Poles as their country's legitimate government, Stalin let it be known that he now favored the self-styled "Union of Polish Patriots," composed of Polish Communists living in the Soviet Union and newly formed under Soviet auspices.

During and after the Moscow conference of foreign ministers, there was not the slightest doubt in anyone's mind that Stalin fully intended to keep the 77,620 square miles of Polish territory he had grabbed during his partnership with Hitler. What worried Eden at Moscow was the very real possibility, given weight by Stalin's hostile behavior toward the London Poles, that the Soviet Union meant to establish a puppet Communist government in all of postwar Poland.

Eden tried to persuade Secretary Hull to join in an appeal for Soviet assurances but barely got an audience. "I don't want to deal with these piddling little things," Hull told an associate. "We must deal with the main issues."

Reluctant to force the Polish issue without wholehearted U.S. support, Eden let the matter fester until Teheran.

Even before the Teheran Conference got under way, Stalin made it quite clear that he meant to have his way in small things as well as in large. Roosevelt did not like the

A GIFT OF STEEL
TO THE STEEL-HEARTED

In a dramatic sidelight to the Big Three conference at Teheran, Churchill solemnly presented Stalin a ceremonial sword fashioned by an 83-year-old smith (left) at the command of King George VI. The Sword of Stalingrad, it was called, and its gilded bronze blade was inscribed in English and Russian: "To the steel-hearted citizens of Stalingrad, the gift of King George VI in token of the homage of the British people."

Stalin took the blade from its velvet cushion. "There were tears in his eyes," Roosevelt later said. "I saw them myself. He bowed from the hips swiftly and kissed the sword, a ceremonial gesture of great style which I know was unrehearsed."

Seconds later, the emotional moment came to an abrupt end: Stalin handed the sword to an aide, Marshal Kliment Voroshilov, who dropped it.

Tom Beasley of the Wilkinson Sword Company tests the sword's edge at his forge. The 50-inch blade was set in a gold-wire grip.

Stalin, backed by a Red Army honor guard, kisses the Sword of Stalingrad. The ceremony took place in the Soviet Embassy in Teheran.

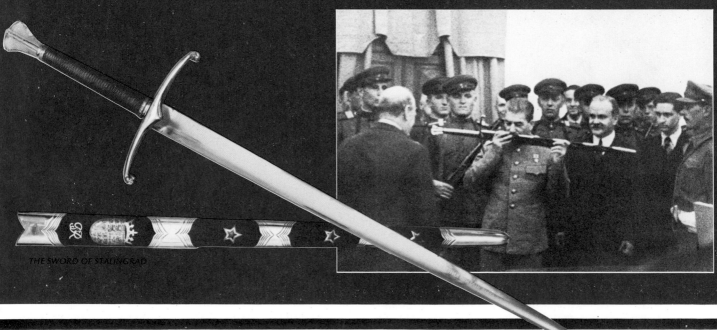

THE SWORD OF STALINGRAD

choice of Teheran as the conference site; he preferred a more accessible location and had suggested that the Big Three might meet at Cairo or aboard ship in some eastern Mediterranean port. Stalin was adamant because Teheran had proper telephone and telegraph links with Moscow, and it was only there, he insisted, that he could rely on secure lines over which to direct Stavka's operations.

At plenary sessions, at private meetings, at banquet tables heaped with caviar and awash with vodka, Josef Stalin towered over Teheran. When he chose, he was amiable. He even agreed to let the Western Allies use three Soviet air bases in the Ukraine for shuttle-bombing attacks on Axis targets beyond normal bomber range. But he budged not an inch on issues of substance and, as in the past, he was occasionally crude, abusive and arrogant. Once, when Roosevelt spoke to him while he was reading a document, Stalin snarled at the President of the United States: "For God's sake let me finish my work!"

By agreement between the Soviet and American leaders, Churchill was excluded from several meetings between Roosevelt and Stalin; neither man wanted to be impeded by the assertive Prime Minister. When Churchill was around, Stalin took pleasure in making the Prime Minister the butt of his dark humor. At a Soviet Embassy dinner when the Big Three were discussing the future of Germany (which they left unsettled for the time being), Stalin suggested that the best solution might be to liquidate between 50,000 and 100,000 German officers. Churchill flushed with anger and roared, "I would rather be taken out into the garden here and now and be shot myself than sully my own and my country's honor by such infamy."

Roosevelt, who also liked a good tease, suggested slyly that 49,000 might be sufficient. At this Churchill stalked out of the room.

Stalin and Molotov, both grinning, followed the Prime Minister and assured him that it had merely been a jest. Churchill allowed them to mollify him, but he was no less convinced that Stalin had meant precisely what he said.

Teheran formalized the main agreements made at Mos-cow. On behalf of the United States and Great Britain, Roosevelt read a statement guaranteeing the opening of the Second Front: "We will launch *Overlord* during May, in conjunction with a supporting operation against the South of France." In return, Stalin signed a Big Three document that proclaimed: "We recognize fully the supreme responsibility resting upon us and all the United Nations to make a peace which will command the good will of the overwhelming mass of the peoples of the world, and banish the scourge and terror of war for many generations."

But Poland remained an open sore. Stalin was disinclined to discuss the subject at all. When pushed, he said only that the Soviet Union must retain its previously occupied Polish territories, but that he would be willing to compensate the Poles by moving the Polish frontier with Germany west to the Oder River. That was agreeable to Churchill. Using three matches, which represented the Soviet Union, Poland and Germany, to illustrate his point, Churchill said that he would like to see Poland moved westward in the manner of soldiers at drill.

Roosevelt was willing to go along—but only if his approval was kept secret. In a private session with Stalin, Roosevelt gave the Soviet dictator a lecture on the realities of American politics. There would be a presidential election in 1944, he explained, and although he had no desire to run again, the winning of the War might require him to stand for a fourth term. There were, he continued, between six and seven million Polish-American voters, and their good favor might decide the election. Therefore, although he personally approved of shifting the Polish border westward, it meant trading away eastern Polish lands and he could not "publicly take part in any such arrangement."

Perhaps the most important statement on Poland was an offhand remark by Stalin: "There is no need to speak at the present time about any Soviet desires," he said. "But when the time comes, we will speak."

It seemed to the Western Allies that Stalin was trying to be amenable. They left Teheran believing that genuine cooperation with the Soviet Union was now possible.

OPERATION "SCORCHED EARTH"

Against a background of ruined and burning homes, Germans prepare to blow up a railroad overpass near Izyum during the Nazi retreat in October 1943.

A VAST EVACUATION OF MEN AND MATÉRIEL

Early in September 1943, when Hitler authorized a belated retreat of German armies on the Russian front, he instructed his commanders to implement a plan as old as warfare itself and as Draconian as its code name implied: Operation *Scorched Earth*. His armies, the Führer decreed, would leave nothing in their wake but a wasteland.

Behind this harsh policy lay sound military reasoning. In their 150-mile withdrawal from the Donets River westward to the Dnieper River, the Germans would vacate some of the Soviet Union's richest land, an area of fertile farms and enormous coal fields, which would provide sustenance for Soviet soldiers and their war machine. By devastating this territory, the Wehrmacht hoped to impede the enemy offensive long enough to allow the German troops to cross the Dnieper, a natural defensive barrier where Hitler's commanders planned to make a stand.

The German commander in the sector, Field Marshal Erich von Manstein, marked a 15-mile zone on the east bank of the Dnieper for especially harsh treatment. Reasoning that the Russians would impress any available men into their advancing armies, Manstein ordered his troops to clear the area of every able-bodied Russian. Thousands of women, who might soon be drafted for Soviet war work, were brought along. In the milling confusion that followed, caravans of peasant carts, raising billowing clouds of dust, moved slowly westward in a gigantic exodus.

Manstein's Army Group South stole more than Russian manpower. The retreating Germans herded along with them more than a half million head of livestock and hauled away everything else of value that they could lay their hands on: farm tractors and threshing machines, industrial tools, grain, fruit and vegetables. And as the locomotives pulled the last trainloads of booty across the Dnieper, the Germans uprooted the tracks behind them. Then German rear guards laid waste to anything that was left.

In summing up the withdrawal, Manstein called it "an immense technical achievement," and without doubt, Operation *Scorched Earth* contributed importantly to its success. Yet when Manstein's retreating armies crossed the Dnieper, the Soviet forces were still pressing remorselessly on their heels.

Retreating German soldiers carrying shepherds' staves herd Russian cattle toward the Dnieper River. In addition to some 200,000 head of cattle, the Germans evacuated more than 150,000 horses and 270,000 sheep in an attempt to deny food to the oncoming Soviet armies.

In seemingly endless numbers, Russian civilians trudge single-file across a Dnieper River bridge alongside a column of Wehrmacht vehicles. A German lieutenant wrote home: "This trek is exciting and unreal, curious and grim at the same time. A country and an army are on the move."

FIERY RUBBLE IN THE GERMANS' WAKE

When Hitler called for the creation of "an uninhabitable desert," German troops put entire towns to the torch. Power plants, factories and bridges were blasted into rubble; roads were mined. Nearly a million tons of grain and 13,000 head of cattle were destroyed.

Even forests that might provide cover for the Russians were set ablaze. In less than a month, almost all of the once-flourishing 440-mile-long strip along the river had been reduced to a smoking no man's land.

Flames engulf a factory section of Smolensk that was set ablaze in September of 1943 by German troops. The once-thriving industrial city of some 150,000 inhabitants was almost entirely destroyed by the fire.

Walking away from a village he has just helped set on fire, a German soldier in a stubbled field smirks for the camera of a comrade. The photo was found in an officer's picture album after he had been captured.

German engineers put charges in place on a wooden bridge.

On the run, soldiers touch off explosive charges laid among tracks in a Soviet railyard.

An ingenious German device, the "trackwolf," rips up railroad ties.

As two officers watch, German demolition troops lay mines along a village road.

In the city of Orel, to the northwest of Kursk, a cluster of buildings explodes skyward in a towering cloud of smoke and dust.

In the aftermath of the fighting in Taganrog, a port on the Sea of Azov, residents emerge from shelter to identify dead relatives.

A mother and her two small children, killed in the course of the Germans' withdrawal from Taganrog, lie sprawled on a beach on the outskirts of the town.

On the bank near the 2,500-foot-long Zaporozhye Dam, First Panzer Army commander General Eberhard von Mackensen (center) listens to his aides' plan for the demolition of the dam's vital power station.

The east bank of the Dnieper River smolders in the wake of the German retreat. The fires did little to slow the Russians; they swarmed across the river in boats and later on bridges concealed just below the surface.

CRIPPLED PAWN OF WAR: THE ZAPOROZHYE DAM

The lone exemption from Hitler's policy of retreat and devastation on the east bank of the Dnieper River was the Soviet hydroelectric showpiece, the Zaporozhye Dam, Europe's largest, and the source of electricity for the whole western Ukraine. The Germans desperately needed its power to run factories west of the Dnieper, and Hitler ordered the dam defended at any cost.

A German army dug in at Zaporozhye, site of the dam on the southern Dnieper. The Soviets sent an entire army group smashing into them. Outnumbered 10 to 1, the Germans held out during heavy bombardment while they planted 200 tons of dynamite in the power station.

On the night of October 14, 1943, as the last of the German defenders were ferried across the river to safety, the great dam blew skyward in a massive explosion and the waters of its reservoir gushed forth. Ironically, the only structure that Hitler wanted saved became the most dramatic example of Operation Scorched Earth.

A RAGING GUERRILLA WAR

Heavily armed partisan leaders in the Kursk region prepare to take a brigade of guerrilla fighters on a raid behind the German lines in March of 1943.

CRIPPLING RAIDS BY LEGIONS OF PARTISANS

On July 22, 1943, an explosive charge detonated a gasoline tank car in the railyard of Osipovichi, a vital supply junction for the German Wehrmacht near Minsk. In seconds the entire train of tank cars became an inferno, igniting in turn a nearby ammunition train, a supply train and finally a fourth train that was loaded with Tiger tanks. The artful sabotage was the work of Russian partisans, and it was far from an isolated incident.

By the summer of 1943, the Russian partisan movement had burgeoned to a force of more than 200,000 fighters—an irregular army operating behind enemy lines. Partisan bands carried out a hit-and-run campaign of demolition and espionage so widespread that the German armies, overextended and undermanned, were powerless to stop it.

The guerrilla fighters concentrated wherever they could hide—in the enormous Pripyat Marshes and the vast forests around Bryansk, and in similarly forbidding terrain in the north near Latvia. The partisan strongholds were situated within striking distance of the primary German supply network of roads and rail lines. And those strongholds were so huge—one unit controlled some 3,000 square miles of territory—that they had their own airstrips, some of them capable of handling even large C-47 transport planes.

These airstrips were key to the emergence of the partisan movement as a well-trained and powerfully armed branch of the Red Army. Partisan leaders were flown by light plane to the nearest Army headquarters to interpret intelligence reports and to coordinate their activities with Soviet units in the area. High-ranking Army officers, shuttled to partisan camps by Red Air Force transports, trained the brigades and in many instances led them into battle. The same transports, most of them American-made C-47s, brought to the partisans teams of Red Army demolition experts as well as an abundant supply of weapons—mortars, antitank guns and other light artillery. With such firepower, the partisans were able to overwhelm weak German rear-area garrisons and wrest control of villages and whole towns from the Occupation forces.

Chosen as a mark of the Red Army's esteem, three partisan leaders carry the medals of slain General Nikolai Vatutin at his funeral in 1944.

In an attempt to curtail partisan sabotage attacks, Germans in an armored train patrol the tracks leading through the extensive Pripyat Marshes in 1944.

A Red Army instructor demonstrates to partisans at a training center the way to fling a hand grenade.

An armored carrier with young partisans riding on its deck emerges from a forest hide-out for a raid.

TRAINING AND FIGHTING ALONGSIDE THE RED ARMY

The partisans' close relationship with the Red Army strengthened their fighting efficiency and bolstered their morale. Partisan brigade commanders were often accorded the rank of full colonel, and those who could get Red Army uniforms and insignia wore them proudly into combat.

The brigade leaders were encouraged to reward their guerrilla fighters for bravery and daring with Army decorations. Frequently medals were flown in for ceremonies in partisan strongholds. Such a system of reward promoted a sense of national unity that reached its peak when partisan soldiers, late in the War, fought side by side with troops of the Red Army.

In a joint operation, uniformed partisans and Red Army regulars attack through a glade in the Carpathian foothills during the drive into Rumania in 1944.

A German prisoner captured near Kursk in 1943 is interrogated by Red Army staff members at a partisan headquarters.

Following a partisan raid, German soldiers attempt to salvage their tanks from a blazing shed. They saved only one.

A boy about 12 years old (far left), already a veteran guerrilla, stands guard with other youthful partisans over the captured garrison of an enemy stronghold.

DISRUPTING GERMAN RULE BEHIND THE FRONT

When partisan brigades raided enemy garrisons and strong points and liberated Russian villages, the Germans who survived the attacks were often allowed to live. Those taken prisoner were pumped for military intelligence and then put to work at menial tasks, or escorted through the lines to the Red Army rear areas.

But the partisans reserved a special hatred for their countrymen who had worked with the German occupiers. When a Russian village was liberated, the partisans rooted out collaborators and routinely executed every one, from town officials to women informants.

After a village had been cleared of Germans and their puppets, the underground fighters often drafted all the able-bodied men and childless women into their brigade. The punishment for many civilians who refused to leave their homes and take up arms could be as harsh as that dealt to collaborators—death. In the world of the partisan fighters, wrote Russian-born historian Alexander Werth, "human life is terribly cheap."

A partisan firing squad, including a 13-year-old boy (top), marches a Russian collaborator through his village, then executes him in an open field nearby.

Wielding pitchforks, Russian peasant women jab savagely at another collaborator (top) as he is marched to his death by firing squad outside the village.

Four hardy, well-armed partisan women enter Minsk; which was liberated with partisan help in July of 1944. As Red Army units advanced, some partisan brigades fought alongside them while others moved farther to the west, staying behind the Germans and harassing their retreat.

Returning to his liberated village near Moscow, a young partisan gets a hero's welcome from his mother, other relatives and several boys from the village. Soviet propaganda hailed the partisans as national saviors.

3

A Soviet army treads on thin ice
"Shell-pitted, bullet-riddled, scarred Leningrad"
Hitler calls for "the lion of the defense"
Fifty-six thousand Germans in a Witches' Caldron
A message from the anti-Nazi League of German Officers
A watery ordeal at the Gniloi Tikich
The Führer's hopeless "heaven-bound missions"
Ukrainian "bandits" bag a Soviet general
"Someone must lay his head on the block"
Fiasco at the Khersones beachhead

In November 1943, Hitler and OKH agreed on a policy for the Eastern Front that could only accelerate the yearlong decline of the Wehrmacht in the Soviet Union. The policy was prompted by an event that loomed in the future—exactly when or where, the Germans did not know. Hitler explained the situation to his generals: "For the last two and a half years, the severe and costly fight against Bolshevism has claimed the utmost of the mass of our military strength and effort. This has now changed. The danger in the East remains, but a greater one is appearing in the West: the Anglo-Saxon landing!"

Hitler and his generals agreed that the Wehrmacht could afford to lose some additional ground in the immense East without endangering the German homeland. But an Allied bridgehead on the Channel coast would bring the enemy to the threshold of Germany. To meet that threat, Hitler ordered that all further fresh supplies of men and matériel be sent to the Western theater. His armies in the East would have to make do with what they already had, at least for the winter. This policy of deprivation, in combination with Hitler's insistence on fighting for every inch of ground despite the cost in flesh and guns, was bound to hasten the Wehrmacht's defeat in the East.

In contrast, the prospects of the Russians had never looked brighter. At the end of 1943, they could look back on a pivotal year in their struggle with the German invaders, a year studded with military accomplishments. On New Year's Day, 1944, in a speech to the Soviet people, Mikhail I. Kalinin, chairman of the Presidium of the Supreme Soviet, celebrated the triumphant counteroffensives that had turned the tide against the enemy and regained a million square miles of sacred Russian soil, half the Soviet territory that the Germans had occupied. Kalinin then reminded his countrymen of the next task they faced: clearing the Germans from all of the Soviet Union.

To that end, Stalin and his high command had spent much of the fall laying the groundwork for three separate winter offensives, to be launched at roughly the same time: on the southernmost flank, a drive aimed at clearing the Crimean Peninsula; in the Ukraine, a thrust westward from the Dnieper River; and in the north, an attack to lift the siege of Leningrad. These offensives would come to be known in the Soviet camp simply as the "three blows."

THE "THREE BLOWS"

The liberation of Leningrad was no longer a strategic necessity. The opposing forces had been in stalemate for two years, and neither showed signs of gaining the initiative. The elaborate fortifications and trenchworks that both sides had been able to build during their long face-off gave the front lines an air of permanence that evoked the static warfare of World War I. More to the point, Leningrad was no longer cut off. In January of 1943, the Russians had succeeded in opening a six-mile-wide rail corridor that linked the city to the rest of the Soviet Union and provided a life line for the city's inhabitants.

It might have been more profitable for the Red Army to let the German Army Group North languish on the city's doorstep for a while longer. But the plight of Leningrad and the heroism of its citizens surpassed strategic considerations and demanded the liberation of the city.

For the people of Leningrad, life was a seemingly permanent nightmare of exploding shells. The poet Nikolai Tikhonov reported: "Once I watched for hours as shells burst every three minutes in a district where I happened to find myself. This went on for seven hours. They fire in various ways—every hour or so they send over four shells per minute, which cut into walls and streets. They fire now at dawn, now in the daytime, now in the evening. Sometimes they fire at night.

"Oh, those streets of Leningrad flowing with blood! Yet, half an hour after the last shell falls, the blood has already vanished from the pavements, the dead and wounded have been removed, the interrupted streetcar traffic resumed."

Despite their expenditure of energies in the siege, the Germans would have relinquished Leningrad without so much as a fight but for a few ill-chosen words and an Army commander's bravado. During the summer and fall of 1943, Army Group North's best fighting units had been drained away to the more active sectors in the south, and their replacements had been inadequate. To counter this erosion of strength, the army group's commander, Field Marshal Georg von Küchler, planned an elaborate withdrawal from Leningrad 150 miles southwest to the so-called Panther Position, a partially completed segment of the projected East Wall. A 50,000-man force supplied with 100 carloads of construction materials a day had built 6,000 bunkers, laid 125 miles of barbed-wire entanglements, and dug tank traps and trenches. During the autumn months, Army Group North had shipped to the Panther Position a million tons of grain and potatoes, and half a million cattle and sheep; together with military supplies, the shipments amounted to 4,000 trainloads.

At the end of the year, Küchler and his staff anticipated pulling back to this bulwark in an orderly, even leisurely, manner in mid-January. All that they needed was the deciding word from Hitler. Expecting to receive the order, Küchler reported everything ready at the noon situation conference in the Führer's East Prussian headquarters on December 30. In passing, he remarked that General Georg Lindemann, who commanded the Eighteenth Army on the front around Leningrad, had "naturally" asked to have his army stay put. In answer to a question from Hitler, Küchler replied that Lindemann's front was actually very well fortified after the almost two-and-a-half-year siege but that the army did not have enough troops to man all of it. Hitler then ended the conference without mentioning a withdrawal; hating any withdrawal on principle, he had decided against this one as soon as he learned that Lindemann had spoken for staying in place.

Unfortunately for Lindemann, his notion to stay at Leningrad had been based on intelligence reports that seriously underestimated Soviet strength. The Soviet forces in the area—the Leningrad Front on the north and the Volkhov Front to the south of it—had swelled with reinforcements during the autumn and outnumbered the Eighteenth Army by at least 3 to 1 in men and artillery, and 6 to 1 in tanks, self-propelled guns and aircraft. The German intelligence officers, moreover, had misinterpreted unusual shipping activity 20 miles west of Leningrad at the port of Oranienbaum, around which the Russians held a bridgehead on the Gulf of Finland. The ships they had seen plying back and forth between Leningrad and the Oranienbaum pocket were not merely supplying the garrison in the pocket, as the Germans thought; they were bringing in a new and powerful offensive force, the Second Shock Army.

With such forces at their disposal, the two Soviet commanders, General L. A. Govorov of the Leningrad Front and General Kirill A. Meretskov of the Volkhov Front, intended to redeem their somewhat shadowed reputations. For suspected political unreliability, Govorov had been under a cloud as late as 1941 and had been spared from being sent to a labor camp or an even worse fate only by the outbreak of the War. Meretskov had been chief of the Army General Staff in 1940 and had lost his post as well as Stalin's confidence when he failed to give a satisfactory explanation for a war game in which the Soviet side was defeated. Both Govorov and Meretskov had held their commands in the Leningrad area for two years. They had made a number of attempts to free the city, but they had succeeded only in making life uncomfortable for the Germans.

This time the two generals planned to use their overwhelming strength in a gigantic two-pronged assault to liberate Leningrad and destroy the German Eighteenth Army. On the north, the Leningrad Front's Second Shock Army would drive out of the Oranienbaum bridgehead; its Forty-second Army would attack from the Pulkovo Heights in the Leningrad suburbs. These forces would then converge and sweep southward, driving the Germans away from the besieged city. In the meantime, 100 miles to the southeast, the Volkhov Front's Fifty-ninth Army would knife into the German flank at Lake Ilmen, capture the city of Novgorod, and plunge westward toward a rendezvous with the Leningrad Front forces coming from the north. When the two Soviet army groups linked up, the German Eighteenth Army would be trapped.

In the early-morning hours of January 14, rising temperatures brought an unseasonable thaw and a heavy fog that grounded all aircraft. The Soviet commanders opened their Leningrad assault an hour before daylight with more than 6,000 guns, among them the cannon of two Baltic Fleet battleships and the cruiser *Lützow*, which Hitler had sold to the Soviet Union in 1940. In 65 minutes, 100,000 shells of all calibers crashed down on the German line. When the bombardment lifted, infantry units of the Second Shock Army moved out against the 10th Luftwaffe Field Division, which started to crumble almost at once. By dark, the attack had penetrated more than two miles.

The next day dawned clear, and Soviet warplanes joined the artillery in preparing for the Forty-second Army's attack from the Pulkovo Heights south of Leningrad. In a bombardment that lasted an hour and a half, more than 200,000 shells rained down on the German positions and 500 bombing sorties leveled what was left of the suburban towns of Pushkin, Krasnoye Selo and Dudergof. Then the Soviet infantrymen advanced across the shell-cratered fields and the bombed-out trenches.

The Forty-second Army gained as much as three miles in the course of the day, but its commander, Lieut. General I. I. Maslennikov, was not satisfied; he cursed and threatened his subordinates for not doing better. On the German side, Generals Küchler and Lindemann were not particularly worried; past experience had shown that penetrations only a few miles deep could always be cleaned up later, and their underestimation of Soviet strength encouraged

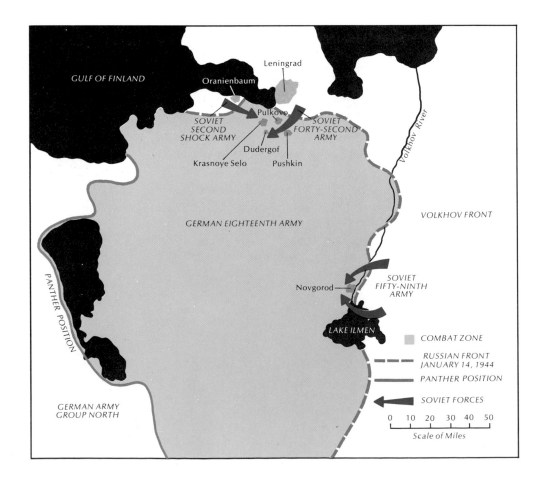

In January 1944, Red Army forces mounted a huge two-pronged assault (arrows) aimed at lifting the siege of Leningrad and trapping the bulk of the German Eighteenth Army. From the Oranienbaum pocket and from the suburbs of Leningrad, the Soviet Second Shock and Forty-second Armies were to attack southward toward a linkup with the Soviet Fifty-ninth Army, which was simultaneously pushing west from Lake Ilmen and the city of Novgorod. The German fallback line was the strong defensive Panther Position.

them to suppose that the enemy attack would soon peter out for lack of reserves.

Well to the southeast, the thaw played havoc with Meretskov's offensive. His spearheads had to cross the Volkhov River north of Novgorod and the tip of Lake Ilmen to the south, and then slog over mostly swampy, roadless terrain to reach the city. Almost as soon as the attack began, Meretskov said, "part of the armor got stuck in the marshes; the thaw turned the tussocky, ice-covered fields into a sea of ooze." The lake caused even worse trouble. The thawing ice was less than a foot thick, and horses and heavy equipment began falling through it. The Germans added to Meretskov's difficulties by bombing the ice, opening holes that had to be bridged.

The warm weather also tormented the Germans at Novgorod and Leningrad. Their trenches filled waist-deep with mud and frigid water; unlike their foe, the Germans did not have enough troops to allow reliefs that would enable the men to warm up and dry out. By the fourth day, Küchler's and Lindemann's early optimism had faded. On the morning of the 18th, Lindemann reported that the lines east of Oranienbaum and west of Leningrad were collapsing—as much from the troops' exhaustion as from anything else.

That same day, the Soviet Forty-second Army took Krasnoye Selo, the former summer retreat of the Czars and a base for German siege guns shelling Leningad 10 miles away. After dark, Soviet tanks roared out of Krasnoye Selo toward a linkup with the Second Shock Army's vanguard six miles to the west. Just north of the town, the colonel commanding the German 126th Infantry Division watched helplessly as tracers from the Soviet machine guns cut through feeble resistance from his disorganized division. From his vantage point, he saw the two Soviet armies meet at 10 p.m. and realized that German forces to the north were trapped. In two hours he regrouped his division and, by the light of his own and Soviet flares and tracers, broke out to the south, bringing his own troops and most of the 9th Luftwaffe Field Division with him.

German troops at Novgorod were in deep trouble, too. Almost surrounded by the Russians on January 19, the Novgorod garrison was fighting desperately to hold open a slender corridor. Hitler had refused several times to permit a withdrawal, saying Novgorod had "extraordinary symbolic significance." But Küchler called Hitler and begged him to give the garrison in Novgorod what would certainly be their last chance. The Führer finally relented, and the troops made their escape under cover of night.

When Soviet soldiers entered the city the next day, they found it a shambles. "Its silent streets were strewn with heaps of broken masonry and bricks," Meretskov reported. "Only about 40 buildings were undamaged. The famous old monuments, the pride and glory of ancient Russian architecture, were blown up. Intending to hand over the Novgorod region to East Prussian settlers, the Nazi command had taken steps to erase all traces of its Russian past."

After losing Krasnoye Selo and Novgorod, Küchler and Lindemann changed their minds about withdrawing to the Panther Position; now they were eager to go there. But Hitler, who might once have allowed them to pull out, had now changed his mind. "I am against all withdrawals," he said heatedly. "We will have crises wherever we are. The battle must be fought as far as possible from the German border." On January 27, in a meeting in Königsberg, East Prussia, the Führer chastised Küchler and told him the Eighteenth Army was not fighting hard enough. Küchler returned to the front a broken man. His chief of staff said that he talked incessantly about attacking with more determination, although he knew that all he could do was retreat.

Whether Hitler approved or not, the Eighteenth Army was on the run. By January 27, Leningrad was out of the reach of the longest-range German guns. That night, the people were summoned into the streets to hear the announcement of the liberation over the loudspeakers. "Suddenly Leningrad emerged from the gloom before our gaze," wrote poet Olga Berggoltz. "To the last crack in its walls, the city was revealed to us—shell-pitted, bullet-riddled, scarred Leningrad, with its plywood windowpanes. And we saw that despite all the cruel slashes and blows, Leningrad retained its proud beauty. In the bluish, roseate, green and white of the lights, the city appeared to us so austere and touching we could not feast our eyes enough on it." And Leningrad's artillery fired a salute of 20 volleys from 324 guns.

On the 31st of January, the Führer summoned Küchler to the Wolf's Lair and relieved him of his command. Walter Model, who was known to the German High Command as "the lion of the defense," would replace him. After receiving his instructions, General Model telegraphed ahead: "Not a single step backward will be taken without my express permission."

Model brought with him a new theory that he and Hitler had devised. It was called *Schild und Schwert* (Shield and Sword), and it asserted in essence that retreats were permissible only if one intended later to strike back in the same or a different direction in a kind of parry-and-thrust sequence. How much Model actually believed in the theory was open to question, but Hitler's confidence in his ability gave this general what Küchler had not possessed—the authority to make decisions.

After inspecting the battlefront, Model began to order piecemeal withdrawals up and down the line. He sent the Eighteenth Army into a controlled retreat and began to withdraw the Sixteenth Army from its line south of Lake Ilmen. He made his moves with such deliberation that before long, Hitler was urging a speed-up. On March 1, Army Group North took its final step back into the Panther Position, where Küchler had wanted to go before the fight that obliterated three German divisions. The arrival of the army group in the heavily fortified line coincided with a spring thaw that finally brought the Soviet advance to a standstill. A lull settled in on the northern end of the Eastern Front.

As Soviet forces pressed their struggle to liberate Leningrad, the Red Army far to the south was leveling a crushing blow against the German Army Group South in the Ukraine. The Soviet offensive in that region, a continuation of the sweep that had brought the Russians to the Dnieper River in the early fall of 1943, began as a general thrust straight westward by three Soviet army groups; the objective was to liberate the remainder of the Ukraine and pin the German Army Group South against the Carpathian Mountains. Two of the Soviet units, however, quickly altered their plan of attack when they saw the opportunity to stage another Stalingrad—that is, to surround a whole army and force its surrender. This time the Soviet tactics, combined with Hitler's stubborn prohibition of withdrawals, produced the Cherkassy pocket, a hellhole that was known to the Germans inside it as the Witches' Caldron.

The Soviet offensive got under way on Christmas Eve,

1943. The commander of Army Group South, Field Marshal von Manstein, was spending the day with one of his divisions behind the threatened line when word arrived that the enemy First Ukrainian Front was on the move against the German Fourth and First Panzer Armies west of Kiev. At first, the news did not worry Manstein. It hardly seemed possible to him that the Russians could crank up again so soon after their exhausting trek of the fall. Moreover, the warm and wet weather had turned the roads to slop—crippling conditions for a mechanized offensive.

The First Ukrainian Front commander, General Vatutin, had the bulk of five armies rolling westward and southwestward. One wing of the attack force headed for Vinnitsa, Manstein's headquarters on the upper Bug River. Five days later and 100 miles to the southeast in the sector held by the German Eighth Army, Marshal Ivan Konev's Second Ukrainian Front surged west toward Kirovograd, a key industrial city; from there, it would head for Pervomaisk on the lower Bug River.

And on January 10, on the southernmost end of the line, the Third Ukraininan Front moved out against German Army Group A, which then mustered only the Sixth Army.

Since Vatutin's thrust was obviously the more dangerous one, Manstein on December 27 proposed to give way against Konev and shift as much strength as he could to his left to hit Vatutin. When Hitler heard this, he fell into a rage, declaring that Manstein was only trying to make himself look good by "pompous talk of counteroperations" and that he ought to label his proposal by its real name, "running away." By the end of the second week in January, Vatutin had gone 60 of the 100 miles he originally had to cover to reach Vinnitsa. Konev had captured Kirovograd and covered 30 of the 90 miles to Pervomaisk on the lower Bug. In the daytime, rain and snow and temperatures well above freezing turned the roads into viscous mud. At night and during cold spells lasting two or three days at a time, the mud became covered with slick ice. The Russians' wide-tracked T-34 tanks and powerful American Lend-Lease trucks gave the Soviet troops more mobility in mud and over ice than the Germans, but not enough to sustain continuous thrusts under those conditions.

As a consequence, Vatutin and Konev pondered a change in tactics. One feature of the enemy line seemed ripe for exploitation: Between the flanks of their two army groups, Vatutin and Konev had created a German-held salient that pressed down on the Dnieper River at Kanev like a giant thumb. While the salient was merely inconvenient to the Russians, its long, exposed, horseshoe-shaped line was a hazard for the Germans. But Hitler, imagining that he might somehow find a way to attack toward Kiev from there, insisted on hanging onto the salient and the fragment of the Dnieper line that was left.

The Soviet High Command was usually reluctant to alter tactics. Its standard practice was to stick with a plan through thick and thin, on the assumption that when performance fell short after thorough preparation, improvising could only make things worse. But Stalin could be flexible. When Marshal Zhukov had dinner with him in January and proposed to turn the First Ukrainian Front's attack south and the Second Ukrainian Front's north to cut off the German salient, Stalin agreed. The First Panzer and Eighth Armies were crammed back to back in the salient, and Soviet thrusts of only 30 miles from both sides would complete the encirclement.

Early on the morning of January 24, after several days of colder-than-usual weather, a Second Ukrainian Front reconnaissance force hit the German line north of Kirovograd, in a 12-mile-long sector where the Eighth Army had no more than one infantryman per 15 yards of front. Before the day was over, what had begun as probing attacks had struck deep in a number of places. On the following morning, the Fourth Guards Army, with support from the Fifth Guards Tank Army, opened a full-scale push northward and broke through with 12 divisions.

A German commander, General Nikolaus von Vormann, found himself and his 23rd Panzer Division directly in the path of the Soviet onslaught. "Regardless of losses—and I really mean regardless of losses—masses of Soviets about midday streamed westward past the German tanks which were firing at them with everything that they had," Vormann wrote later. "It was an amazing scene, a shattering drama. There is really no other comparison—the dam had burst and a huge flood was pouring over the flat land, past our tanks, which, surrounded by a few grenadiers, were like rocks towering from the swirling flood. Our amazement was even greater when, later in the afternoon, the cavalry forma-

tions of three Soviet divisions galloped through our defensive fire in close order. It was something I hadn't seen for a long time—it just seemed unreal."

Sensing disaster, the Eighth Army commander, General Otto Wöhler, asked for permission to begin drawing his forces away from the Dnieper. He could not get permission from Hitler.

The next day, two mechanized corps of the Soviet Sixth Tank Army ripped through the First Panzer Army line and raced south without waiting for the infantry to catch up. While the First Panzer Army commander, General Hans Hube, joined Wöhler in pleading for permission to evacuate the salient, both Soviet thrusts gained speed. Getting a negative answer, Hube, who had distinguished himself in the Stalingrad battle, observed dolefully: "One can only obey, even in the deepest anxiety."

On January 28, the Soviet spearheads met, trapping two corps of the Eighth Army in a 1,200-square-mile pocket near the city of Cherkassy. From a captured position map, Zhukov estimated the bag at 11 German divisions, approximately 85,000 troops. But the German penchant for exaggerating troop strength on paper threw Zhukhov's estimate off. Actually, the Russians had cut off only six divisions, or about 56,000 troops.

The best move for the trapped 11th and 42nd Corps would have been a fast breakout, but Hitler refused to give ground. In fact, there was still a possibility of reestablishing contact with German troops outside the pocket and restoring the German lines. Probably because they overestimated the size of the trapped German force, Vatutin and Konev concentrated on tightening their grip on the pocket rather than pushing their main front westward. Consequently, a German relief force would not have to travel much more than 25 miles to reach the pocket.

With Hitler's permission, Manstein had readied a relief force: the 3rd Panzer Corps, which he had been building up to stop Vatutin's drive toward Vinnitsa, and the 47th Corps. These corps were made up of the 1st, 16th and 17th Panzer Divisions, the SS Leibstandarte Adolf Hitler Division and the Heavy Panzer Regiment "Bäke." The heavy panzer regiment, led by a daredevil tank veteran, Lieut. Colonel Franz Bäke, had 47 Panthers and 34 Tigers and was tailor-made for the job it faced—spearheading an armored charge.

The relief column jumped off on February 4, a bright, clear day with temperatures well above freezing. In spite of the Russian mud, the relief force made good progress on the first day. But by the next day, the tanks had used up their fuel churning through the mud, and rations and ammunition were running low. Resupply by truck was impossible, so the army ordered the 3rd Panzer Corps to mobilize all the civilians in its area as porters and to requisition all the horses and sledges that could be found. Twenty-four hours later, the relief force was moving again. But the tank crews were bringing up their gasoline in buckets and the infantrymen were slogging barefooted through the gluey, knee-deep mud, finding this less exhausting than having to stop and retrieve their boots every few steps. And Soviet resistance was growing stiffer with every yard.

By the third day the 47th Corps had given up, and Manstein and his commanders also realized that the 3rd Panzer Corps probably would not be able to punch through to the pocket in time to relieve the trapped forces. Lieut. General Wilhelm Stemmermann, 11th Corps commander, was now assigned to command both corps inside the pocket. He did a masterly job of juggling his troops to plug gaps in the line and blunt the strong Soviet stabs, but he could not hold out much longer.

General Wöhler had already sent an officer courier by air to alert the two corps to the possibility of breaking out to meet the relief force. Hitler pondered the possibility for 12 hours and then gave his reluctant approval.

On February 11, the 3rd Panzer Corps pushed to the southern edge of the large village of Lysyanka, which straddled the narrow but deep and fast-flowing Gniloi Tikich River. There it had to stop to bring up supplies, particularly more gasoline, which the tanks were consuming at three times the normal rate because of the mud.

Stemmermann's attack westward out of the pocket started shortly before midnight that night and went a mile or so to the villages of Khilki and Komarovka before being stopped by counterattacks. The 3rd Panzer Corps remained stalled throughout the following day as rain and mud frustrated its efforts to bring up ammunition and refuel the tanks.

But on the 14th, the panzer corps had a piece of extraordinary good luck: The 1st Panzer Division captured a bridge on the Gniloi Tikich in Lysyanka and established a bridgehead on the other side. Only two more Soviet positions, the village of Dzurzhentsy and close beside it Hill 239, blocked

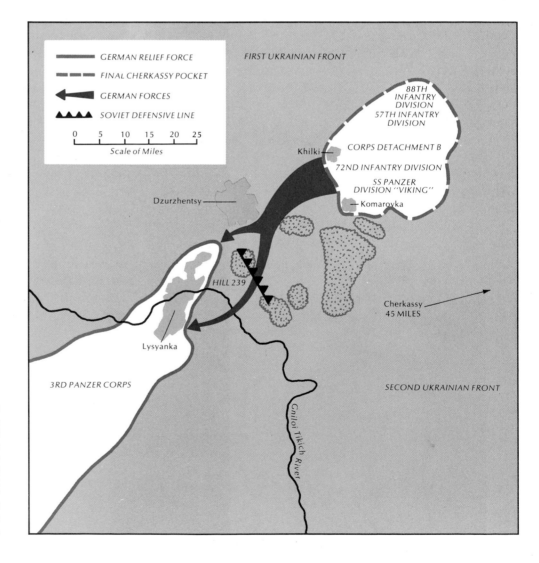

In late January of 1944, spearheads of the Red Army's First and Second Ukrainian Fronts converged to trap the remnants of two shattered German corps in a pocket near Cherkassy. In an effort to rescue the encircled units, spearheads of the 3rd Panzer Corps attacked the Soviet ring from the southwest, while troops in the pocket made an attempt to link up with the relief column. Key points in the final struggle were a German bridgehead on the Gniloi Tikich River, the village of Dzurzhentsy and Hill 239.

the way to the pocket. The hill was the key. Protruding above the otherwise gently rolling terrain, it would provide fields of observation and fire all the way across the remaining four miles to the pocket. It had to be taken first.

The Russians were no less aware of the importance of the hill. Their artillery bristled on its slopes and their T-34s swarmed around it.

From the German bridgehead on the Gniloi Tikich, the 1st Panzer Division and the Heavy Panzer Regiment Bäke moved out in a blinding snowstorm to capture the village and the hill. They met intense opposition immediately and were halted.

But a few of their compatriots in the pocket managed to claw their way into Dzurzhentsy in fierce house-to-house fighting, only to be repelled by a Soviet counterattack. "Suddenly machine-gun fire rattles at us," a German soldier reported. "Tank engines get into lower gear and whine like frightened babies. Through the blizzard the outlines of enemy tanks show themselves. Our artillerymen and infantrymen run around screaming. They throw away their arms, fall down and are crushed by the heavy caterpillar tracks. Some stop and put their hands up to signal their surrender, but the next moment they're mowed down by the whipping machine-gun fire."

The soldier and a comrade ran from the T-34s, which raced by, raising a dense cloud of snow. "In one place we have to throw ourselves down and let the tanks roll over us, as they told us to do in the training manual. Panic-stricken, we press ourselves down. Rumbling, rattling, and whirring, the vast tonnage of a T-34 thunders over us, while the screaming, clanging chains roll past us on both sides.

"You're no longer normal when something like this hits you. You shake and tremble. Your speech is confused and slurred. You can't believe you're still alive."

The battle seesawed between Lysyanka, Hill 239 and Dzurzhentsy. The distances were short, but for the Germans so was time, and on February 15, Manstein decided a relief was not going to be possible. He told Stemmermann he was going to have to get the whole pocket on its feet and make a grand run toward Hill 239 and Dzurzhentsy. Stemmermann answered that he would do it an hour before midnight the next night.

The Russians, in the meantime, tried to cajole the Germans into surrendering. Letters to Stemmermann, to Major General Theobald Lieb of the 42nd Corps and to other officers, calling on them to abandon the Nazi cause, were air-dropped into the pocket or even hand-delivered by German prisoners. They bore the signature of Lieut. General Walther von Seydlitz-Kurzbach, who had been captured at Stalingrad and had become the leading figure in a Soviet-sponsored, anti-Nazi League of German Officers. By radio, Seydlitz also appealed to the troops to lay down their arms. He had no success.

Early on the 16th the three-day snowstorm ended, leaving the mud blanketed with wet snow as much as three feet deep. The snow had brought the Germans in the pocket a respite, but now it was over.

In the early afternoon, the Russians retook Komarovka, which was to have been the southern anchor of the breakout front, and Stemmermann had to redeploy his troops. During the day, the 1st Panzer Division, with Heavy Panzer Regiment Bäke in the lead, tried again to take Dzurzhentsy but could not push beyond the northern tip of Lysyanka. The heavy panzer regiment managed to get three tanks atop Hill 239; then fire from the flanks forced them back 400 yards. By nightfall, nothing more could be done. The First Panzer Army had brought hospital trains up to the closest station behind the front line and had Junkers-52 transports standing by to take on wounded at the airfield at Uman, 50 miles southwest of the pocket.

It was now up to the trapped Germans to free themselves. Stemmermann assigned positions along the line of departure in the pocket: Corps Detachment B, the collected remnants of three burned-out divisions, on the north in Khilki; the 72nd Infantry Division in the center; and the SS "Viking" Division on the south. Each division placed a regiment with artillery in the vanguard. Stemmermann took personal command of the rear guard, the 57th and 88th Divisions. A sixth division, the 389th Infantry Division, had ceased to exist a week earlier; its last 200 men were attached to the 57th Division. The total German strength in the pocket now stood at about 45,000, including 1,500 wounded who were to be left behind.

The breakout began at 11 p.m. sharp. Jumping off in silence and using only knives and bayonets, the three vanguard regiments cut through the enemy outpost line and main screening line before the Russians knew what was happening. The lead regiment of Corps Detachment B did not meet any more Russians until it arrived at the line between Dzurzhentsy and Hill 239, which it pushed through easily. Thereafter, it followed white signal flares fired by the 1st Panzer Division and reached the northern edge of Lysyanka at 5 o'clock.

The regiment of the 72nd Infantry Division did even better. At a road running into Dzurzhentsy from the southeast, the infantrymen had a nighttime encounter with four Soviet tanks and a column of trucks moving toward the village. When a German soldier yelled "Halt!" in Russian, the tanks stopped and obligingly let the whole German regiment cross the road. The infantrymen then made their way to the 1st Panzer Division sector north of Lysyanka.

The SS regiment was not so lucky. Passing to the east of Dzurzhentsy, it ran into heavy fire from the village and from Hill 239. After one battalion was diverted to engage the Russians, the main force turned due south. To reach Lysyanka by that route, it had to cross the Gniloi Tikich one and a half miles south of the 3rd Corps's bridge; the only way to get to the other side of the river was to swim. The SS men had carried their field guns, mortars and machine guns this far. Now they had to leave them behind on the east bank; indeed, most of the troops discarded their rifles while swimming across. Even so, many of them drowned. They were the first of hundreds, perhaps thousands, whose lives would be claimed by the icy water that day.

As succeeding waves of troops started their march out of the pocket, Stemmermann stayed at his command post in Khilki trying to maintain an orderly withdrawal amid increasing chaos. He had ordered all vehicles destroyed except for those that would be needed to make the breakout. But tanks, self-propelled guns, trucks and wagons got stuck and caused traffic jams. Many of the vehicles that made it past Khilki had to be abandoned farther on.

At 4 a.m., Stemmermann and his staff followed the last troops of Corps Detachment B out of Khilki, intending to set up a new command post about halfway to Dzurzhentsy. The general never arrived there. South of Khilki, in the tangle of troops and vehicles, he became separated from his staff. A soldier later reported he had taken Stemmermann aboard his wagon just before it was blown to pieces by a Soviet antitank shell.

General Lieb and his staff officers of the 42nd Corps, all on horseback, had followed the last echelon of the 72nd Infantry Division out of the pocket at 3:30 a.m. Half an hour later they crossed the muddy gully south of Khilki, which by then was filled with mired vehicles that were rapidly being ground into unrecognizable junk by Soviet tank and antitank fire from Komarovka.

Dawn overtook the last German columns due east of Dzurzhentsy. The troops could hear the sound of heavy fighting coming from the village and from Hill 239 and woods to the south. By the time they drew up to the hill, it was full daylight and the Russians were now wide awake, with a clear idea of what was happening. Their machine guns, mortars, rockets and artillery raked and pounded the exposed Germans, who drove their vehicles hard in an effort to escape dozens of Soviet tanks.

"In this frantic race, vehicles were overturned, throwing

Soviet troops search for salvage in this composite view of the dead soldiers and ruined equipment left behind by the Germans in their breakout from the Cherkassy pocket in February 1944. The debacle cost the already strapped Wehrmacht almost 26,000 men, and heavy equipment for twice that number.

wounded in confusion to the ground," recalled Leon De-grelle, the commander of an SS brigade composed of Belgian volunteers. "A wave of Soviet tanks overtook the first vehicles and caught more than half of the convoy; the wave advanced through the carts, breaking them up one by one like boxes of matches, crushing the wounded men and the dying horses."

The German retreat dissolved into chaos. To escape the withering fire, troops dived into ravines and gullies. Units became completely intermixed, discipline collapsed, and it was every man for himself. Since the fire was heaviest from the direction of Hill 239 and Dzurzhentsy, the Germans from the pocket veered south to meet another test of survival, the icy Gniloi Tikich.

When Lieb and his staff reached the Gniloi Tikich in the afternoon, they found a scene of utter horror. Thousands of German troops crowded toward the 50-foot-wide river and pushed down the steep, slick east bank to swim across. Soviet T-34s on the east bank several hundred yards upstream fired high-explosive shells into the milling mass of soldiers. Driven to desperation, groups of Germans leaped into the Gniloi Tikich. Although the temperature was 23° F., many of the soldiers stripped and tried to throw their clothes and weapons across, but most of the bundles and guns fell into the water. Thousands of men attempted to swim. But they were battered by ice floes swirling in the strong current. The frigid water sapped the strength of hundreds before they reached the far shore. Their bodies and the carcasses of horses drifted downstream, rolling and bobbing amid the chunks of ice. Some of the men who made it across the river collapsed on the far bank and froze to death.

Throughout the day, Lieb and other officers struggled to restore order at the river crossing. A tractor was driven into the river to serve as a base for an emergency bridge. It was swept away by the current. So were farm carts that had been submerged for the same purpose. Human chains, composed alternately of swimmers and nonswimmers, tried to span the river but were swept away. One coolheaded and hardy German sergeant fashioned a lifesaving harness from belts, and in three trips across the river, pulled as many nonswimmers to safety. Two other noncoms tied their unit's wounded to planks and towed them across the river.

In the late afternoon, after the tank fire subsided, Lieb and the surviving members of his staff swam the river and joined the long lines of Germans, most unarmed, many naked and all shivering violently as they scrambled up the snowy slope toward the cottages of Lysyanka.

In all, 30,000 of the 45,000 troops who had been in the pocket on February 16 made good their escape. Manstein and the two army commanders were pleased and relieved that so many had been extricated. Even Hitler did no more than grumble briefly over the lost equipment. But the men who had escaped were shattered by the experience, and their condition was shocking even to other German soldiers inured to the viciousness of the Eastern Front. Manstein decided he would have to send all the survivors back into Poland to rest and recuperate.

The repercussions of the battle of the Cherkassy pocket extended far beyond the loss of territory and the thousands of men who had been killed, wounded or captured. The relief operation had siphoned off soldiers, supplies and equipment that were sorely needed elsewhere in the Ukraine.

When Manstein committed his armored reserves at Cherkassy, the Soviets took advantage of the resultant weaknesses on the German line to the north and to the south. The Soviet forces drove deep into Manstein's northern flank along the edge of the Pripyat Marshes. On his southern flank, the Third and Fourth Ukrainian Fronts attacked Field Marshal von Kleist's Army Group A and shoved it back 70 miles, almost entirely out of the Dnieper bend. Army Groups South and A had now lost all of the Dnieper line except for a 60-mile stretch at the lower end.

For two weeks following the breakout at Cherkassy, an ominous quiet prevailed on the southern flank of the Eastern Front. Behind the Wehrmacht forces, about 50 miles apart, were three more rivers, the Bug, the Dniester and the Prut. Kleist and Manstein, supported by the chief of the Army High Command, Zeitzler, proposed withdrawing to the Bug while they could still go back on their own terms. Hitler equivocated. His mind was elsewhere.

In early March, he issued an operations order introducing to the Eastern Front a major new tactical concept, the "fortified place." He would designate specific cities and towns, usually astride communications lines, to be garrisoned and fortified in order, he said, to "perform the same functions as forts did in the past." Beneath the fancy definition, the fortified places had a single, simple mission: to hold out to the last man. The commandants, whatever their rank, received the authority of a corps commander, which meant that they could convene courts-martial of officers and men and could impose the death penalty. Initially, Hitler singled out 26 cities and large towns in still-occupied Soviet territory as fortified places. In the parlance of the German soldiers, assignments to defend these strongholds were aptly known as *Himmelfahrtskommandos,* or heaven-bound missions.

On their side, the Soviet commands needed the lull to regroup. The battle of the Cherkassy pocket had diverted the First and Second Ukrainian Fronts from their original lines of attack toward Vinnitsa and Pervomaisk on the lower Bug. That was, in fact, the only advantage the Germans derived from the entire affair, but it was a temporary one.

Although Cherkassy had distracted the Russians, it had in no way impaired their power. The weather, not the German resistance, was their problem. The unstable winter was giving way to an early, wet spring—and more mud. And the Soviet forces were encountering another problem in the western Ukraine, something that previously had been an exclusively German concern: partisan warfare. Ukrainian separatism was strong in the area. It had smoldered under the German Occupation, and it burst into a blaze around the returning Soviet armies. Ironically, the Russians called the anti-Soviet partisans by the same name the Germans used for the Soviet partisans—"bandits."

On February 29, Ukrainian partisans claimed one of the best Soviet generals. While on his way to an Army headquarters in the western Ukraine, Vatutin was wounded in a guerrilla attack, and he died six weeks later. He was buried with honors in Kiev and given a funeral salute by the Moscow artillery.

Zhukov replaced Vatutin as the commander of the First Ukrainian Front and on March 4 resumed the offensive. The Second Ukrainian Front joined in the following day and the Third Ukrainian Front the day after that. Their orders were sweeping: to drive the Germans off all Soviet territory between the Pripyat Marshes and the Black Sea. Zhukov and Konev found themselves engaged in a race to the Rumanian border.

In a style befitting Soviet marshals, the two commanders started out with equal forces. Between them they had all of the Soviet tank armies: Konev the Sixth, Second, and Fifth Guards, and Zhukov the First, Fourth, and Third Guards. Both marshals aimed to cut across all of the three remaining river lines and crush Army Groups South and A against the Carpathian Mountains.

Konev, who put all of his tank armies into the opening attack, smashed through between the First Panzer and Eighth Armies on the first day. Zhukov made a breakthrough between the First Panzer and Fourth Panzer Armies on the second day. To the south, General Rodion Malinovsky's Third Ukrainian Front had no tank armies, and its attack on the German Sixth Army on the third day was less powerful than those of Konev and Zhukov. But against its weak opponent it was overwhelming anyway. By the 8th of March, the Soviet fronts were rapidly rolling all four German armies back toward the Bug River and toward Hitler's fortified places: Ternopol, Proskurov, Kovel, Vinnitsa, Pervomaisk.

Konev's tank armies blasted their way across the Bug without a pause and were crossing the Dniester by March 22, having covered 120 muddy miles in 17 days. On the south, the German Sixth and Eighth Armies were pinned to the Bug by Hitler's orders. If they did not withdraw farther, they were sure to be crushed. On the morning of March 26, Kleist defied the Führer by taking personal command of the Eighth Army and giving both armies an order to retreat to the Dniester. "Someone," he told OKH chief Zeitzler, "must lay his head on the block." Hitler chose not to countermand Kleist's order, but he did not forgive him.

Konev's Fortieth Army was already cutting deep behind the First Panzer Army on the southeast when, on the 21st of March, 200 of Zhukov's tanks broke through the German unit's left flank from the northwest. When the Soviet tanks passed Chortkov, they cut the panzer army's main artery, a single-track railroad. When they crossed the Dniester and fanned out to meet the Fortieth Army's elements already on the other side, the First Panzer Army was encircled.

On March 25, Manstein flew to Berchtesgaden, where Hitler was taking his spring vacation, to persuade the Führer to let the First Panzer Army break out of the trap. Hitler refused to approve a breakout. He claimed Manstein had "dribbled away" all the divisions he had given him, and accused Manstein of always wanting to retreat but never being able to make a stand anywhere.

Later that day, however, the Führer's mood inexplicably changed. At midnight, the hour at which he customarily held the main situation conference of the day, Hitler received Manstein again and, without more argument, authorized the breakout. Having done so, he also gave Manstein four divisions with which to stage a relief drive from the west: one infantry and one light infantry division, and two SS panzer divisions. The release of the SS divisions, both new and fully equipped, represented a significant departure from the reinforcement ban, but Manstein soon learned that the apparent turnabout did not signify restored confidence in his generalship.

While Manstein was in the air the next day on the way back to his headquarters in Lvov, Konev's armor reached the Prut River, which was also the Rumanian border. Konev had won the race, and Moscow honored the Second Ukrainian Front that night with a first category salute, 24 volleys from 324 guns. As the guns were firing, Konev's troops were crossing the river with scant opposition. The Rumanian Army, assigned to defend its own frontier, showed little desire to fight. As a precaution, many of the Rumanian officers had already stopped wearing their German decorations.

On March 30, in a truly unusual gesture, Hitler sent his personal Condor transport to pick up Kleist at his headquarters in Tiraspol and Manstein at Lvov. That night, at the midnight situation conference, he awarded them each the swords to the Knight's Cross of the Iron Cross—and relieved them of their commands. Obviously straining to appear to be parting with them amicably, Hitler told them he approved of everything they had done in the past months but had concluded that, on the Eastern Front, the day of the master tacticians was past and what he would need henceforth were generals who could drive their troops to the utmost and extract the last ounce of energy from them.

On their way out, Manstein and Kleist passed their successors, Walter Model, promoted to field marshal, and Ferdinand Schörner, newly advanced to colonel general, waiting in the anteroom. Model, the defensive specialist called in from Army Group North, would take over from Manstein. Schörner, Kleist's replacement, was an autocrat who, during

German soldiers trudge through blinding April snow in an attempt to break the Soviet ring around Kovel, which Hitler had designated a "fortified place" to be defended to the death. But once again, as so often in the past, Hitler himself was forced to rescind the designation, and the Germans retreated to a more defensible line 15 miles farther west.

a tour of duty in northern Finland, quieted his troop's complaints about the bitter weather with a simple order: "The Arctic does not exist."

To make the break with the past complete, Hitler also renamed the two army groups. Army Group South became Army Group North Ukraine, and Army Group A became Army Group South Ukraine.

Meanwhile, General Hube's task of extricating the encircled First Panzer Army remained onerous and perilous regardless of who commanded the army group. To break through the Soviet ring, he had to take the army west along the left side of the Dniester, through the rear lines of Zhukov's tank armies and across two tributary rivers, the Zbruch and the Seret. The whole pocket would have to move like a giant amoeba, contracting on the north and east and stretching to the west. The first crisis would come at the Zbruch. The fate of the army rested on whether it could cross the river in the first place and then on whether it would have strength enough to go any farther.

Hube secured two bridgeheads on the Zbruch on March 29. During the next two days, his lead elements headed for the Seret, and the rear drew in to the Zbruch. The first crossing was then assured, but Zhukov was ranging a phalanx of armor on the west bank of the Seret, and Hube doubted that his army could fight its way through on the paltry supplies it had, plus what it was getting by air.

On March 31, a blizzard swept over the battlefield, and it proved to be the army's salvation. The Luftwaffe transports kept flying through the worst of the three-day storm, giving Hube the ammunition and supplies he needed for a powerful push to safety. To brighten the First Army's picture further, the two SS divisions earmarked for the relief completed their train trips through Poland and arrived at the front at the turn of the month.

On April 2, covered by the storm, the First Panzer Army secured a bridgehead on the Seret. The next day, when the weather began to clear, Zhukov rushed in more tanks, but they were too late. The German bridgehead expanded. During the night of April 4, sixty Junkers transports loaded with ammunition and fuel landed in the pocket, and on the following morning the SS panzer divisions attacked out of the Fourth Panzer Army line. In two days, they had made contact with the pocket. In four more days, 600 tons of supplies

had been transported in through the corridor the SS divisions had opened, and Hube brought his rear guard behind the Seret. He then maneuvered his army upstream, northwest toward Lvov.

Hube's masterly extrication of his army from the jaws of the Soviet trap did not go unrewarded. At the Berghof on the night of April 20, Hitler decorated him with the swords and diamonds to the Knight's Cross of the Iron Cross. Then, suddenly, the brilliant panzer general was no more. Taking off before daylight on the following morning, the pilot of Hube's plane made a wrong turn and crashed into a mountain in the Austrian Alps. Hube and all the others aboard the plane were killed.

The survival of the First Panzer Army was only a flicker of light in what had been a disastrous season for the Wehrmacht in the Ukraine. By mid-April, the German Fourth Panzer Army, licking its wounds, was pinned to the Carpathian Mountains, its line dipping into Rumania for a 120-mile stretch. Farther south, the Sixth and Eighth Armies, which arrived at the Dniester River line on April 14, were in a shambles. By the time the troops pulled behind the river, the Rumanian railroads on which they relied for supplies had broken down entirely, and the two armies found themselves stranded, without clothing or food. The wounded had to be left in the open at the empty sidings. The daily ration was reduced to 200 grams of bread.

As Army Group South was reeling from the second of the Russians' three blows, Soviet armies were aiming the third one at the Crimea. This was not to be a distinguished campaign. For weeks, in fact, the main question seemed to be which side would defeat itself first.

The Soviet command began pondering a Crimean invasion in October 1943, when its front line was approaching the peninsula. Some strategists favored bypassing the peninsula and sealing it off, which would have spared the effort and expense of an invasion. The prevailing opinion, however, was that the Crimea had to be retaken to prevent the enemy from using it as a base for attacks on the surrounding Soviet territory. Perhaps prestige was what actually counted most. The Soviet Union could not assert its predominance in the Black Sea until it controlled the Crimea.

In the first two weeks of November, the Soviet forces took

steps toward reclaiming the Crimea. On the northern edge of the peninsula, the Fourth Ukrainian Front, commanded by General Tolbukhin, blocked the Perekop Isthmus, the principal access to the mainland, and took several small beachheads on the south shore of the Sivash, the shallow fringe of water lying between the peninsula and the mainland. At the same time, the Independent Maritime Army, under Lieut. General Ivan Y. Petrov, who had commanded Soviet forces during the German siege of Sevastopol in 1941-1942, took a beachhead on the easternmost neck of the peninsula, where it abuts the mainland at the Kerch Strait. The stage had been set for a two-pronged drive into the peninsula from the north and the east, and Stalin sent Marshal Kliment E. Voroshilov, a member of the Soviet High Command and the State Defense Committee, to coordinate Tolbukhin's and Petrov's operations.

Two years had passed since Voroshilov had last been in the field—on a brief stint as the High Command's representative to the Volkhov Front. His name was well known in the Army, since he was an old crony of Stalin's and one of those regularly mentioned in the newspapers on ceremonial occasions; but his military abilities were dubious and Stalin sent along as his adviser Lieut. General Sergei Shtemenko, chief of operations of the General Staff. During the train trip to the south, Voroshilov showed himself to be more interested in discussing music and literature than military affairs, and he passed the time testing Shtemenko's knowledge of opera, composers and Russian classical authors. In the evening, Voroshilov liked to have his aide read to him from the works of Chekhov or Gogol. "The aide read well," Shtemenko said, "and Voroshilov's face wore an expression of bliss."

On reaching the Crimea, Voroshilov cautiously set out to organize the reconquest of the peninsula. He, Petrov and Shtemenko all agreed from the first that the beachhead could not accommodate all the men and equipment necessary for a full-scale offensive and would have to be expanded with another landing farther to the west. Expanding the beachhead was going to require joint operations by the Army, Navy and Air Force of a sort that had produced mixed results in the past. And planning for the operation was hampered from the outset by bickering between the various commanders over their areas of responsibility.

Voroshilov could have resolved the issue, but in so doing he would have established himself as a partner in the operation, and the senior one at that. Instead, he avoided the risk of assuming responsibility and presented himself as a mediator. After lengthy negotiations the commanders settled on a compromise battle plan. Ten officers signed the protocol, with the senior one, Voroshilov, appearing merely as a "participant."

After about six weeks' preparation, the landing was made under cover of darkness on January 10. The Germans laid down murderous fire on the beaches. A planned linkup with the original beachhead could not be made, and after two days the whole operation had to be abandoned because the landing force ran out of ammunition.

On February 3, without prior notice either to Voroshilov or to Petrov, General Andrei I. Yeremenko arrived from Moscow with orders to take over command of the Independent Maritime Army. Petrov and Shtemenko were summoned to Moscow, Petrov to be relegated to the command reserve pool, Shtemenko to receive a dressing down from Stalin for not having given Voroshilov, who outranked him by two grades, stronger guidance. Stalin was particularly angry about the signed protocol. "Like some collective farm!" he scolded. "You didn't hold a vote on it by any chance? Voroshilov can be forgiven for a thing like that—

Assault troops of the Fourth Ukrainian Front ferry horses across the Sivash, or Putrid Sea, whose briny shallows separated the eastern Crimea from the Ukrainian mainland. The April 1944 attack opened up the Crimea to Soviet forces, which then traversed the 156 miles to Sevastopol in just one week.

he's not a staff officer. But you should have known how things are done." As for Voroshilov, Stalin sent him to take over as Tolbukhin's Stavka representative on the mainland approaches to the Crimea—where he would be under the watchful eye of Marshal Aleksandr Vasilevsky, chief of the General Staff.

Meanwhile, on the German side Zeitzler, Kleist and Colonel General Erwin Jaenecke, commander of the Seventeenth Army, had agreed that Jaenecke's troops ought to quit the Crimea. The army's five German divisions and seven highly unreliable Rumanian divisions (about 90,000 German and 60,000 Rumanian troops) were not enough to withstand a determined attack for more than a few days anywhere except at Sevastopol. And, even there, the effort could not affect the situation on the mainland front in any useful way.

The Russians, for their part, were giving the Germans plenty of time to clear out. Vasilevsky, without consulting Voroshilov (whom he considered most notable for his "geniality and hospitality"), decided to put off the invasion of the Crimea until troops could be spared from the more important operations in the Dnieper bend. In February and through March, while Voroshilov busied himself as best he could aboard his private railroad car, Vasilevsky and Tolbukhin worked intermittently on a plan for the Crimea.

All winter long, Hitler refused—as was to be expected—to allow the Seventeenth Army to budge.

On April 7, General Schörner, the newly appointed commanding general of Army Group South Ukraine, completed his inaugural inspection of the Crimean defenses, pronounced them in excellent shape and made one of history's shortest-lived military prognostications—that the peninsula could be held "for a long time."

The next day Tolbukhin's Fourth Ukrainian Front drove into the Perekop Isthmus and across the Sivash. By the time Yeremenko's Independent Maritime Army joined in from the east three days later, the issue had already been decided. The isthmus and Sivash battlefronts had collapsed after one day, and Hitler, in a rage at Jaenecke, whom he accused of having lost his nerve, had been forced to permit a retreat to the Gneisenau Line, an arc of trenches centered on Simferopol 40 miles east of Sevastopol. But the German retreat enabled Tolbukhin and Yeremenko to bring most of their combined total of 470,000 troops and 560 tanks and self-propelled assault guns into play and to crack the Gneisenau Line on April 12. Four days later, only a small jump ahead of the Russians, the German Seventeenth Army went into the Sevastopol line.

Everybody in authority on the German side, including Hitler, had previously believed that once the retreat began it would inevitably proceed to the final stage—evacuation. Schörner, backpedaling from his earlier optimism, had reported that resistance in the Gneisenau Line and Sevastopol together could be sustained no longer than the three to four weeks it would take to complete a sealift to the mainland. When the first German supply convoys to arrive had to fight their way in and out through light units of the Soviet Black Sea Fleet swarming off Sevastopol, even Schörner's latest estimate began to look excessively optimistic. But Hitler now insisted on holding Sevastopol.

The Russians gave the Seventeenth Army one last chance to escape. Having come up on Sevastopol much faster than they had anticipated, they needed the last half of April and most of the first week in May to regroup. But Hitler refused to take advantage of the opportunity.

Late in the month, Hitler called Jaenecke to the Berghof and promised him "generous" reinforcements. On learning that the reinforcements, in fact, amounted to only four battalions of half-trained recruits, Jaenecke angrily submitted a

Rescued from Sevastopol, troops of the German Seventeenth Army dock at Constanta, Rumania, in May 1944. They were among the few lucky ones; more than 100,000 German and Rumanian soldiers were killed or captured in the Crimea, and another 42,000 drowned when Soviet air attacks sank their ships while they were crossing the Black Sea.

letter requesting that the Seventeenth Army be placed directly under the Army High Command, which would have made Hitler personally responsible for the destruction of the army when it came. In response to the affront, Hitler declared that Jaenecke had demonstrated he was no longer capable of commanding at Sevastopol, gave the army command to Lieut. General Karl Allmendinger, one of the corps commanders, and ordered that Jaenecke was not to be allowed to return to the Crimea.

Physically, Sevastopol was the most defensible spot on the whole Eastern Front. Rugged terrain and lines of ridges, most notably the Zapun Heights of Crimean War fame, gave natural protection to the city and the harbor. The Germans also had three successive lines of trenches and bunkers.

The Seventeenth Army's problem, though, was manpower, not fortifications. Its strength, German and Rumanian combined, was under 65,000 when Allmendinger took command—scarcely enough troops to man an outer line of 27 miles plus an inner line 18 miles long. Tolbukhin, on the other hand, had three armies, the Second Guards, the Fifty-first and the Maritime Army.

Early on May 5, the Second Guards Army hit the northern quadrant of the outer line. This was where the Germans had placed their main effort two years before, and they had expected the Russians to do the same because the lie of the ground and the road system were better for an offensive than in the south. But the Second Guards Army's attack was a feint. Vasilevsky and Tolbukhin did not launch their main effort until two days later, after Allmendinger's small reserves were thoroughly tied down. Then the other two Soviet armies drove out of the southeast past Balaklava and toward the Zapun Heights.

By nightfall, the Fifty-first Army and the Maritime Army had smashed through both German lines and scaled the Zapun Heights, which gave them a clear field of observation over the whole beachhead out to Cape Khersones, its westernmost tip. In the night, "the sky above Sevastopol is a glowing red," a Soviet correspondent reported, "filled with the droning of motors and roar of explosions, as if the mountains were cracking asunder. The Germans have set up antiaircraft guns and the curtain of fire they raise at night is so thick it seems as if a many-colored rainstorm has burst over the city. But our planes penetrate this fire curtain, dump their missiles in the bay and sink ships at sea, while Ju-52 transport planes are shot down as they take off from the airfield."

On the night of April 8, after the Russians had wrested control of the harbor, Hitler gave the order to evacuate.

During the next four nights, convoys with enough ships to take all of the surviving troops aboard stood off Cape Khersones, but some turned back to the Rumanian port of Constanta empty, and others embarked only a fraction of the men they could have carried. The Navy claimed that the whole cape was shrouded in smoke and the ships could not go inshore. The Seventeenth Army chief of staff insisted that visibility had been sufficient for ships to navigate into the inlets, but that several whole convoys had failed even to try. The result was a fiasco, and the majority of the troops who had made their way out to the cape, more than 26,000, were left on the beach to be taken prisoner.

"The promontory," Shtemenko wrote later, "was literally packed with German tanks, vehicles, guns, and mortars. There were signs of Soviet bombing and shelling everywhere. All kinds of stores had been abandoned in the ravines and on the steep slopes leading to the shore. The human corpses had been cleared away, but a nauseating stench still hung in the air. As far as the eye could scan, the sea was covered with swollen carcasses of horses that were slowly rolling over in the waves and bursting in the heat."

By then Hitler had decided where to place the blame for the debacle at Sevastopol. Neither Jaenecke nor Allmendinger would ever be given another command.

By the spring of 1944, the Russians' three blows had pounded and twisted the German line and driven it westward as much as 300 miles. In the north, the German line had been pushed back almost to the borders of the Baltic States. In the south, from the Pripyat Marshes to the Black Sea, the immense westward protuberance of the line bespoke the Germans' loss of the entire Ukraine and the restoration of the pre-1939 Soviet boundary with Rumania and Poland.

Only in the center, Belorussia, had the German armies been able to hold their line during the first few months of 1944, and that only because the German Army Group Center had not been challenged there. For that group of armies, the trial of blood and steel was still to come.

THE RED AIR FORCE REBORN

Soviet aircrews prepare for a mission over German lines in their twin-engined Il-4 medium bombers. The Il-4 was a work horse of the resurgent Red Air Force.

BUILDING AIR POWER AMID DISASTER

In a 1942 speech, the brilliant Soviet aircraft designer Sergei V. Ilyushin proclaimed his government's view of air power, which ran counter to that of the Western Allies: "We have never accepted the doctrine of winning a war by massive long-range bombardment. We have always thought the main role of aviation was the support of the ground forces."

But Ilyushin was dissembling about the past. Through the late 1920s and early 1930s, the U.S.S.R. had competed with Great Britain and the United States in developing large four-engined bombers, intended for strategic bombardment of an enemy's homeland. Then Stalin, impressed by the nimble, hard-hitting German fighter-bombers in the Spanish Civil War, had decided to revamp the Red Air Force. Henceforth, the concentration would be on tactical air war and the construction of fighter planes and attack bombers.

The Soviet Air Force was still in a vulnerable transition when the Germans launched their sudden attack. In the first week of the June 1941 invasion, more than 4,000 of the 7,700 Soviet planes in the West were destroyed. The old bombers flew suicidal missions against the Wehrmacht; of the 800 on hand, only 266 were still flying in December. Soviet fighters were shot down in job lots by faster, higher-flying Messerschmitts. Inexperienced Soviet pilots resorted to the desperate tactic of trying to ram Luftwaffe planes.

By late 1942, however, the new Red Air Force was rising phoenix-like from the ashes of the old. Aircraft plants that had been hurriedly moved to the Soviet interior were turning out thousands of the new models Stalin had ordered; in addition, hundreds of British and U.S. Lend-Lease fighter planes (left) were being ferried to the Soviet Union. The new Soviet planes were made largely of wood, plywood and synthetic compounds because of the scarcity of aluminum, but they gave the pilots confidence and encouraged aggressiveness and experimentation in fighter operations.

By mid-1943, the Red Air Force boasted no fewer than 8,300 frontline aircraft and close to half a million men and women. It was fast being transformed into a juggernaut that would match the Red Army.

Ace Aleksandr Pokryshkin is congratulated by fellow pilots after one of his 59 victories. For each kill, a star was painted on his American-made P-39.

Women pilots of the 46th Guards Night Bomber Regiment are briefed for a mission. During the War, the women of this regiment flew 24,000 night missions and won from the Germans the name "night witches."

A PO-2, acting in its courier role, brings dispatches from Army headquarters to an artillery battery on the Eastern Front in 1942.

Beside a PO-2 ambulance plane, medics lift a wounded Soviet soldier into a compartment made from the observer's seat. Only these light planes were able

A PESTIFEROUS FIVE-CYLINDER RELIC

The PO-2 looked and performed like a relic of the First World War. It was tiny and slow—60 miles per hour—and in fact it dated back to 1927. Yet this ancient wood and canvas crate, with a putt-putting five-cylinder engine, was a plane of many roles in the hard-pressed Red Air Force of 1941 and 1942. It served as a primary trainer, a scout plane, an aerial ambulance and a liaison taxi that transported couriers to field headquarters and evacuated important prisoners captured at the front.

Amazingly, the PO-2 was even used as a night bomber. The Soviet pilots, many of them women, would cross the German lines one at a time at low altitudes and seek out an enemy in the dark. Since the little planes were largely nonmetallic, they often escaped detection by German radar, and the pilots frequently preserved the element of surprise by gliding in with engines off. They would drop a few light bombs or grenades and then slip away before German fighter planes could rise in pursuit.

Such raids did little damage, but their nuisance value was considerable. Each attack forced the enemy troops to fall out, man their antiaircraft guns, take shelter in trenches—and grumble over the hours of lost sleep. So regularly were the Germans awakened by the pestiferous PO-2s that they called the plane the "duty sergeant."

Soviet crewmen warm up the engine of a PO-2, hidden from German patrol planes in a snowy wood.

to use the rough fields close to the battlefront.

On patrol, PO-2 pilots inspect a Soviet tugboat steaming through the Kerch Strait with a supply barge.

Paratroopers on a training mission file aboard a TB-3, an obsolete heavy bomber used only as a transport plane after 1941.

A multipurpose Il-4, loaded with a torpedo, warms up its 1,100-horsepower engines for a raid on shipping near Murmansk.

A TRIO OF TOUGH TACTICAL BOMBERS

The Red Air Force that finally emerged in 1943 packed a devastating tactical punch: two versatile twin-engined bombers, the Pe-2 and Il-4, and a great single-engined attack bomber, at its best in direct support of the Red Army's infantry and tanks.

The single-engined Il-2 Stormovik, designed by Sergei Ilyushin, was called the "flying tank" because it was difficult to shoot down; its vital machinery was encased in steel plate.

Late models of the Stormovik carried a rear gunner to ward off German fighters and could stop a panzer column with their arsenal of weapons: two 37mm cannon, three machine guns, eight wing-mounted rockets or 1,325 pounds of bombs.

Pe-2 dive bombers release their 2,200-pound bombloads over a rail junction.

Six Il-2 Stormoviks, flying at treetop level after their approach dives, blast a German position in the Crimea with incendiary and fragmentation bombs.

119

FROM SITTING DUCKS TO BIRDS OF PREY

An I-153 taxis before takeoff in 1941. The craft was the last biplane fighter in any major air force.

In 1941, the two main Soviet fighters pitted against the Luftwaffe—the I-16 *(below, left)* and the I-153 *(left)*—were almost a decade old and hopelessly outclassed. Neither plane was able to match the high-altitude performance of the rival Messerschmitts, and the Soviet fighters' top speed fell about 100 miles per hour short of the Me-109's 350 miles per hour. German fighter pilots, pouncing from above and pursuing with deadly effectiveness, ran up fantastic kill records. One ace, Major Erich Hartmann, was credited with shooting down more than 300 Soviet planes.

But by early 1942, help was on the way. During a design competition held in 1939, three aircraft designers—Semyon Lavochkin, Vladimir Gorbunov and Mikhail Gudkov—had gotten together to produce a fighter plane that was identified with their initials, the LaGG. The first three models were underpowered; their airframes, made largely of wood, were too heavy for the planes' liquid-cooled engines. But the LaGG became a stunning success when a potent radial engine was installed. Rechristened the La-5 *(below, right)*, it battled the Messerschmitt on even terms.

Stubby I-16 monoplanes fly in an outmoded tight formation that the Germans found easy to attack.

A LaGG-3 warms up before a winter mission in 1942. Because it was prone to spin and crash, the LaGG was called the "varnished coffin" by Soviet pilots.

One of the War's better fighters, the La-5 combined the sturdy LaGG airframe with an ASh-82 air-cooled engine, which produced 1,510 horsepower.

The MiG-3 was dangerously unbalanced by its long, heavy nose and its short rear section. Designed as a high-altitude interceptor, the plane proved to be ineffective at lower levels.

A high-performance Yak-3 rolls into a climbing turn. Luftwaffe fighter pilots were told to avoid this sleek Yak model, identified by the lack of an air intake under its "chin."

A BEAUTIFUL FAILURE AND A SOLID SUCCESS

Of the fighter planes that emerged from the 1939 design competition, one was so tricky that Soviet pilots feared to fly it, and the other turned out to be the most reliable Soviet fighter of the War.

The plane that failed was the beautiful MiG-3 *(above)*, designed by Artyom I. Mikoyan (brother of Politburo member Anastas) and Mikhail Gurevich. The MiG-3's main trouble was an engine too powerful and heavy for its short, light airframe. It was also feebly armed with three machine guns—not nearly enough to do battle with cannon-firing Messerschmitts.

The success was the Yak. The designer and namesake of the plane, Aleksandr S. Yakovlev, freely borrowed features from early models of the Me-109 and British Spitfire and incorporated them in a rugged, cannon-firing plane that was maneuverable and easy to fly. Yakovlev tirelessly worked to refine and improve upon his basic Yak-1. The Yak-3 *(left)* could climb and match speed with the best German fighters, and the Yak-9 *(right)*, fitted with extra fuel tanks, could escort bombers on 1,300-mile missions. Ultimately the Soviet Union built more than 30,000 Yaks—58 per cent of all its wartime fighter planes.

Patrolling Yak-9s of the elite Sixth Guards Army fly over the Crimea in 1944. The planes had 37mm cannon in their propeller hubs.

Trailing black smoke, a riddled Messerschmitt wings over and dives toward earth as the victorious Soviet pilot, a captain named Tarasov, follows in his Yak

fighter. This kill, Tarasov's 19th, was recorded in late 1943, when Soviet airmen were at long last equipped with aircraft able to compete with the Germans'.

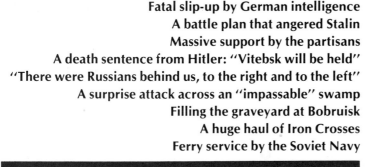

4

Fatal slip-up by German intelligence
A battle plan that angered Stalin
Massive support by the partisans
A death sentence from Hitler: "Vitebsk will be held"
"There were Russians behind us, to the right and to the left"
A surprise attack across an "impassable" swamp
Filling the graveyard at Bobruisk
A huge haul of Iron Crosses
Ferry service by the Soviet Navy

In May 1944, when the Soviet winter offensives finally bogged down in spring mud, the only large chunk of Soviet territory still under German control was Belorussia, a great domain of forested and lake-studded lowland lying between the Baltic States and the Ukraine. Here, the front lines of Field Marshal Ernst Busch's Army Group Center ran along the upper reaches of the Dnieper River and bulged to within 300 miles of Moscow. The situation in this area had not changed significantly since 1941, when the Germans were rolled back after reaching the gates of the Soviet capital.

Although Soviet advances to the north and south had left Army Group Center's flanks dangerously exposed, Busch had little fear of a major Soviet attack. The German Eastern Intelligence Branch had predicted that the big Soviet summer offensive of 1944 would take place in the south, toward the Balkans.

Hitler agreed. As he saw it, Stalin could not pass up the opportunity to grab Rumania, Bulgaria and Hungary—countries long coveted by the Russians. Besides knocking these already shaky German allies out of the War, a Soviet drive through the Balkans would deprive Hitler of vital Rumanian oil, something that repeated Allied air raids on that country's wells and refineries had failed to accomplish. It would also give the Red Army a direct route into Austria and southern Germany along the Danube River valley.

With these factors in mind, Busch did not complain as Hitler stripped units from his Army Group Center in order to reinforce the southern sector of the Russian Front. During May 1944, Busch gave up 15 per cent of his divisions, 33 per cent of his heavy artillery, 50 per cent of his tank destroyers and 88 per cent of his tanks. Army Group Center, at one time a force of nearly one million men, was reduced to 400,000 men—and left perilously open to attack everywhere along its 450-mile front.

Hitler, it turned out, had made a mistake—a monumental strategic blunder. Since April 1944, the Soviet High Command had been meticulously preparing a major blow against the German line in Belorussia, and the Führer had played right into the Russians' hands.

The Belorussian Bulge, as the German salient came to be known, represented both a threat and an opportunity to the Russians. It threatened the flanks of any Soviet advance into the Baltic States or Poland. On the other hand, it was inher-

CLEARING THE RUSSIAN LAND

ently vulnerable. If Stalin could nip off the bulge with a powerful pincers attack from north and south, his forces could strike at will toward the Baltic States, East Prussia and central Poland without worrying about the security of their flanks or rear.

In focusing his attention on the German center, Stalin had not overlooked the possibility of strategic gains in the Balkans to the south. Nor had he failed to consider how his allies might view his ambitions for that region. Ever since the Teheran Conference in November 1943, he had suspected the British and Americans of plotting a move he called the Balkan Variant—a preemptive Allied landing in the area to keep the Russians out. At the first sign of an Allied move into the region, Stalin intended to grab the Balkans himself. But with the invasion of Normandy scheduled for the spring of 1944, the Balkan Variant did not seem to be in the cards, and Belorussia could safely take precedence.

Stalin named and timed the offensive against the Belorussian Bulge with heavy-handed historical symbolism. He code-named the attack Operation *Bagration,* after Peter Bagration, a Russian warrior-prince who had won fame fighting another Western invader, Napoleon. And he set the start of the offensive for June 22, the third anniversary of Hitler's invasion of the Soviet Union.

The planning and coordination were turned over to Marshals Vasilevsky and Zhukov, the architects of the smashing victories at Stalingrad and Kursk. They worked through May and June to assemble a force of 2.5 million men for Operation *Bagration.* Of these, more than 1.2 million were combat troops, organized into 166 infantry, armored, motorized and cavalry divisions. The infantrymen were supported by 5,200 tanks and self-propelled guns, 7,000 fighter planes and bombers, and more than 31,000 field guns and mortars. For several weeks before the opening of the attack, 100 trainloads of ammunition, food and fuel arrived daily at the Soviet forward areas. A huge fleet of trucks—many of them American Lend-Lease vehicles—was assembled to supply the advancing armies once the assault began. And some 300,000 hospital beds were readied for the expected flood of wounded.

The Germans did not detect any unusual activity opposite Army Group Center until the end of May, when the Ninth Army reported heavy traffic on the opposite bank of the Dnieper. Thereafter, the portents of trouble multiplied rapidly. Busch's Third Panzer, Fourth and Ninth Armies identified new enemy units in their sectors. A downed Soviet pilot confirmed rumors picked up by German agents that Marshal Zhukov was commanding in the field—a sure sign that something big was in the works. But when Busch told the Führer of this activity, Hitler dismissed it as Soviet deception, nothing more. It was only to be expected, Hitler said, that the Russians would feed some reinforcements into the Belorussia area in order to pin down Army Group Center while they attacked in the south.

The strategy developed by Vasilevsky and Zhukov was a classic envelopment that would bag or smash most of Army Group Center. Marshal Rokossovsky, commanding the First Belorussian Front, would thrust toward Minsk from the southeast. Simultaneously, the Third Belorussian Front, under Lieut. General Ivan D. Chernyakhovsky, would attack toward Minsk from the northeast and link up with Rokossovsky. Chernyakhovsky would have the help of General Ivan K. Bagramyan, whose First Baltic Front would assist in the initial breakthrough and protect Chernyakhovsky's northern flank. The Second Belorussian Front, under the newly promoted General Matvei V. Zakharov, would serve as the link between the two arms of the Soviet pincers, driving the encircled Germans forward into Rokossovsky and Chernyakhovsky's trap.

The Soviet field commanders agreed wholeheartedly with the overall plan of attack, but there were some sharp differences of opinion concerning the precise methods of execution. Rokossovsky's forces, for example, would have to capture or neutralize the fortified town of Bobruisk before the southern arm could advance on Minsk. Bobruisk sat at the northern edge of the immense Pripyat Marshes, which restricted armored vehicles to relatively narrow corridors of dry ground. Rokossovsky decided that conditions in the Pripyat Marshes dictated a double-pronged attack on Bobruisk. This was in conflict with Soviet tactical doctrine, which always called for a single, massive blow at the beginning of an offensive.

Rokossovsky's heretical tactics became the subject of sharp debate during a May 22 meeting in Moscow. He carefully presented his plan and described its advantages to Stalin and members of the Soviet State Defense Committee, including Foreign Minister Vyacheslav M. Molotov and Secretary of the Central Committee Georgy M. Malenkov. At the first mention of a two-pronged advance, Stalin interrupted Rokossovsky.

"The defense must be breached in one place," Stalin declared firmly.

"If we breach the defense in two sectors," replied Rokossovsky, "we can bring more forces into the attack, whereupon we deny the enemy the possibility of transferring reinforcements from one sector to another."

"And that's what you call advantages?" asked Stalin contemptuously. "Go out and think it over again."

Rokossovsky went to an adjoining room and reconsidered his plan of attack. The more he thought about it, the more certain he felt that the terrain demanded a dispersal of forces; a single strike could cost unnecessary loss of life if his soldiers were trapped in a narrow corridor. His conviction renewed, Rokossovsky returned to Stalin's study.

"Have you thought it through, General?" asked Stalin. "Yes, sir, Comrade Stalin."

"Well then, that means we'll strike a single blow?" Stalin asked rhetorically, already tracing the path of advance on a situation map.

"Two blows are more advisable, Comrade Stalin," replied Rokossovsky. The other generals in the room looked on in stunned silence.

Stalin studied the map, then said, "Go out and think it over again. Don't be stubborn, Rokossovsky."

In the adjoining room, Rokossovsky was soon joined by Molotov and Malenkov.

"Don't forget where you are and with whom you're talking," warned Malenkov. "You are disagreeing with Comrade Stalin."

"You'll have to agree, Rokossovsky," added Molotov. "Agree—that's all there is to it."

Rokossovsky was again ushered into Stalin's presence.

Relentlessly the dictator asked, "So what is better—two weak blows or one strong blow?"

"Two strong blows are better than one strong blow," replied Rokossovsky.

"But which of them should be primary, in your opinion?"

"They should both be primary."

For a few tense moments, Stalin simply smoked his pipe and said nothing. Then he walked over to Rokossovsky, put a hand on his shoulder and remarked to the others: "You know, Rokossovsky is right. And generally I like a commander who sticks to his guns. I confirm your decision, Comrade Rokossovsky."

Now it was up to Rokossovsky to prove his point on the battlefield.

The Soviet forces unfolded Operation *Bagration* over a three-day period, attacking the German northern flank on June 22, the central sector on June 23 and the southern end on June 24. The piecemeal attacks confused the Germans, just as Zhukov and Vasilevsky had intended. Not until the offensive was three days old did Hitler recognize the terrible truth: The Russians were throwing an all-out offensive at the weakest point on the German line.

At Army Group Center headquarters in Minsk, Field Marshal Busch listened with growing alarm to radioed reports of Soviet breakthroughs. But there was little he could do to stop them. Belorussian partisans had set off 10,500 explosive charges behind the German lines, crippling the vital railroad network needed to move reinforcements and supplies up to the front; they claimed to have derailed 147

trains in a three-day period. Busch had only five understrength, half-trained reserve divisions, and the Luftwaffe's Sixth Air Fleet, supporting Army Group Center, had only 40 operational fighters on the day of the attack. Worst of all, eight of Busch's best divisions were tied down in so-called fortified places along the front line, and only a direct order from Hitler could release those units for Busch's use.

The four Soviet army groups had slammed into the Germans at six separate points along the 450-mile front. In the Vitebsk area, Colonel General Georg-Hans Reinhardt's Third Panzer Army was hit by General Bagramyan's First Baltic Front and by General Chernyakhovsky's Third Belorussian Front. Under furious assault, Reinhardt's 9th and 6th Corps fell back in confusion, leaving the northern and southern approaches to Vitebsk wide open. By the 23rd of June, the First Baltic Front had driven 10 miles deep into the German lines.

Reinhardt telephoned his superior, Field Marshal Busch, and asked for his permission to evacuate Vitebsk immediately. But Busch, mindful of the Führer's orders to stand firm, refused to grant the request. Nor would Busch permit Reinhardt to reinforce his disintegrating flanks with the four inactive divisions of the 53rd Corps that were being used to garrison Vitebsk.

By June 24, the situation had become so serious that Reinhardt went over Busch's head with an appeal to Hitler himself. In a telephone conversation with General Zeitzler, Hitler's chief of staff, Reinhardt said that his 53rd Corps, numbering 35,000 men, would soon be encircled in Vitebsk by the advancing Soviet spearheads. If its four divi-

Phalanxes of trucks, assembled for the Red Army offensive in Belorussia, stand in a depot outside Moscow in May of 1944, waiting to be dispatched to the front lines. All in all, 12,000 trucks transported Soviet soldiers and supplies to the site of the enormous battle.

In the decisive battle of the summer of 1944, the 166 divisions of four Soviet army groups attacked the German Army Group Center at six separate points (small arrows) in Belorussia, with orders to sweep toward Minsk (large arrows) and envelop the enemy's 38 divisions. The German defense plan was to tie down Soviet strength with do-or-die stands at four towns: Vitebsk, Orsha, Mogilev and Bobruisk.

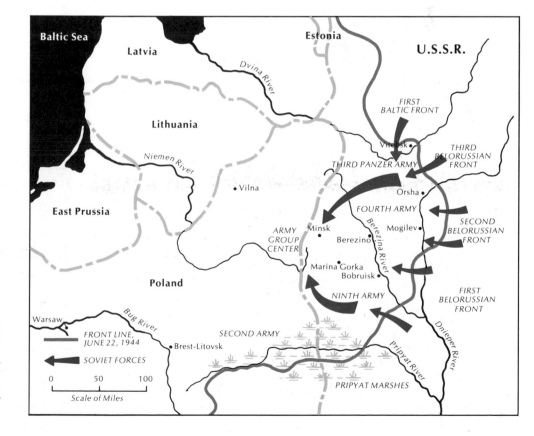

sions were to be saved from destruction, they would have to be withdrawn immediately.

Zeitzler told Reinhardt to hold the telephone line open while he talked to Hitler. After 10 minutes, Zeitzler reported the Führer's order: "Vitebsk will be held." Minutes later, the exasperated Reinhardt learned that the Russians had begun closing the only remaining road from Vitebsk to the German positions in the west.

Three more hours passed before Hitler realized the gravity of the 53rd Corps' plight. In a radio message at 6:30 p.m. on June 24, he belatedly gave permission for the 53rd Corps to withdraw. But there was a catch: "One division," read Hitler's order, "will remain in Vitebsk and continue to hold out. The name of the commander is to be reported to me." Reinhardt reluctantly chose the 206th Infantry Division, under Lieut. General A. Hitter, for this sacrificial role.

Hitler's change of mind had come too late. The commander of the 53rd Corps, Major General Friedrich Gollwitzer, tried to lead three of his divisions out of the Soviet trap. But there was no escape. On the afternoon of June 25, Gollwitzer reported to Reinhardt by radio: "Situation drastically changed. Totally encircled. 4th Luftwaffe Field Division no longer exists. 246th Infantry Division and 6th Luftwaffe Field Division engaged in heavy fighting in several directions. Fierce fighting in the built-up area of Vitebsk."

For the next two days, the remnants of Gollwitzer's corps were squeezed from all sides by the Soviet infantry, mercilessly hammered by artillery fire, and bombed and strafed by the Red Air Force. A German sergeant major later described the confusion and terror of the encircled troops: "No one knew what was going on. There were Russians behind us, to the right and to the left. Rumor had it that men who lost touch were abandoned by headquarters. We were told we were in the midst of Russian positions. We wanted to break out. We fired. My God, but it was useless. It was like firing at the ocean waves with the tide coming in."

On the morning of June 27, Reinhardt received a final report from Gollwitzer. His troops, still trying to fight free, were 10 miles southwest of Vitebsk and making some progress. But they were running out of ammunition and were under constant air attack. After this message, the radio channel was silent.

Soviet witnesses later reported that some 8,000 men of the 53rd Corps had succeeded in breaking out of the Soviet encirclement. But they were quickly surrounded again. On June 27, Gollwitzer accepted a Soviet ultimatum and surrendered to General Chernyakhovsky's forces. In captivity, Gollwitzer voiced his frustration and bitterness over the catastrophe that had befallen his corps: "The responsibility for what has happened is not the Army's," he told General Chernyakhovsky. "It's Hitler's."

While Gollwitzer's three divisions were being destroyed in their battle to break out of the ring, Hitler preoccupied himself with the suspicion that Hitter's 206th Division might not fight to the last bullet for Vitebsk. On June 25, he ordered Reinhardt to have a staff officer parachute into the surrounded town to deliver a written order to Hitter.

This was the last straw for Reinhardt. He pointed out to Busch that the Führer's orders had already been sent by radio and acknowledged by Hitter. Reinhardt saw no point in sacrificing one more life in Vitebsk. Busch, predictably shocked by this display of insubordination, pointed out that the suspicious Führer was waiting for the name of the officer and the time of his dispatch. Reinhardt replied that if Hitler really insisted on his order, he would go himself.

Reinhardt's bluff worked. Within an hour, Hitler withdrew his order. But Hitler's commands could no longer alter

At the headquarters of the First Belorussian Front, commanding officer Konstantin K. Rokossovsky carries on a phone consultation with the aid of a map while preparing for the enormous Soviet offensive that netted Belorussia and eastern Poland in the summer of 1944. Rokossovsky's political commissar, Lieut. General K. F. Telegin, looks on at right.

the fate of the 206th Infantry Division. On June 26, as the town of Vitebsk disintegrated under Soviet artillery fire and bombing, Hitter took matters into his own hands and ordered a breakout after darkness fell. His men loaded their numerous wounded on horse-drawn carts and an artillery tractor. Shortly after 10 o'clock that night, Hitter's advance guard found an opening in the Soviet ring and began leading the tattered division through it.

The Russians soon detected Hitter's nocturnal movement. Troops of General Chernyakhovsky's Thirty-ninth Army rushed to intercept and encircle the grim column of Germans. In desperation, Hitter ordered his men to charge the Soviet lines with fixed bayonets. Chernyakhovsky's troops mowed down the weary Germans as they advanced and then rounded up Hitter and a handful of survivors hiding in a nearby forest.

As the Russians were entering Vitebsk on June 26, the fortified towns of Orsha and Mogilev were under attack by General Zakharov's Second Belorussian Front and units of the Third Belorussian Front. Two divisions of General Kurt von Tippelskirch's Fourth Army already had been destroyed in the fortified towns, and the remainder of the Fourth Army was falling back in chaos and confusion. Soon, few units existed as cohesive formations. Along the Germans' front lines, everyone pitched in and tried to halt the Soviet juggernaut—engineers, military police, medics, cooks and baggage handlers.

In this sector, the Soviet infantry received invaluable support from the fighter planes and bombers of General K. A. Vershinin's Fourth Air Army. Vershinin's primary targets were the Germans' big 88mm guns, which Tippelskirch had moved up to the front line to compensate for his shortage of tank destroyers and antitank weapons. But the guns had been emplaced in the open to give them good fields of fire, and they were utterly unprotected against air strikes.

Vershinin's pilots had a field day. They destroyed the guns with pinpoint bombing, strafed the crews with machine guns and knocked out the German command bunkers with cannon fire. Afterward, during the Germans' retreat, the pilots inflicted heavy casualties and destroyed about 3,000 vehicles. "We have not had targets like this," exulted Vershinin, "since the Crimea."

Tippelskirch ordered one of his reserve units, the Feld-

herrnhalle Panzer Grenadier Division, to rush forward and plug "the hole east of Mogilev." The division commander, Major General von Steinkeller, promptly reported to the Fourth Army's 39th Corps commander, General Martinek. "Precisely what hole are you supposed to stop?" asked Martinek incredulously. "We've got nothing but holes here. Your place is back on the Berezina River, so that we have an interception line there when we can't hold onto the Dnieper any longer. And that will be pretty soon."

Under the strain of combat, battle-hardened German officers began to crack up. Soviet correspondent Ilya Ehrenburg reported that a German general was found wandering aimlessly in a patch of woods near Mogilev, carrying a mortar and repeating to himself: "I'm a German, not a louse." Other German officers tried to rationalize the catastrophe. Among them was a German major who stumbled out of the woods near Mogilev and surrendered to Ehrenburg. "At the present you may have the advantage," the prisoner told Ehrenburg. "Germany is forced to fight on two fronts. But you must admit that the techniques of the tank breakthrough and encirclement are great achievements of German strategy. You're only following in our footsteps."

At the southern end of the battle line, Marshal Rokossovsky was taking a leaf from the German book as his First Belorussian Front launched its two-pronged assault on the fortified town of Bobruisk. But Rokossovksy's strategy of encirclement included some peculiarly Russian refinements designed to catch Lieut. General Hans Jordan's Ninth Army off guard: Rokossovsky's advance would be aided by the Soviet Navy's fresh-water Dnieper Flotilla, whose ships would sail up the Berezina River to Bobruisk and disrupt any German attempts to escape across the river.

Rokossovsky had prepared his attacks with characteristic thoroughness. Planes of his supporting Sixteenth Air Army photographed the German positions, pinpointing the locations of German guns and strong points for the Red Army's artillery. Reconnaissance parties raided the German trenches, capturing prisoners and documents for Rokossovsky's intelligence units. Engineers carefully dug up and disarmed 34,000 German land mines along the main routes of attack.

Rokossovsky's artillery, its guns zeroed in on the German positions, opened fire at 4 a.m. on June 24. Soviet correspondent Vasily Grossman observed the bombardment from a nearby village: "The pounding blows of the headquarters artillery, the thunder of the divisional cannon, the heavy strokes of the howitzers, the sharp, rapid reports of the regimental guns merged in an uproar that shook the very foundations of the earth. Through the rumble of the artillery came a piercing whistle, like an enormous locomotive letting off steam. Hundreds of fiery sickles rose into the air and fell into the German trenches: The trench mortars of the Guards had opened fire. A cat ran down the deserted village street, dragging its tail in the dust. It must have been mewing desperately, but its cry could not be heard. The leaves were trembling on the Belorussian maples, oaks and poplars. In the deserted houses windowpanes were shattered, brick stoves fell crumbling to the floor, and doors and shutters swung wildly."

Lieut. General P. I. Batov's Sixty-fifth Army, spearheading the southern arm of the attack, made rapid progress. Batov had chosen for his main advance a 500-yard section of swampy ground that the Germans considered impassable. He ordered his infantry to weave willow branches into lightweight wooden frames resembling snowshoes. With these frames fastened to their boots, Batov's men crossed the swamp without sinking into the ooze. Nearby, a tank corps rumbled through the swamp on a corduroy road of logs and tree branches that Batov's engineers had laid under cover of smoke screens.

The Ninth Army's 41st Panzer Corps, caught off guard by the unexpected direction of the attack, was soon reeling under the Soviet blows. By noon, the Soviet infantry had overrun all the Germans' frontline trenches, and the I Guards Tank Corps was slicing toward Bobruisk, followed by other fast-moving mechanized and cavalry divisions.

Rokossovsky's northern spearhead, with Lieut. General Aleksandr Gorbatov's Third Army in the lead, ran into unexpectedly heavy resistance. After four hours of bitter fighting, Gorbatov's men had reached only the second of six German trench lines. Gorbatov called for support from the Sixteenth Air Army. "The sky was in tumult," wrote correspondent Grossman, "with the rhythmic roaring of the dive bombers, the hard, metallic voices of the attack planes, the piercing whine of the Yakovlev fighters. Fields and meadows were splashed with the darting outlines of

The Stalin II, an improved version of the Josef Stalin heavy tank, was a surprising and deadly combination of extremes. It weighed only 45 tons—as much as 20 tons less than other heavy tanks. Yet it was armed with the biggest main gun of any World War II tank and was protected by some of the heaviest armor.

The Soviet engineers pulled off these feats by giving the tank a low profile (8 feet 11 inches); this saved weight and made the Stalin II an especially hard target to hit. More weight was saved by their canny positioning of the armor, skimping in some places but piling it on—up to six inches thick—in the frontal areas most vulnerable to attack. A panzer commander who confronted the Stalin IIs was dismayed to discover that "although my Tigers began to hit them at 2,200 yards, our shells did not penetrate until half that distance."

Of course, the Stalin II tank paid a price for these advantages. With its low profile came cramped quarters for the four-man crew. Space was at such a premium that the tank went into battle with only 28 rounds for its main gun, 56 fewer than Germany's Tiger, and it carried two fuel tanks in a dangerously exposed position on the hull behind the turret.

hundreds of planes." By nightfall, the warplanes of the Sixteenth Air Army had logged 3,200 sorties against the German positions.

Gorbatov's infantry then resumed the attack, and by noon of the following day the Germans' last trench line had fallen to the Russians. The Soviet IX Tank Corps followed the infantry through the enemy lines, and headed for Bobruisk from the north.

On June 27, Batov's and Gorbatov's forces linked up to the west of Bobruisk. Rokossovsky's two-pronged strategy had succeeded. Five corps of the German Ninth Army—an estimated 100,000 men in all—were trapped in Bobruisk or on the east bank of the Berezina River. The Dnieper Flotilla supported the Soviet troops along the Berezina by preventing the Germans from using the bridges, while at the same time ferrying men, horses, guns and trucks across the river. In a three-day period the ships ferried 66,000 troops into combat.

With a fearlessness born of desperation, the Germans repeatedly attempted to hack their way out of Rokossovsky's encirclement. One assault, on the northern edge of the pocket, was met by General P. A. Teryomov, commanding

Aiding the Soviet advance, Polish underground fighters assemble in winter camouflage for a harassing attack on the German rear near Vilna in January of 1944. But the Red Army showed these non-Communist guerrillas little gratitude. After Vilna fell in July, the underground leaders attended a Soviet staff conference—and none of them returned.

Rokossovsky's 108th Infantry Division. "About 2,000 enemy officers and men supported by fairly strong artillery fire attacked our positions," Teryomov reported. "Our guns opened fire from a range of 700 meters, and machine guns joined in from 400 meters. The Nazis continued to advance. Shells exploded in their midst, and machine-gun fire mowed them down. Still they came forward, stepping over the bodies of their men. They came on blindly. There was nothing heroic in it. There was in the movement of this enormous mass of men more of the mulish stubborness of the herd than of fighting men intent on forcing their will on the enemy at all costs."

The scene was reenacted many times within the 15-mile-wide pocket around Bobruisk. "The whole area," Rokossovsky wrote later, "soon began to look like a huge graveyard strewn with mauled bodies and mangled machines." To the southeast of Bobruisk, the Germans lost more than 10,000 men dead and 6,000 taken prisoner in just two days. Only on the southern edge of the pocket did the Germans succeed in cracking the inexorably tightening ring of infantry and armor.

As the Russians closed in on the town of Bobruisk on June 29, units of the 20th Panzer Division made a breach in the Soviet blocking forces. After bitter fighting, some 30,000 men of General Jordan's Ninth Army escaped across the Berezina River, abandoning 5,000 of their wounded comrades in Bobruisk. In all, some 50,000 of Jordan's men had been killed, and 20,000 others were captured by Rokossovsky's forces.

Bobruisk was the fourth fortified place to be captured by Soviet forces in as many days. Hitler's strategy of defending these towns to the last man in an effort to retard the Soviet advance had once again proved disastrous: The attacking Russians had merely encircled the towns with their infantry while the main tank and mechanized forces pushed on toward Minsk.

On the 28th of June, the day before Bobruisk fell, Hitler searched for and found two scapegoats for the disaster that was rapidly consuming Army Group Center. General Jordan, who through no fault of his own had presided over the dismemberment of the Ninth Army, was dismissed and replaced by General Nikolaus von Vormann. The same day

Hitler sacked Field Marshal Busch and turned his armies over to Field Marshal Model, commander of the neighboring Army Group North Ukraine. Model retained Army Group North Ukraine, and he immediately stripped it of four infantry and four panzer divisions to plug the gaps in his new command.

Model would have liked to fight a battle of movement, hitting the Russians hard with swift panzer units, then pulling back to regroup before striking again in another sector. But Hitler was still committed to a rigid defense. On the morning of Model's appointment, he fixed a new defense line running north and south from the town of Berezino on the Berezina River, 60 miles east of Minsk. In an order telegraphed to Army Group Center headquarters, Hitler authorized the surviving units of the Third Panzer, the Fourth and the Ninth Armies to pull back to the new line, but not a step farther.

By the time the order was issued, most of the survivors of the Third Panzer and Ninth Armies were already west of the new defense line. On June 28, General von Tippelskirch moved his Fourth Army command post to Berezino over the same road that his army would have to take. The trip, a distance of 30 miles, took nine hours. The road was packed solid with columns of trucks barely inching along. Between sunrise and sunset, Soviet aircraft attacked the Berezina River bridge at Berezino a total of 25 times. Large numbers of German soldiers worked frantically to keep the approaches to the bridge clear of dead and wounded men and horses and burning vehicles.

In the meantime, Rokossovsky's and Chernyakhovsky's armored spearheads were closing in on Minsk. As the tankers raced along the main Moscow-Minsk highway in the north and the Bobruisk-Minsk road in the south, they came across deserted German field kitchens with soup still warm on the stoves. In abandoned German headquarters, the Russians gleefully examined boxes of unawarded Iron Crosses and enemy maps that showed German units still advancing eastward.

Behind the tanks came the infantry, mopping up enemy units that had been bypassed by the tanks. Soviet officers exhorted the weary foot soldiers, "Don't give them any respite, keep fighting!"

Most of the men needed no encouragement. As they ad-

vanced, the Soviet soldiers uncovered more and more evidence of German atrocities: countless razed villages and mass graves. During their three-year occupation, the Germans had killed an estimated one million Belorussians. Said a Soviet general, "The infantry has its own mechanization now: its heart. They see what the Germans have done and they're in a hurry."

Thousands of Germans, dazed by the catastrophe that had befallen them, now surrendered or wandered off. Army Group Center's chain of command and communications collapsed. When Ninth Army headquarters attempted to rally German stragglers into a defense force at Marina Gorka, 30 miles to the southeast of Minsk, the officers and men disappeared as fast as they could be assembled. Many of the Germans simply turned themselves in to the nearest Russian. Correspondent Evgeny Kreiger saw a Belorussian farmer, who was armed only with an ancient rifle, herding a group of 750 German prisoners toward the rear. They had stumbled out of forests and swamps and surrendered to women farm workers, who had locked them in barns until they had run out of room.

In Minsk, there was panic among the Germans as the Soviet pincers began closing around the city on July 2. Soldiers piled onto tanks, trucks and self-propelled guns—anything that was moving westward. They fled on foot when the vehicles got bogged down in enormous traffic jams. Officers threw away their uniforms and tried to disguise themselves as privates or civilians. A resident of Minsk watched in amazement as a German soldier paused at a corner, smashed his rifle against a wall and then rushed off to join his fleeing comrades.

On July 3, Rokossovsky's and Chernyakhovsky's forces linked up west of Minsk. With the closing of this armored pincers, an additional 100,000 Germans were trapped in a gigantic pocket east and southeast of the city. The figure included most of General von Tippelskirch's Fourth Army, which was still retreating from the Berezina River, and some of the 30,000 Ninth Army troops who previously had escaped from the Soviet encirclement at Bobruisk.

Even those Germans who had managed to escape from Minsk gained only temporary deliverance from the Soviet steam roller. On July 4, Stalin assigned his commanders new and ambitious objectives. Chernyakhovsky's Third Belorussian Front was ordered to push northwest from Minsk toward Lithuania, while Rokossovsky's First Belorussian Front was sent southwest toward Brest-Litovsk on the Bug River. Zakharov's Second Belorussian Front was left behind to mop up the remains of Army Group Center.

By the 11th of July, when Zakharov's troops finished combing the forests and swamps for survivors, the dimensions of the German defeat had become clear. The Soviet forces had destroyed Army Group Center, ripping a hole 250 miles wide in the middle of the German line. Twenty-eight German divisions had ceased to exist, and between 300,000 and 350,000 men had been killed or captured. These men could not be replaced. In the same way that the Battle of Kursk had broken the back of the German panzers, the Battle of Belorussia had broken the back of the entire Wehrmacht in the East.

Two ravishing possibilities now beckoned to Stalin. He could send Soviet forces due west into Poland through the gaping hole in the German center. Or he could send his southern armies into the Balkans, where the Germans had been greatly weakened as Hitler siphoned off units to feed into the great battle in Belorussia. He did both.

The Soviet High Command had begun preparing for the Balkans operation in May, but Stalin had held back, waiting for his forces in the south to be strengthened. Finally, in late summer, he was ready: The 10 Soviet armies of the Second and Third Ukrainian Fronts burst into Rumania on a 250-mile front and soon fanned out into Bulgaria, Yugoslavia and Hungary. By then, even more powerful Soviet forces had swarmed across the border into Poland—on their way, said Marshal Zhukov, "to invade Nazi Germany and complete its destruction."

A column of 57,600 German soldiers—all of them captured during the Soviet Army's stunning victory in Belorussia—marches through Moscow on the 17th of July, 1944. The grim procession, led by 19 German generals and liberally photographed from a special press truck, was staged primarily to correct a mistaken impression of American and British journalists, who had been speculating that the Germans had withdrawn most of their troops from Belorussia before the Soviet offensive began.

YEAR OF VICTORIES

Shouting and brandishing a submachine gun, a Soviet officer waves his men forward during the offensive that broke the siege of Leningrad in January 1944

"SWEEPING FORWARD LIKE A MIGHTY RIVER"

Red Army soldiers of the Second Ukrainian Front put up a "U.S.S.R." sign on the Rumanian border after their triumphant thrust to the Carpathians.

"Our troops are sweeping forward like a mighty river that knows no barriers and washes away all obstacles, clearing the mud and the filth from a vast area." So wrote a Soviet correspondent in 1944, the year the Red Army drove the last Germans from Soviet territory. Marshal Konstantin K. Rokossovsky, whose First Belorussian Front helped crush Hitler's Army Group Center and opened avenues of attack into Poland and the Balkans, described the 6.5-million-man Soviet onslaught with unabashed relish. "At last the time had come when the enemy began to experience what the Red Army had experienced in the beginning."

All along the Eastern Front, from the Baltic Sea in the north to the Black Sea in the south, Soviet armies slashed at the Germans with preponderant strength. When resistance was heavy, the Russians brought their artillery to bear on a few breakthrough points and leveled the German positions. Then an infantry vanguard poured through the gap to clear the way for the tanks. Armored columns drove behind enemy lines, cut off the German strong points and destroyed them piecemeal. "Our units whittle down the German defenses village by village," wrote a Red Army war correspondent. "We attack from four sides and grind them to pulp."

"Our fury and thirst for revenge are more intense than ever," a Red Army soldier wrote. "Even in the days of our retreat, it was never like this." At Lysyanka in the Ukraine hundreds of retreating Germans were trapped in a field and crushed by Soviet tanks, and those who escaped the tanks were hunted down and hacked to death by saber-wielding cavalrymen. The Soviet troops had little time or inclination to take prisoners, and when a German soldier surrendered he knew that he might be shot on the spot.

Fear of the Russians drove most Germans to fight. But their determination and skill rarely won the day against the foe's huge numbers of tough peasant fighters. "Behind the tank spearheads rolls a vast horde," a German general said of the Russians. "Each soldier carries a sack on his back with dry crusts of bread and vegetables collected from the fields and villages. You can't stop them."

Racing across the snow, Red Army foot soldiers enter the grounds of a czarist palace located in the historic village of Pushkin, just to the south of Leningrad.

Infantrymen of the Soviet First Baltic Front scramble from beneath a freight train during a skirmish with Germans on the Shyaulyai-Telshai railway in northern Lithuania.

Soviet artillerymen rush their guns to new firing positions during the battle for Klaipeda in western Lithuania in November of 1944.

A Soviet photograph shows three Red Army soldiers charging across a field near Riga. They are in the line of fire of their comrades in the foreground, suggesting the scene was staged.

Positioned behind a snowbank, an artillery
unit of the First Belorussian Front shells a
German strong point before a predawn attack.

Soviet T-34s laden with troops rumble through
the dust toward Minsk. The Soviet forces
trapped 100,000 Germans in this campaign.

Supported by Red Air Force planes, infantry
and armor of the Soviet Sixty-fifth Army move
out to seize a rail junction near Osipovichi.

*Troops of the Soviet Third Guards Tank Army
enter a Ukrainian village in January 1944.
They took part in a pincers assault that trapped
56,000 Germans in the Cherkassy pocket.*

*A field-artillery unit of the Second Ukrainian
Front waits to be rafted across the Dniester
River in the western Ukraine. The bridge had
been destroyed by the retreating Germans.*

Riding tanks and hauling howitzers, troops of the First Ukrainian Front ford the Western Bug River en route to the Hungarian border.

Soviet infantrymen creep through a castle's deserted salon during house-to-house fighting for Jassy, Rumania, in August of 1944.

In pursuit of fleeing Germans, saber-wielding cavalrymen of the Third Ukrainian Front leap a stone fence in a village near Odessa.

A squad of Red Army infantrymen storms a Black Sea village during the Soviet campaign to rid the Crimean Peninsula of enemy troops.

Emerging from a battered house, the last survivor of a German unit is taken prisoner at bayonet point by a Soviet infantryman.

SWIFT SUCCESS IN SEVASTOPOL

Jubilant Red Army soldiers fire a victory salute on a rocky beach in Sevastopol, whose harbor is littered with ruined German ships.

Soviet troops swarm through the ruins of Sevastopol in May 1944. They recaptured the Black Sea port in just four days' fighting.

5

A new Polish government, made in Moscow
Invitation to revolt against "the Hitlerite vermin"
Deceptive victories for the insurgents
A brigade of looters and murderers
The boy martyr of Napoleon Square
Cross-town sweeps and open-air massacres
Kaminski captures a vodka distillery
Stalin's sudden change of heart
Token help from the Americans
The battle for the sewers

Josef Stalin had plans for Poland. The shortest distance to Berlin was a straight line across that war-battered country, and Stalin intended to use the route for his war-winning drive against Germany. It was a route made to order for offense: great plains stretching all the way from the Soviet border to Berlin. The retreating Wehrmacht—that is, the sketchy remnants of it that were left after the smashing Soviet victory in Belorussia in June 1944—would find no important natural defenses save the Vistula and Oder Rivers.

Stalin was interested in Poland for other reasons. Its plains were fertile and its industry promising; postwar trade between the Soviet Union and Poland would be logical, easy and essential. While planning a drive into the huge Silesia industrial region, Stalin placed his hand on that section of the map and told his generals, "Gold!"

Stalin intended to install in Poland a government perfectly attuned to Soviet political, social and economic arrangements. He considered this essential; he could not and would not have an unfriendly wartime regime in his Army's rear area as it advanced on Berlin, and after the War he wanted a cooperative and populous nation interposed between the Soviet Union and a possibly resurgent Germany. Poland would be Communist. As the dictator told Yugoslavia's Marshal Tito, "Everyone imposes his system as far as his army can reach. It cannot be otherwise."

In Poland as in the Balkans, Stalin would use the Red Army as a political weapon, wielding it or withholding it to serve his purposes. His political maneuvers, together with the logistic difficulties of his Army, would soon lead to one of the War's greatest tragedies—the bloody and abortive Warsaw Uprising.

The campaign for Poland began in mid-July, 1944, with an enormous two-pronged assault by Marshal Rokossovsky's First Belorussian Front. While Rokossovsky's right flank was advancing beyond Minsk, the left flank—six Soviet armies including the so-called First Polish Army, a force made up mostly of onetime Polish prisoners of war and Russians with Polish surnames—stood poised near the 1939 Soviet-Polish border. Rokossovsky's next objectives in Poland were Lublin, 60 miles beyond the border, and Warsaw, 105 miles northwest of Lublin.

In the predawn darkness of July 18, General Vasily Chui-

THE DOOMED UPRISING

kov, commander of the Soviet Eighth Guards Army, prepared to launch the offensive from his forward command post on a hill facing the German-held town of Kovel. "The night was uncommonly quiet," Chuikov later wrote. "Now and then, far behind the night-enshrouded forest, flashes lit up the sky and the rumble of explosives could be heard as Soviet bombers hammered targets deep in the enemy rear. In the meantime, under cover of darkness, intensive work was in full swing: The regiments and battalions were taking up assault positions."

At 5:30 a.m., the Soviet artillery opened up. "On some sectors," said Chuikov, "we had more than 200 guns per kilometer of frontage. The ground trembled. The thunder of guns gained in volume as guns of the largest caliber spoke up, wreaking havoc on enemy positions. Chaos reigned in the forward defense line as flames and smoke and fountains of earth and sludge rose into the air, eclipsing the sun. The morning light faded as the artillery hurricane raged on." Later, Chuikov learned that the artillery had pumped 77,300 shells into the enemy positions in 30 minutes.

At 6 o'clock, the assault infantry, following in the wake of mine-clearing tanks, reached the first enemy trenches. Then Chuikov ordered the main body of his army into action.

The Eighth Guards Army swept ahead. By the second day, vanguard divisions were crossing the Bug River into Poland on a wide front. On the morning of July 22, Soviet tanks rammed past Chelm; they entered Lublin the next afternoon. The capture of Lublin was a simple matter. Hitler had designated the city a fortified place, which meant it had to be defended to the death. But it was manned by only 900 troops, and the Russians easily overwhelmed the garrison.

On July 22, Radio Moscow had announced the formation of a Polish Committee of National Liberation. The Lublin Committee, as it became known, was portrayed by Soviet authorities as a broadly representative group with only three Communists among its 15 members, and it was therefore said to be a more worthy government for a liberated Poland than the Polish government-in-exile in London under Prime Minister Stanislaw Mikolajczyk.

To solidify the Lublin Committee's claim to legitimacy, the Soviet government signed an agreement giving it "full responsibility in matters of civil government" behind Red Army lines. The Lublin Committee came out wholeheartedly in favor of a Soviet-Polish border proposed by Moscow, a border that was unacceptable to the London Poles because it would give the Soviet Union about 40,000 square miles of the territory of prewar Poland.

The Soviet forces left Lublin and slashed ahead. The Second Tank Army veered northwest toward Praga, a district of Warsaw on the eastern bank of the Vistula River. Meanwhile, to the south, Marshal Konev's First Ukrainian Front had crossed the Polish border and swiftly advanced to the Vistula 75 miles south of Warsaw.

On July 26, units of Rokossovsky's army group came within 60 miles of Warsaw. Four days later, they had fought 55 miles closer. Rokossovsky later said that it was time for a pause: "Our supply lines were stretched out over hundreds of kilometers and could not provide all that was needed to maintain our successful advance." Besides, his troops found the going slower and harder: The Germans had suddenly committed five divisions to battle along the Vistula, three of them panzer divisions. At the same time, German troops who had been leaving Warsaw began coming back. These new German moves had just been ordered by Hitler; he had decided to stop the Soviet steam roller on the east side of the Vistula. And he had pronounced Warsaw a fortified place.

At 8:15 p.m. on July 29, a Moscow station named after the 18th Century Polish military hero Tadeusz Kościuszko broadcast the first of many appeals to Warsaw, urging an uprising against "the Hitlerite vermin."

"No doubt Warsaw already hears the guns of the battle that is bringing her liberation," said Radio Kościuszko. "Those who have never bowed their heads to the Hitlerite power will again, as in 1939, join battle with the Germans, this time for decisive action." The broadcast ended with the cry, "Poles, the time of liberation is at hand! Poles, to arms! There is not a moment to lose!"

The same exhortations were issued in a communiqué signed by Soviet Foreign Minister Molotov and the chairman of the Lublin Committee, Edward Osóbka-Morawski. Leaflets with the text of both the radio broadcast and the communiqué were dropped on Warsaw by Soviet planes.

These clear and urgent calls for an uprising were specifically addressed to the People's Army, sponsored by the underground Polish Communist Party. But the People's Army, as Moscow and the Lublin Committee knew, could do very little. It was a small force with a potential fighting strength in Warsaw of only about 500 men and women. Any uprising would have to come from a stronger underground.

By far the strongest resistance group in Poland was the Home Army. Its national commander, General Bór (the *nom de guerre* of Tadeusz Komorowski), claimed its membership totaled 380,000. The commander in Warsaw, Colonel Monter (Antoni Chruściel), had 40,000 fighters in the city. The Home Army was the fighting arm in Poland of the Mikolajczyk government in London. As the chief rival of the Communist underground, it had been repeatedly subjected to Soviet condemnation as reactionary and collaborationist.

General Bór and his associates heard of the Moscow broadcast and read the air-dropped leaflets. But, having planned an insurrection of their own since the German conquest, they were more interested in the Red Army's progress toward Warsaw than in Moscow's propaganda. The Home Army leaders were determined to liberate Warsaw as a matter of national pride and also political pragmatism; they wanted to establish the authority of the Mikolajczyk government in the capital before the Red Army could arrive and install a Communist government. Bór calculated that they would have to strike soon, for it seemed certain that the Soviet forces would enter Warsaw within a week; and they would have to win quickly, for German reinforcements were bound to arrive after the shooting started. The exact moment to start the uprising would have to be chosen by the "feel" of the situation.

On July 31, evidence mounted that the time was right. The Hermann Göring Division crossed the Vistula to defend Praga, and German engineers began emplacing demolition charges on the bridges. The noon news broadcast of the German armed-forces radio reported a general attack southeast of Warsaw, and a Moscow communiqué announced that the commander of the German 73rd Infantry Division had been captured just outside Praga.

Late that afternoon, while Bór was meeting with his chief of staff and operations chief in an apartment in downtown Warsaw, Colonel Monter burst in with the news that Soviet tanks were approaching Praga; a number of towns close to the capital—Radość, Milosna, Okuniew, Wolomin and Radzymin—were already in Soviet hands, he reported.

The officers agreed that now was the time to begin the up-

rising; it seemed that they would have to hurry to take the city before the Red Army arrived. Although Bór had been authorized by Mikolajczyk to start the uprising on his own judgment, he called in and briefed Jan S. Jankowski, the civilian representative of the London government. Jankowski said, "All right. Go ahead." Bór then gave Monter the order: "Tomorrow, at 1700 hours, you will go into action."

On the morning of August 1, Warsaw was unusually active. Men and women were busily smuggling arms, ammunition and food to assembly points. Excitement ran high—much too high—among the members of the Home Army. Scattered shooting broke out at 3 p.m., two hours ahead of schedule. By 5 p.m., fights were raging all over the city. The uprising was off to an enthusiastic if haphazard start.

Waclaw Zagórski found himself involved in a spontaneous action much like many others. He was in his basement counting a batch of propaganda leaflets when he heard gunfire outside. He poked his head out the window in time to see a car full of German soldiers go speeding by, followed by another car full of young men in black raincoats who were firing at them with revolvers. Emboldened by the sight, Zagórski and two companions armed themselves with pistols, hand grenades and two homemade bombs and went out in search of a battle.

They saw some Germans guarding a factory but decided there were too many of them to take on. Suddenly a group of men came into the street, some wearing the red-and-white arm bands of the Home Army. They were looking for something to do, and though only a few were armed, they joined Zagórski and his companions in an attack on the factory. A few shots were exchanged, but as soon as the insurgents broke down the factory gates, the Germans surrendered. By the time the prisoners had been locked up, it was dark and starting to rain.

Zagórski and most members of the Home Army that night were completely out of touch with events anywhere but on their own street. But on Zagórski's street and numberless others throughout the city, German rule had, for the moment, come to an end; the Poles controlled the heart of Warsaw—the Old Town, the Inner City and the Vistula quarter. Wherever they held sway, the insurgents began constructing a maze of cobblestone barricades and passageways, breaking through cellar walls and opening up manholes that led to Warsaw's labyrinthine sewer system.

Around 8 o'clock that evening, a member of the Home Army burst into General Bór's headquarters, an abandoned factory near the old Jewish ghetto, and asked Bór to accompany him to the roof of the factory. "The flag, the Polish flag," shouted a spotter on duty on the roof. "Our flag—right in the middle of the city."

Through the smoke that billowed up from countless fires that had shrouded the city in gray, Bór saw the flag—flying from the 16-story Prudential Building in the center of the city. "I concentrated my gaze," Bór recalled. "No; it was not a Nazi flag. Now I could see the white and red. After five years, the Polish colors were once more floating defiantly over the city. Similar flags were already flying from the cupola of the Post Office Savings Bank, from the tower of the Town Hall and from other buildings."

The flags gave Bór his first notion of how the battle for Warsaw was proceeding. But they were deceptive. The ragged beginning of the revolt had alerted the 13,000 German troops on both sides of the Vistula and had given them time to prepare for action at crucial places. Everywhere, except at one food and clothing supply dump in the former ghetto, the Germans beat back assaults on their main installations, thus denying the insurgents the weapons and ammunition they desperately needed. The insurgents had failed to take any of the Vistula River bridges. Furthermore, the uprising across the river in Praga had collapsed in a matter of hours, and the Germans had regained full control.

Yet for the first few days it seemed the Home Army might triumph. About 8,000 German troops were pinned down guarding bridges, factories and other installations. The Warsaw commander, Lieut. General Reiner Stahel, was himself besieged in his headquarters, a historic palace in the Inner City. Thus only 5,000 German soldiers were available for immediate counteraction against the insurgents. Furthermore, Stahel, an Austrian who had come to Warsaw just five days earlier to convert the city into a fortified place, lacked the experience to deal with an urban insurrection.

In fact, such was the tangled German military bureaucracy that Stahel—whose force was part of the Ninth Army—actually did not have responsibility for fighting the insurgents. The man who did was Heinrich Himmler, who, as chief of the SS, was responsible for counterinsurgency and antipartisan warfare.

Himmler instantly saw a bright side to the uprising. It would give the Germans, he told Hitler, a chance to destroy Warsaw, "the head, the intelligence of this 16 to 17 million Polish people, this people that has blocked us in the east for 700 years." Starting the destruction in a small way, Himmler had General Stefan Rowecki, Bór's predecessor as head of the Home Army and a German prisoner since June 1943, taken out and executed on the first day of the uprising.

To do the dirty work of putting down the uprising, Himmler on August 2 selected SS General Erich von dem Bach-Zelewski, who had made a reputation fighting partisans in Belorussia. On taking over his new post, von dem Bach was not as optimistic as Himmler about the job ahead. Except for two battalions of the Hermann Göring Division and the 4th East Prussian Grenadier Regiment, the only combat-experienced units he had within reach were two of the most disreputable in the German armed forces: the SS Dirlewanger Brigade and the Kaminski Brigade.

SS Colonel Oscar Dirlewanger, the commander of the brigade that bore his name, was a notorious drunkard and liar who was said to have been convicted of rape, robbery and several other crimes. But he was well regarded by Hitler and Himmler and thus could operate with impunity. Most of his troops had been recruited from the concentration camps. Originally, he had selected convicted poachers be-

Nearly a million pairs of shoes, taken from Jews who perished in Nazi gas chambers, fill an immense warehouse discovered when troops of the First Belorussian Front captured the death camp at Majdanek, two miles east of Lublin, on July 23, 1944. An estimated 1.5 million people were put to death at Majdanek, the first of six such camps found by the Russians in their drive across Poland.

cause they were good shots. But by 1944, common criminals predominated, with a sprinkling of Communists and other political prisoners. For most of the men, the term of service was short. The brigade had about 900 troops when it went into Warsaw and required 2,500 replacements during the fighting.

The Kaminski Brigade was an unruly force of mercenaries led by Mieczyslaw Kaminski. A political adventurer, drunkard, womanizer and hater of Poles, Kaminski had attracted Himmler's attention in 1942 by organizing a locally successful antipartisan movement in the Bryansk Forest area of central Russia. After the Bryansk Forest area was lost in the summer of 1943, Kaminski's 7,000-man brigade and more than 20,000 camp followers had drifted westward with the retreating Germans, marauding as they went. The brigade had wound up in East Prussia, where the Germans were hard put to think of what to do with it next. From it, von dem Bach took the best-armed regiment—2,500 men with a number of Soviet heavy machine guns and eight Soviet antitank guns—to help put down the uprising.

Kaminski, Dirlewanger and their minions arrived piecemeal in the first days of the uprising and swung into action immediately.

In Warsaw, from August 2 through August 4, fighting flared and subsided. Small parties of Germans attacked the barricades; they were devastatingly effective when they had a tank or two along, but they were not strong enough to mount a real offensive. The insurgents could not do that either, yet the battle seemed to be going in their favor. A Home Army radio station trumpeted, ''Poles! People of Warsaw! We call upon you to join the fight against the German criminals. Warsaw is fighting and her streets blossom with the fresh graves of her heroic soldiers.'' The people responded. Children carried messages over the barricades and through the sewers, and some of them even fought.

One small boy attacked the last German pillbox covering the Central Post Office on Napoleon Square. ''The boy sneaked out of the gate,'' recalled a nurse in the Home Army. ''Flat on his belly he crawled toward the spluttering machine-gun nest. He pushed a square flagstone out of the sidewalk pavement ahead of him.

''Breathlessly I watched him crawl, measuring the distance. 'Good Lord, let him kill them,' I prayed. My fists were clenched.

''Now the boy was right near the pillbox, too close for the machine-gun bullets to stop him. Slowly, cautiously, he began to get up. He pulled out the grenades.

''The boy rose to his full height. He thrust his grenades into the death-spitting mouth of the pillbox. Instantly the explosion hit the whole square. The pillbox went up in smoke and fire.

''We ran out from behind the gate and made for the boy. I was not conscious of the sudden silence until I came to the small body lying in a heap out there.''

In Zoliborz, Mokotów and the other districts, Home Army contingents enjoyed some success in individual skirmishes. In Zoliborz, they were bolstered by a group of 35 Communists from the People's Army. But pockets of Germans were holed up in the Old Town, the Vistula quarter and the Inner City, and they could not be dislodged. Those inside the walls of the Warsaw University grounds beat back attacks from all four sides.

On Saturday, August 5, the Germans took the offensive. After consultations with the Führer, Himmler had issued straightforward orders: All captured insurgents and noncombatants, women and children included, were to be killed and the city was to be leveled. The Ninth Army, stationed in Wola, had introduced a complication by insisting on having a road opened through the city to one of the Vistula bridges so it could regain contact with its units in Praga.

According to plan, Dirlewanger's men would go on a bloody sweep from the west to the Kierbedz Bridge in the Old Town, while Kaminski's force would attack from the southwest through the Ochota district. Although this plan called for no great tactical finesse, von dem Bach was far from certain that his commander in the field, SS Major General Heinz Reinefarth, would be capable of carrying it out. Reinefarth, a lawyer in civilian life, had won a Knight's Cross in the 1940 French campaign and had been doing desk duty in Berlin ever since. Understandably, he detested Dirlewanger and Kaminski, and avoided contact with them, but this boded ill for the assault.

The working-class district of Wola was the first target for both brigades. Dirlewanger's troops and four companies of police and reserves—more than 6,500 men in all—moved out at 9:30 a.m. on August 5. Kaminski's brigands began their attack, as Ninth Army records sarcastically reported, "according to plan, two hours late." An armored train on a railroad spur that passed through Wola and Ochota gave artillery support to both groups, as did some tanks and self-propelled assault guns.

As the Germans pressed into Wola, they ordered the inhabitants to assemble in the streets for "evacuation to the rear." The rear proved to be the nearest open space—a park, a square, a cemetery. There the Poles were crowded together by the hundreds and thousands and shot. No one counted the men, women and children who were killed in Wola that day. The Poles later estimated that 38,000 died there and in Ochota.

Kaminski's share of the total killed was relatively small; he and his troops gave priority to liquor, loot and rape and paid no attention to exhortations from Reinefarth, who made the mistake of trying to control them by radio while he stayed with the main force in Wola. In the afternoon, Kaminski came upon a vodka distillery, and that crucial objective halted his advance. (For this and numerous other derelictions, the Germans shot him several weeks later.)

The Germans' tactical gains on the first day of the assault were small. Dirlewanger's column had advanced only about half a mile into Wola; Kaminski had penetrated no more than a few hundred yards. Von dem Bach quickly realized that the Dirlewanger and Kaminski Brigades were capable of little more than murder and looting. New troops and new tactics would be needed. That night, as much for efficiency as for any humanitarian reasons, von dem Bach disobeyed Himmler's order and prohibited the shooting of women and children—a prohibition that was in turn repeatedly disobeyed as the fighting went on.

Moscow, meanwhile, had fallen silent. No more appeals for an uprising were heard, and the radio and newspapers made no mention of the one going on in Warsaw. But radio reports from General Bór to his government in London told of the insurgents' worsening situation and asked for help.

Prime Minister Churchill appealed to Stalin to aid the Poles. On August 5, Stalin replied: "I think that the information given you by the Poles is greatly exaggerated and unreliable. The Home Army consists of a few detachments miscalled divisions. They have neither guns, aircraft nor tanks. I cannot imagine detachments like that taking Warsaw."

At Churchill's urging, Mikolajczyk had flown to Moscow on July 31 in hopes of negotiating a political accommodation with Stalin. But Stalin proved to be uncooperative, and when Mikolajczyk begged him to help Warsaw, the dictator answered with a question: "Can you give me your word of honor that there is fighting going on in Warsaw? The Lublin Poles tell me there is no fighting at all."

For General Bór and the Home Army command, the rude indifference shown Mikolajczyk in Moscow marked the end of a dream. Their heroic effort to liberate their capital had turned into a lonesome, doomed struggle. Bór had a direct radio link with London but not with his own subordinate commanders; communication with them was through London or by messenger. Furthermore, the orders he gave were based mainly on guesswork and on the little he could see from the roof of his headquarters in the Old Town.

The insurgents were still handicapped by a lack of basic weapons. Bór repeatedly radioed pleas for help to London, and some supplies did come. On August 4, the British air base at Brindisi in southern Italy sent 14 bombers, seven of them flown by Polish crews, on the journey north laden with machine guns, Sten guns, rifles, pistols and ammunition. The round trip to Warsaw was 1,200 miles—much of it over German-held territory.

The planes that reached Warsaw parachuted supplies in 10-foot-long, cigar-shaped metal cylinders, each containing several weapons and a stock of ammunition. The insurgents particularly treasured the Piats—British-made, bazooka-like rocket projectors that gave them something better than Molotov cocktails to use against the German tanks. The weapons were wrapped in articles of military and civilian clothing, and the leftover space was filled with cigarettes, coffee, chocolate and other items that most of the Poles had not seen since long before the uprising.

The cost of the airlift was very high, however. On the first mission, five of the 14 British planes failed to return. The British terminated their flights to Warsaw after the first mis-

Two soldiers of the Soviet-backed First Polish Army attack a German position in Praga, just across the Vistula River from Warsaw. The sign on the streetcar says "For Germans Only" in German and Polish.

sion, but the Poles' vehement protest prompted them to resume the flights four days later. Despite heavy losses, they continued flying until September 21.

The Americans wanted to send the Poles supplies from England by long-range B-17 Flying Fortresses. But the distance to Warsaw and back—about 1,800 miles—was beyond the B-17s' range, so the planes would have to fly on past Warsaw and land at Soviet bases in the Ukraine to refuel. As authorized by Stalin at the Teheran Conference a year before, U.S. and British planes had used these bases on shuttle bombing missions (opposite). But when Averell Harriman, Ambassador to the Soviet Union, requested the Kremlin's approval for the supply flights, he was informed, "The Soviet government does not wish to associate itself directly or indirectly with the adventure in Warsaw." Molotov later told Harriman that nothing could be done to save the Warsaw fighters from their own folly. When Harriman reminded him of Moscow's radio appeals for an uprising, the Soviet Foreign Minister denied having heard of them.

Meanwhile, von dem Bach decided to prepare for his next attack with a bombardment far too heavy for its purpose. The weapons he deployed included a Gargantuan howitzer that fired a concrete-piercing shell nearly two feet in diameter, and radio-controlled Goliaths, miniature tanks that could—on the rare occasions when they worked—carry 200 pounds of explosives to the enemy's doorstep.

Von dem Bach's first targets were the heart of the resistance, the Old Town and the Vistula quarter.

On August 12, the attack on the Old Town began behind heavy shelling and dive bombing. Then, from the southwest corner of the district and from the Citadel to the north, German troops followed a wave of Goliaths and self-propelled guns toward the center of the Old Town. The drive was slow work: The insurgents defended many thick-walled, medieval buildings that withstood heavy punishment.

Day after day, the bombs and shells kept falling. Steadily the Poles gave ground—and their misery increased. No rain had fallen in 10 days; drinking water was scarce and dust was everywhere. The sky was clear and the sun was so hot it softened asphalt pavement. The dead, unburied or in shallow graves, decomposed quickly, filling the air with a stench and attracting flies—billions of fat, greenish-blue

flies. With the flies came an epidemic of dysentery. Food supplies dwindled and even healthy people weakened.

On August 19, the Germans launched their heaviest assault to date, hitting the Old Town with a whirlwind of dive bombers and artillery, followed by infantry sweeps. When Bór looked across the Old Town the next day, all he saw was heaps of rubble and the shells of bombed-out buildings. "The ancient houses," he wrote later, "had collapsed across streets, forming gigantic barriers of hundreds of thousands of bricks. Nothing but ruins now remained." Two days later, with his radio link to the outside world failing, Bór and his headquarters withdrew to the Inner City, taking the safe, stinking route through the sewers.

On August 20, eight days after the start of the German assault on the Old Town, President Roosevelt and Prime Minister Churchill addressed a joint plea to Stalin. They asked him either to have his planes deliver supplies to the beleaguered insurgents or to "agree to help our planes in doing it very quickly." In reply, Stalin called the leadership of the Home Army "a handful of power-seeking criminals" who had gulled the people of Warsaw into fighting a battle they could never hope to win. All the uprising was doing, he added, was drawing German attention and strength to Warsaw, thereby creating difficulties for the Soviet forces.

The fighting in the Old Town ended on September 2. The surviving Home Army men—about 3,500 out of an original 7,000—went over to the Inner City and the Zolibórz quarter by the same route Bór had used. Several thousand wounded and about 40,000 civilians stayed behind. It was estimated that 30,000 had been killed in the Old Town.

On September 3, the Germans attacked the Vistula quarter, lying south of the Old Town between the Inner City and the river. Von dem Bach flogged his troops onward; impatient rumblings were coming from the Führer's headquarters in East Prussia. After three days of fighting, the Germans reached the broad, north-south boulevard that separated the Vistula quarter from the Inner City. They now controlled the approaches to all five bridges; the Home Army, reduced to defending the Inner City and the Zolibórz and Mokotów quarters, was surrounded.

The rapid collapse of Polish resistance in the Vistula quarter made it appear to the Germans—and possibly to the Poles as well—that the uprising was coming to an end. On

FLYING FORTRESSES ON THE EASTERN FRONT

Three Ukrainian airfields where American B-17s refueled after air-dropping supplies to the Warsaw insurgents had been built so that U.S. bombers could hit eastern European targets too far from their bases in Britain or Italy for nonstop round trips. On June 2, 1944, the baptismal flight of bombers landed at the Poltava airstrip after attacking a German base in Hungary. The airmen were accorded a hero's welcome.

But just three weeks later, the Poltava field was the scene of a disaster. The Luftwaffe launched a surprise night raid that caught the Soviet air defenses completely unprepared. Forty-seven Flying Fortresses were destroyed, and 30 Russians and two Americans were killed.

Many U.S. airmen were angry at their losses—so angry that their commanding officer, Major General Robert Walsh, officially silenced them to prevent disrupting inter-Allied relations. Just five more missions were flown from the bases before the Red Army's westward advance removed the strategic reasons for the shuttle bombing. Although Poltava remained open until the end of the War, the U.S. flight that landed there after the Warsaw airdrop was the last to use the base.

Soviet antiaircraft tracers and German flares light up the Poltava airfield during the Luftwaffe's destructive night raid. The Soviet gunners failed to down a single enemy plane.

American crewmen stand in front of their B-17 bomber—whose name, North Star, is printed in Russian—with Brigadier General Alfred A. Kessler (back row, left), U.S. Army Air Forces deputy commander in the U.S.S.R.

September 7 and 8, during brief truces arranged by the Polish Red Cross, the Germans allowed noncombatant women and children to cross the barricades and leave the areas held by the Home Army. About 45,000 did; most stayed. On September 9, after having ignored numerous German ultimatums and offers in the previous five weeks, Bór sent a delegation to discuss surrender terms with the Germans.

Stalin also perceived that the uprising was about to end—apparently too soon to suit his purposes. Now, in several ways, he encouraged the Home Army to continue the fight.

On September 11, Stalin informed the British and Americans that they could, after all, use the Ukraine air bases for supply flights to Warsaw. By then, the Soviet Forty-seventh Army and units of General Zygmunt Berling's First Polish Army had given a mighty heave against the German bridgehead around Praga; one day later, Soviet troops were on the riverbank across from Zoliborz, the Old Town and the Vistula quarter. The Germans in Praga had retreated to the west bank and blown up the last of the bridges behind them.

On the night of September 14, Radio Moscow broadcast an appeal in the name of the Lublin Committee, exhorting the Poles to fight on. "The hour of liberation for heroic Warsaw is near. Your suffering and martyrdom will soon be over," read an announcer. "The Germans will pay dearly for the ruins and blood of Warsaw. Help is coming. Victory is near. Keep fighting."

The armies' arrival convinced General Bór that Stalin had changed his mind about helping the insurgents, and he broke off negotiations with the Germans. And still more help was forthcoming from Moscow; Stalin ordered Soviet planes to drop supplies to the Warsaw insurgents.

To prepare for the airdrops, a few pilots flew low over the Inner City and Zoliborz, scattering instructions on how to mark the boundaries of insurgent-held areas for supply planes. Thereafter, antiquated PO-2 biplanes—the Germans called them "sewing machines" after the stuttering sound of their motors—dropped 55 tons of supplies, including 15 tons of food. Each plane could carry only 200 pounds. The drops were made by tossing the cargo over the side without parachutes. Nothing landed in good condition.

In yet another gesture, Stalin sent units of Berling's Polish Army across the river by ferry on the night of September 16 to establish a bridgehead on the southeastern corner of the Vistula quarter. The Germans paid scant attention to the force, whose strength they estimated at no more than a few companies—not the six battalions claimed in Soviet battle reports. Berling's troops held out for a week and then retreated to the east bank.

It was September 18 before the Americans could mount a supply flight from England. That morning, 110 B-17s took off from four airfields, each plane carrying 12 containers filled with weapons, ammunition, explosives, food and medical supplies. Flying in three groups, they headed east.

In the early afternoon, Waclaw Zagórski was at his command post in the Inner City when a sentry warned him of approaching aircraft. Zagórski went out to look. "There, straight ahead to the north and very high up, I saw aircraft coming over," he recalled. "They looked like silver birds in the blue sky lightly scattered with little clouds. I counted 12 of them, then more and more until I lost count. The roar of their engines grew, for they were coming straight toward us.

"Everyone ran out into the street and scrambled up on the rubble to try to get a better look. I don't know where they had all sprung from. It was as though the dead had risen from their graves.

"Then dozens of little clouds opened out around the aircraft as the German antiaircraft opened fire. Shrapnel began falling around us, and I shouted to everyone to take cover, but no one heeded. Then three black dots fell away from the leading planes, to be followed at once by more and more, while little colored circles appeared over the dots—parachutes were opening out.

" 'Parachutists!'

"Everyone went mad. They jumped up and down, waving, hugging one another.

" 'No, it isn't parachutists—it's arms! They're dropping arms.' "

Of 1,284 containers dropped, only 288 were recovered; the rest fell into German hands. Nonetheless, the mission brought the insurgents at least twice the total of 55 tons dropped by the Soviets. But it was the last U.S. airdrop; Stalin withdrew permission for the B-17s to land at the Ukraine bases, which were never used again during the War.

Although the token help from the Allies gave the insurgents a glimmer of hope, it also put the Germans under increased pressure to end the uprising quickly. After a good deal of nervous buck-passing between the Wehrmacht and the SS, units of the Hermann Göring Division and other elements of the Ninth Army began driving into Mokotów on September 24. The plan was to finish off Mokotów, then Zolibórz. If those two operations were not sufficient to quash the resistance, the Inner City would be stormed.

Two days later about 600 Poles tried to escape to the Inner City through the sewers. But the Germans were on to that trick by now and quickly set off smoke bombs and tear gas in the tunnels. They also used the *Taifun-Gerät,* or typhoon apparatus, a device that could pump explosive gas into an enclosed space and set it off.

When the insurgents found the passages blocked, some became lost in the underground labyrinth, some were killed by the gas and some returned to Mokotów. Their reappearance, half-dead and filth-caked, shook the morale of those who had stayed. On September 27, Mokotów surrendered.

Zolibórz, although it was within easy range of Soviet artillery across the Vistula, proved even less difficult. Von dem Bach managed to persuade the insurgents and civilians that those who surrendered would be given decent treatment, as had the thousands who left the Vistula quarter during the brief cease-fires arranged by the Red Cross. The drive into Zolibórz began on September 29 and ended shortly after dark the next day when Bór's representative, Colonel Karol Ziemski, met with von dem Bach and arranged for a cease-fire on October 1. That day Ziemski surrendered the district, and the surviving insurgents went into German captivity. A small Communist contingent escaped by boat to join the Soviet forces on the other side of the river.

Meanwhile, from his headquarters in the Inner City, Bór had sent radio messages to Konstantin Rokossovsky's headquarters and to London saying that the insurgents had reached the limit of their endurance, but that they would hold out still longer if the Soviet ground forces would come to their aid soon—very soon. Rokossovsky's station acknowledged the message but did not answer. In London, Mikolajczyk asked the Soviet Ambassador to forward the message to Stalin; he refused. At Mikolajczyk's request, Churchill sent the message to Stalin. Again there was no answer.

The message did evoke a brisk response from von dem Bach, whose monitors were supplying him with transcripts of the insurgents' radio traffic. The last thing that he wanted this late in the game was to see the uprising revived by another Soviet turnabout. Consequently he was willing, even anxious, to grant the insurgents the one victory they could still win from the uprising: an honorable military surrender.

On October 2, under a flag of truce, von dem Bach sat down in his suburban headquarters with a four-officer Polish delegation to negotiate a surrender. Von dem Bach readily agreed to many of the Poles' conditions: prisoner-of-war status, amnesty for acts against the German Occupation before and during the uprising, and a guarantee that insurgents who surrendered would be guarded only by German Army personnel, not by brutal SS or foreign auxiliaries. Under the terms of surrender, the first Home Army regiment would cross the barricades and lay down its arms at nine the next morning.

The surrender was signed at 9 o'clock that night. Von dem Bach then asked the Polish delegates to join him in a moment of silence for the dead on both sides. The Poles had many to remember: about 180,000 civilians and 18,000 Home Army fighters. The Germans had lost 10,000 men dead, 7,000 missing, and another 9,000 wounded, many of whom did not survive.

The surrender and departure of the Poles proceeded smoothly. So, in accordance with the wishes of Hitler and Himmler, did the destruction of Warsaw. Demolition work went on for weeks, moving from one district to the next as German troops finished their systematic looting.

None of these activities were interrupted by the Soviet forces. They settled down along the east bank of the Vistula and there they stayed, refitting and resupplying their divisions, until Josef Stalin was ready to renew the offensive. When he did, and when Soviet troops finally entered the Polish capital in mid-January, 1945, Warsaw was dead.

REVOLT IN WARSAW

Men of the Polish underground army, identified by their cloth arm bands, defend a barricade during the Warsaw Uprising against the German Occupation.

A CIVILIAN ARMY TAKES TO THE STREETS

On August 1, 1944, with the sound of Soviet artillery drifting in from the east, 40,000 patriots of the underground Polish Home Army took to the streets of Warsaw to wrest their capital from the German Occupation forces. Their plans were proud and ambitious: They would quickly overwhelm the weak German garrison before the Russians arrived, so they would not owe Warsaw's liberation to the Soviets.

In spite of mounting casualties and dwindling food supplies, Poles of every age, profession and political persuasion joined the battle. "Even the handicapped fought," insurgent leader J. K. Zawodny later wrote. "An armed platoon of deaf-mutes defended their own building, assisted by an elderly priest who served as their interpreter." Morale remained high even when famine took hold and desperate insurgents were driven to eat their pets. "I don't remember feeling hungry," an insurgent later wrote. "Everyone was in great spirits. We were fighting for our freedom."

But from the outset the obstacles were almost insuperable. The fighters were unable to capture the large stocks of German weapons and supplies they needed for the lengthening struggle. Soon the Germans received reinforcements and counterattacked, winning back vital sectors of the city and isolating many Polish units.

At last, the insurgents reluctantly looked east for help from the Red Army. Time passed; no help came.

The Poles reached a bitter conclusion: The Red Army was hanging back because Moscow wished the democratic insurgents crushed. Even Polish Communists were enraged by the Russians' failure to come to Warsaw's aid. In the fourth week of the uprising, Zawodny watched five fighters with Communist arm bands—one of them a woman—dig a grave for a dead comrade. "After a little while," he wrote, "the girl reached into her blouse and brought into the daylight a beautiful white carnation. She kissed the flower and put it beside the dead man's face. And then the composure broke. She turned to the eastern shore of the Vistula, toward the Soviet forces, and exploded with an eerie, high-pitched scream, 'You sons of bitches—you haven't come!' "

A Polish soldier listens to the BBC, which regularly broadcast encouragement and orders to the insurgents from their exiled government in London.

Armed women insurgents—one wearing a helmet taken from a dead German—smile confidently before going to the barricades to fight along with the men.

FURIOUS FIGHTING AND EARLY SUCCESS

"Much of Warsaw is ours again!" a 15-year-old freedom fighter wrote in his diary on the fourth day of the uprising. In heavy fighting, the insurgents had captured three fifths of the city, including the main post office, the central railway station, the gasworks and the water plant.

But the same day, another Pole added a more ominous note: "We are defenseless against aircraft, which come over in increasing numbers." Soon the bombing transformed Warsaw into a flaming pyre, and German artillery systematically turned block after block to rubble.

Sturdily built churches served as strong points for both sides. The struggle for one church was so intense that gunfire was exchanged at distances of only four to eight feet. "The Germans were in the choir and we were downstairs," one Pole recalled. "We killed 26 of them, but more than 20 of us had fallen."

Poles escort a German prisoner captured when they stormed Warsaw's main telephone exchange.

Soldiers of the Home Army sprint across a Warsaw street during the first days of the uprising, when buildings were still largely undamaged by shelling.

168

After driving the Germans out of the Church of the Holy Cross, Poles try to stop a fire from spreading by knocking apart the woodwork of a blazing window.

AN UNDERGROUND LEGION OF GALLANT CHILDREN

Thousands of children took part in the uprising, many of them members of the Boy Scouts or Girl Scouts. Some of the girls served as medics, but most were assigned to carry messages and orders from district to district and house to house.

Avoiding the dangerous streets whenever possible, the messengers used Warsaw's sewer system, sometimes crawling for miles through the narrow passages in the dark, stinking labyrinth. The Germans tried to obstruct the pipes with coils of barbed wire but the agile children still got through, their clothes torn and their cuts infected by the raw sewage.

To deliver one message, a pair of girls had to cross a square defended by a German unit. "There were two of us," one of the girls recounted, "because if one should be killed the other one was supposed to take the message and deliver it. We were caught by cross fire on the streets. At that I was so terribly frightened that I just couldn't move. I froze." Despite her panic, she and her partner got the message to its destination.

Many boys demanded the right to fight for their city, and some as young as 12 were considered good enough soldiers to be given guns or grenades. The youths lived through horrors that made grown men blanch. In one harrowing episode, several boys were crossing German-held territory at night when a faulty hand grenade, dangling from the belt of a youth known as Baron, exploded, inflicting a terrible stomach wound. "Baron begged us to put him out of his agony," a boy reported; "he knew we could not take him with us, and we could not leave him for the Germans to find." The boys had no other choice but to kill their friend.

A barricade of asphalt, capable of stopping small-arms fire but not tanks, protects Home Army troops crossing a bullet-swept street.

Messenger boys enter a hole cut in the wall of a battered building. Their work was exceedingly dangerous, and many of the young couriers were killed by German snipers.

Four girl couriers grin with pride for their perilous work. Somehow they had managed to get hold of a few Polish Army uniforms.

Medics, still functioning in textbook style early in the uprising, carry a neatly strapped casualty to an aid station.

Bodies awaiting burial in a Warsaw square are covered with makeshift shrouds of newspapers held in place with stones.

TENDING THE WOUNDED, BURYING THE DEAD

The Warsaw Poles were ill equipped to cope with the enormous number of casualties in their city—more than 200,000 people died in the fighting and twice that many were wounded.

Aid stations were set up for the military wounded, while civilians were treated in hospitals not occupied by the Germans. But as buildings were shattered and supplies exhausted, doctors began operating wherever they could, often by flashlight or candlelight in unventilated basements, without disinfectants or anesthetics, using ordinary handsaws for amputations.

When Germans overran Warsaw's Old Town section, one doctor was charged with deciding which of the Home Army's wounded could be evacuated through the sewer and which had to be left behind. He knew that if just one man died in the narrow passageway his body might block it for all following. "I shall never forget their eyes," he said, "how they looked at me as at someone who was passing sentence. We knew that some of the manholes were open and that a scream from a wounded man would cause the Germans to throw hand grenades or gasoline, which they would ignite, into the sewer. These were such young boys, such beautifully enthusiastic boys. This was the most difficult and tragic moment of my life."

The dead, piling up by the thousands every day in the hot August weather, had to be buried at once. The city's supply of coffins was quickly depleted, and survivors knocked crude boxes together from tables, beds and chairs. Since the streets were under artillery or mortar fire, burial was always a hasty procedure. "The body was first searched for identification papers which would be put in an empty bottle, sealed with wax from a candle or possibly a cork," one witness wrote. "The bottle with documents was left on the body, and a little cross of sticks was sometimes placed in the hands."

In time the soft earth in the gardens and parks was filled, and the pavements were torn up to provide more room for graves. "As the uprising wore on," the witness said, "the streets accumulated row after row of graves."

Rows of shallow graves marked by crude wooden crosses lie in the bed of an uprooted sidewalk. Funerals were held whenever enemy shelling subsided.

Exhausted civilians rest in the sunshine after hiding for days in the cellars and drainage pipes of Warsaw.

A Pole draws water at a hand-dug well. Water was so rare that pails of it were used in barter.

Polish soldiers grab a load of supplies dropped from an

174

In the desperate last days of the uprising, water was almost as scarce as food and ammunition. The German troops had destroyed the city's main water pumps as well as its water-treatment plant. The Poles responded by attempting to drill wells in streets and backyards, but these makeshift measures provided only a trickle. Breath itself seemed to be almost gone as the people gagged on reeking air. "Warsaw smelled of burning and dust," a woman insurgent remembered. "It was the most pervasive stench."

What little assistance the Allies offered was more frustrating than helpful. British and American bombers made long supply flights from Italy and England, but three fourths of the food and arms they parachuted over the besieged city fell into the hands of the Germans.

On the 26th of September, after the Poles had fought for 57 days, one of their leaders wrote: "We are faced with the specter of capitulation."

American plane. Poles despaired when supplies fell within German lines. "Some watchers cried," one officer said. "Some struck the walls with their fists."

General Bór, the Home Army commander, surrenders to General von dem Bach-Zelewski.

PROUD AND BLOODY IN DEFEAT

In the last days of September, the Polish leaders negotiated a surrender under honorable terms. General Eric von dem Bach-Zelewski, the German commander, was almost affable at the capitulation ceremony. "We must try to save the magnificent soldiers of the Home Army," he said. "It is our common destiny that one day in the future, we Germans and you Poles shall fight against the common enemy."

More than 15,000 Home Army soldiers, including 2,000 women and 550 children, were marched off to POW camps. As the insurgents departed Warsaw under guard, the city's inhabitants lined the streets to see them off. A Polish officer remembered the emotional farewell: "Thousands and thousands of emaciated, dirty, bandaged, bloodstained men and women of Warsaw were crying, shouting, singing the Polish national anthem. They ran from behind the police, hugging, kissing and giving the insurgents gifts."

Some civilians fell to their knees as the columns of departing soldiers passed by, the officer reported. "This was an unforgettable, almost shocking scene," he said, "because in Poland one kneels in reverence only to the Holy Sacrament."

Carrying their paltry possessions, Polish women soldiers leave Warsaw for a

German prison camp. Though they could have melted into the civilian population, they proudly surrendered together, still wearing their insurgents' arm bands.

6

A lugubrious Christmas with Hitler
The Wehrmacht's welcome breathing spell
The greatest Soviet offensive of all
Conflicting stories from a wily dictator
A grim demand for $20 billion
Moving the Polish border westward
A puzzling halt in the drive to Berlin
Terror in East Prussia

On Christmas Eve, 1944, Colonel General Heinz Guderian, chief of the German Army General Staff with responsibility for the Eastern Front, arrived with an unpalatable proposal at the Eagle's Nest, the Führer's headquarters 20 miles north of Frankfurt am Main. Hitler had moved to the Eagle's Nest from the Wolf's Lair in East Prussia to be near his latest adventure: He had scraped up 300,000 troops and, on December 16, had gambled them all on a counteroffensive in the Ardennes region of Belgium and Luxembourg. But the operation—the Battle of the Bulge, it was called by the Americans—was going poorly, and that was what had brought Guderian so far from his own front.

Guderian informed the Führer that in the past 48 hours it had become certain that the Ardennes offensive would fail; the Allies had contained the panzer breakthrough and were moving up reinforcements to attack the flanks of the German-held area. He told Hitler that on the Eastern Front north of the Carpathian Mountains, the Red Army had completed the heaviest offensive build-up of the War. Therefore, Guderian said with what he considered faultless logic, it was time to call off the Ardennes operation and begin moving forces from the West to save the situation in the East.

As Guderian feared, Hitler could not stomach the proposition. He refused to stop the attack in the Ardennes, and dismissed Guderian's report of the Soviet build-up, calling it "the greatest bluff since Genghis Khan." He even refused to consider creating reserves for the Eastern Front by pulling troops from Norway and the Western Front or from the endangered beachhead in Courland, on the Baltic. Himmler echoed the Führer, calling the build-up "a giant bluff."

Despite Germany's unenviable position in the last days of 1944, Himmler and Hitler found cause for optimism. Admittedly, the Ardennes offensive had fallen short of expectations, but it had given the German Army a breathing space; the Allies would take weeks or months to reorganize and refit before continuing their offensive in the West. Despite Guderian's grave concern about a Soviet build-up, the Eastern Front north of the Carpathians had been dormant for two and a half months. And Army Group South, which had nearly been destroyed in August when Soviet armies overran Rumania, had retreated into Hungary and was now holding its own. Army Group E was withdrawing successfully from Greece, Albania and southern Yugoslavia. In

STALIN TRIUMPHANT

northern Italy, Army Group C had stopped the Americans and British at the Gothic Line.

All the same, Hitler was merely fighting for time. On both fronts, Germany's enemies enjoyed overwhelming and still-growing superiority in matériel and men. Heavy bombing of the Ruhr in December had reduced iron and steel production that month to about half of the September level. The bombing also had severely damaged the German railroad system and most of its fuel sources. Oil from Rumania's Ploesti fields was lost. Army Group South still held the Hungarian fields at Nagykanizsa, but the refineries were out of reach at Budapest, now encircled by the Russians. The synthetic oil plants south of Leipzig had been targets of bombing since May and scarcely had time to repair the damage from one raid before they were hit by another. The Luftwaffe had consumed 180,000 metric tons of gasoline in June 1944 trying to contain the cross-Channel Allied invasion and intercept bombing raids over Germany; its supply for the rest of the War would be only 197,000 metric tons.

Worst of all for the Germans, the Wehrmacht was burned out at the core. To defend the Reich, Hitler had activated the *Volkssturm,* a last-ditch militia composed of young boys and old men; but there were no more well-trained, full-strength units left. To disguise his weakness, he engaged in organizational sleight of hand, setting up corps that were actually no more than brigades and brigades that were really no more than two battalions.

By all normal standards, the Third Reich had lost the War. But Hitler had never let himself be governed by normal considerations. Four days after he rejected Guderian's plea to call off the Ardennes offensive, he admitted to a group of generals that the operation had failed and that Germany would henceforth be fighting for existence alone. But in the next breath he told them, ''You should not infer that I am thinking even in the slightest of losing the War. I have never in my life learned the meaning of the word capitulation, and I am one of those men who have worked their way up from nothing. For me, therefore, the circumstances in which we find ourselves are nothing new.''

History, he continued, proved that victory or defeat was not necessarily decided strictly by military events. He cited the ''miracle of the House of Brandenburg'': Frederick the Great of Prussia, despite having been defeated in the Seven Years' War, kept all of the territory he had gained because the coalition against him fell apart. Hitler fully expected just such a miracle: The Western Allies and the Soviet Union would fall out, giving the Reich a new lease on life.

Guderian tried once again to make Hitler face up to realities. On January 9, 1945, after an inspection tour of the Eastern Front, he returned to the Eagle's Nest and warned Hitler, ''The Eastern Front is like a house of cards.'' Army Group A's front on the Vistula—stretching 260 miles from the Carpathians to Modlin, 20 miles north of Warsaw—had been broken by three Soviet bridgeheads south of Warsaw, at Magnuszew, Pulawy and Baranów. In fact, war games conducted by Army Group A a few weeks earlier suggested that the Red Army could break through to a depth of 100 miles in six days. The remnants of Army Group Center, whose line ran northeastward along the Narew River and the East Prussian border to the Baltic, were no better off. The Russians also had bridgeheads on the Narew River at Rozan and at Serock, the latter only 20 miles north of Warsaw; on the East Prussian border, Army Group Center would have to fight with its back to the sea.

The Eastern Intelligence Branch of the Army General Staff predicted—and the army-group commanders agreed—that the Red Army was prepared to make two deep thrusts: one from the Narew to the mouth of the Vistula, which would cut off Army Group Center, and the other from the Vistula to the Oder River and, possibly, to Berlin. General Joseph Harpe, commander of Army Group A, and Colonel General Georg-Hans Reinhardt, the new commander of Army Group Center, replacing Model, could propose nothing better than to pull away from the bridgeheads just before the offensive started, hoping thereby to avoid an encirclement, shorten the front and create a much-needed reserve force.

Hitler, of course, flatly refused to believe Guderian or the intelligence estimate; whoever had concocted that report, he said, ought to be put in an insane asylum. And he rejected Harpe and Reinhardt's proposal on now-familiar grounds, as proof of how foolish it had been to permit retreats in the first place.

Guderian's conviction that Hitler's Ardennes offensive had failed was not shared by the Western Allies. On January 6, Moscow received an urgent message from Churchill. The

British and Americans were worried that Hitler might take troops from the Eastern Front to keep the offensive going in the West, and Churchill asked Stalin if the Western Allies could count on a Soviet offensive during January on the Vistula or elsewhere. Stalin was delighted to put the Allies in his debt. He replied that he was ready "to commence large-scale offensive operations against the Germans along the whole central front not later than the second half of January." In fact, Stalin had planned to launch the offensive on January 20, but he would oblige Churchill by moving up the starting date to January 12.

Preparations for what would be the greatest Soviet offensive of the War had begun in September 1944 on a 300-mile stretch of terrain between the upper Narew River and the Carpathians; the territory was occupied by the Second Belorussian Front in the north, the First Belorussian Front in the center and the First Ukrainian Front in the south. The stage was grand, and Stalin made certain that he was at its center. In November, he moved Marshal Rokossovsky to the Second Belorussian Front and gave Marshal Zhukov the First Belorussian Front. At the same time, he informed Zhukov that a Stavka representative would not be needed: The offensive would be coordinated from Moscow. In other words, Zhukov and Rokossovsky each would get a share of the glory, along with Konev, now in command of the First Ukrainian Front. But the credit for the whole operation would be Stalin's alone.

The Soviet offensive would be launched from five separate bridgeheads on the Vistula. The First Belorussian Front would make its breakthroughs from Pulawy and Magnuszew, south of Warsaw, and move toward Poznań; the First Ukrainian Front would advance from Baranów toward Breslau, and the Second Belorussian Front, at Rozan and Serock,

would strike for Danzig and the mouth of the Vistula. In the meantime, to the north, the Third Belorussian Front was to move west from the Pregel River toward Königsberg, split the German Third Panzer Army off from Army Group Center's main force and surround the Fourth Army in the Masurian lake country.

Stavka calculated that the distances in the first phase of the offensive—200 miles for Zhukov and 140 miles for Konev and Rokossovsky—could be covered in 15 days. In the second phase, for which 30 days had been allotted, Konev would go beyond Dresden to the Elbe River, Zhukov would take Berlin, and Rokossovsky would sweep along the Baltic coast on Zhukov's right. In the meantime, the Third Belorussian Front would mount a subsidiary operation to clean out East Prussia. As Stavka saw it, the offensive would last 45 days and end the War.

In the early hours of January 12, the temperature at the Baranów bridgehead stood a few degrees above freezing. The roads were icy. Low-hanging clouds and fog would keep aircraft grounded that day. Along the bridgehead's perimeter, the German 48th Panzer Corps had placed three divisions, which meant that there was one soldier for every 15 yards of front—far too low an average. Each division had only a dozen self-propelled assault guns, while the corps kept about 100 guns in reserve. Fifteen miles back, the 24th Panzer Corps held four panzer divisions, which were to counterattack wherever breakthroughs threatened.

Konev's First Ukrainian Front, with seven armies and more than 1,000 tanks, opened the offensive just before dawn. His artillery, 420 pieces per mile, laid down a barrage that caught German units advancing beyond their main battle line; they had expected the Russians to wait for better weather. For the next three hours, a pulverizing hail of

Red Army trucks cross the Vistula between Praga and Warsaw over a wooden bridge erected by combat engineers near one of the five spans blown up by the Germans. On entering the capital on January 17, 1944, the engineers had to clear away more than two million mines and unexploded shells— relics of the previous summer's uprising.

shells fell on the German positions. Behind the bombardment, Konev's infantry drove deep; by noon it had opened wide gaps and the Soviet tanks came pouring through.

The three divisions of the 48th Panzer Corps practically evaporated. Before the 24th Panzer Corps could organize a counterattack, two of its divisions were overrun in their assembly areas. By nightfall the next day, the leading Soviet tanks had cut through the rearmost German position and reached the Nida River, 25 miles beyond the Baranów bridgehead. Ahead of them lay only open country and the roads to Cracow, Oppeln and Breslau.

The Third Belorussian Front, under Lieut. General Ivan Chernyakhovsky, launched its drive on January 13 and was stopped at the main German battle line at Schlossberg and Kattenau in East Prussia. Rokossovsky was brought to a standstill a day later in the Rozan and Serock bridgeheads. In both sectors, the Germans' gallant stands were aided in part by a curtain of heavy snow and fog that made it all but impossible to tell friend from foe.

To the south, at Magnuszew and Pulawy, Zhukov waited for the weather to clear before sending his First Belorussian Front to the attack. On the morning of January 14, the mist actually grew thicker, severely reducing visibility. But Zhukov had his troops primed with a rare hot meal and with martial music blaring from loudspeakers, and he decided that the attack would begin that morning, fog or no fog.

The Germans had ringed Zhukov's bridgeheads with three lines of trenches spaced at intervals of about a mile. The Soviet artillery, more than 600 guns to the mile, opened up on the first line at 8:30. After 25 minutes, the artillery stopped and scout patrols moved forward. Outside each bridgehead they found a row of empty trenches. The Germans had anticipated the attack, pulled out of the first line and let the artillery waste its shells on empty trenches.

At 11 o'clock, a heavier artillery strike hit the second line. The Soviet forces smashed through the second line in time to pause for dinner. The third line was broken shortly before dawn on the following day; the vanguards of the tank armies began to roll through.

With the Eastern Front rapidly crumbling, Hitler left his Eagle's Nest headquarters and returned to the Chancellery in Berlin. Lashing out at the "weaklings and traitors" who had failed him, Hitler fired Harpe as commander of Army Group A on January 16. General Ferdinand Schörner was recalled from Courland, given command of the army group and ordered to stem the Soviet tide.

The following day, the First Belorussian Front, including units of General Zygmunt Berling's First Polish Army, encircled Warsaw and entered the city. The Russians found that most of the German garrison had abandoned the city—despite Hitler's orders to defend Warsaw to the death.

Guderian still believed the Eastern Front could be held, and once again he urged Hitler to send help from the Ardennes, which was fast turning into a German death-trap. Surprisingly, Hitler concurred and said he was sending the Sixth SS Panzer Army, which had been badly mauled in the Ardennes. Even more surprising, Hitler told Guderian that the army was being transferred not to Poland—where it might do some good—but to Hungary, where it would try to break through to the oil fields located southwest of Budapest.

Meanwhile, in western Poland, the onrushing Soviet tank armies were taking advantage of a convenience they had never known in their own country: a network of relatively good roads. Traveling in columns, the tanks could easily cover 25 to 30 miles a day, while the infantry was able to do 18 to 20.

The War was coming home to Germany at express-train speed. Northwest of Cracow, in the Upper Silesian industrial area, steel mills and factories were still running full blast as Konev's tanks bore in on them; nobody dared give orders to evacuate because summary execution as a defeatist awaited anyone who did. Nevertheless, the roads leading to the Oder and Germany were filling with refugees, some of them Nazi Party leaders in official cars who had suddenly remembered important business in Berlin. Others tried to save themselves and their property by horse and wagon. Many fled on foot; for the first time, the refugee columns that had long been familiar on the Eastern Front were composed of German civilians. They were propelled by sheer terror, for rumor traveled even faster than the Soviet tanks. And the one rumor everyone had heard—and believed—was that the Russians' revenge on German civilians was swift, personal and brutal.

In fact, the official watchword of the offensive was "Vengeance!'' For weeks beforehand, it had been drummed into the Soviet troops in meetings, by slogans, in articles and leaflets written by prominent Soviet literary figures. Political officers had recounted endless stories of German atrocities, and Soviet soldiers and officers had addressed large groups of troops and told what had happened to their own families. The object had been to give each man the feeling that he had a personal score to settle.

Said a German prisoner of war who served as a translator for the Red Army: ''It seemed as though the devil himself had come to Silesia. From January into April, there raged a seemingly planless regime of looting, rape and murder. Every German was fair game, all German property booty.''

The Germans living in an obscure village in western Poland felt the full weight of Soviet vengeance. German women of all ages were raped; many died after being assaulted by 20 or more men. Those who survived were herded off the following morning toward the east.

On January 18, a group of Soviet soldiers burst into the cottage of a villager named Peter Haupt and rousted his wife and children from their beds. While Haupt and his sons were forced to look on, the soldiers, led by their captain, raped Haupt's wife and his teen-age daughters. When Haupt tried to stop them, the captain shot him in the groin.

On January 24, Konev's armored columns, working their way downstream along the Oder River, reached Breslau. A day later, Zhukov's main force reached Poznań, completing the first phase of Stalin's great offensive a full four days ahead of schedule.

Zhukov had another 140 miles to go from Poznań to Berlin, and the road was wide open. The German Ninth Army, which was supposed to stop him, had been reduced to one corps headquarters and some rear-echelon troops. Two of its divisions were encircled at Poznań and two more at Torun—all of them cut off because Hitler had declared both cities fortified places.

If his speedy advance had continued, Zhukov would have reached the Oder River in three more days. It took him eight days, however, for nature accomplished what the Germans could not. On January 27 and 28, a blizzard dumped several feet of snow over western Poland and eastern Germany. Himmler, not ordinarily a religious man, was moved to declare, ''God has not forgotten the German people.'' Almost immediately, the temperature rose, the snow melted and the ground thawed into a quagmire. The Soviet armor bogged down in the morass.

But by the first day of February, troops and tanks of two fronts, Konev's and Zhukov's, had reached the Oder and were preparing to cross it. The Germans, they reported, were demoralized. Berlin was virtually in Stalin's pocket as he flew south for his fateful meeting with Roosevelt and Stalin at Yalta in the Crimea.

On February 1, 1945, the U.S. heavy cruiser *Quincy* and three destroyer escorts, zigzagging to avoid any German submarines, were steaming through the western Mediterranean toward the island of Malta. Aboard the *Quincy* was President Franklin D. Roosevelt, who was to fly from Malta 1,360 miles to Yalta. He was traveling halfway around the world because Stalin had refused to leave the Soviet Union, citing his need, as supreme military commander, to remain on Russian soil. For the ailing American President—who had been under secret treatment for an enlarged heart and high blood pressure—the conference was going to be a finale. It would be his last chance to resolve the problems discussed at Teheran in 1943: Soviet entry into the war against Japan; the postwar borders and government of Poland; the political freedom of other liberated peoples of Eastern Europe; the postwar treatment of Germany; and the number of seats that the Soviet Union would receive in the United Nations (Stalin was demanding 16, one for each ''free and independent'' Soviet republic).

On board the *Quincy*, Roosevelt remained in his stateroom through most of the voyage; he emerged on January 30, his 63rd birthday, but only long enough to blow out the candles on a birthday cake. He did not study a voluminous report on Yalta issues that had been prepared for him by the State Department.

On February 3, Roosevelt's C-54 transport, the *Sacred Cow*, took off from Malta at 2:30 a.m.; almost seven hours later it landed at the Saki airfield on the Crimean Peninsula. Spectators at Saki were shocked by the President's wan appearance. Lord Moran, Churchill's personal physician, who watched as Roosevelt reviewed the Red Army honor guard from a jeep, described the President as ''old and thin and drawn; he sat looking straight ahead with his mouth open,

Fifty miles from Berlin, Soviet soldiers wrestle a 76.2mm field gun across the Oder River late in January of 1945. In the race to the Oder, Marshal Ivan Konev's First Ukrainian Front managed to beat Marshal Georgy Zhukov's First Belorussian Front by nine days.

as if he were not taking things in." Churchill, himself running a fever, solicitously walked beside the President's jeep.

The third key member of the Anglo-American delegation, Harry Hopkins, Roosevelt's top adviser, had long been debilitated by a chronic blood disease and appeared to be the worst off of the three. "Physically, he is only half in this world," Moran recalled thinking at the time of Hopkins' arrival. "He looked ghastly—his skin was a yellow-white membrane stretched tight over the bones." Hopkins was to spend most of the conference in bed, arising only for the Big Three's daily four-hour meetings.

After reviewing the honor guard, Churchill and Roosevelt—along with a combined retinue of 700 admirals, generals, diplomats, translators and miscellaneous officials—were driven 80 miles across the Yaila Mountains to Yalta. The road to Yalta was lined on both sides by Soviet security men and by soldiers who saluted every car as it passed. "Some of the Russian troops were so tiny," noted Mike Reilly, Roosevelt's Secret Service bodyguard, "that their ancient Springfields were bigger than the warriors who carried them. On closer inspection, these fierce soldiers proved to be girls still in their teens."

The drive took five hours and ended 150 yards from Yalta's Black Sea coast, an area that had been known before the Revolution as the Russian Riviera. To rest and await Stalin, Roosevelt went to his quarters in the Livadia Palace, for-

merly Czar Nicholas II's summer retreat, and Churchill to the Vorontsov Villa, five miles away.

Stalin reached Yalta on the morning of February 4. That afternoon, he conferred privately with Churchill. He told the Prime Minister, among other things, that the Oder River "was no longer an obstacle" because "the Red Army had several bridgeheads across it and the Germans were using untrained, badly fed and ill-equipped Volkssturm for its defense."

An hour later, Stalin had a private meeting with Roosevelt and told him a very different story. Roosevelt had remarked to Stalin that he had made a few bets on whether the Americans would take Manila before the Russians took Berlin. In reply, Stalin said that fighting along the Oder was very heavy and that the Americans would undoubtedly reach Manila first (which they did that same week).

At negotiation, observed British Foreign Secretary Anthony Eden, Stalin was "the toughest proposition of all." The Soviet leader was playing political poker, and the Red Army's position at the Oder was a card he wanted to play to best advantage.

That night, the Big Three held their first working session in the grand ballroom of the Livadia Palace—a session, said Roosevelt, that should be devoted to "the most important front of all, the Eastern Front." General Aleksei E. Antonov, deputy chief of the Red Army General Staff, then read a

lengthy and somber report on the Soviet Union's January offensive. Antonov emphasized statistics: an advance of nearly 300 miles, more than 9,000 tanks employed, 27 German divisions isolated in East Prussia, another 15 encircled and largely destroyed in Hitler's fortified places.

Antonov predicted a stubborn German defense on the Oder. The Germans had, he declared, brought in 16 divisions of reinforcements from the interior of Germany, the Western Front and Italy, and 30 to 35 more divisions were to be expected.

When Antonov had finished, General George C. Marshall, U.S. Army Chief of Staff, outlined the Western Allies' plans to get their march on Germany rolling again. They had recovered the ground lost in the Battle of the Bulge, Marshall said, and would be starting a drive toward the Rhine River four days hence. The Russians asked Marshall if the Americans planned to mount an offensive in Italy at the same time. He told them no, that it would subtract strength needed for the invasion of Germany proper.

Stalin then pointed out that his January offensive had been "a service of pure comradeship." He asked Roosevelt and Churchill how he could "continue to help" them and pledged to press operations on all fronts in March and April. But beneath that veneer of camaraderie lay a portentous implication: The Red Army, poised on the Oder only 40 miles from Berlin, would finish the War on its own terms and its own timetable.

A polite tone of confidence and mutual trust, and a strong undercurrent of uncertainty and suspicion, prevailed for the remaining seven days of the conference. Churchill and Roosevelt had come to settle long-range issues as well as to coordinate the final stages of the War. The issues were not new ones, but as Averell Harriman ruefully pointed out, "trading with the Russians you had to buy the same horse twice"—i.e., the Russians regarded all commitments made to them as binding, whereas any they had made were always subject to revision in their favor.

For example, Stalin's spoken agreement about the need for a free and democratic Polish government had become moot: The Red Army, which had stood by across the Vistula while the Germans in Warsaw destroyed much of the democratic resistance, was now in control of the country and would turn over authority only to the Soviet-fostered

Winston Churchill, Franklin D. Roosevelt and Josef Stalin sit for formal photographs in the ornate courtyard of the Livadia Palace following the final meeting of the Yalta Conference. At Churchill's right, the British Minister for War Transport, Lord Frederick J. Leathers, gazes skyward in apparent dismay at the tedious picture-taking session. Behind the Big Three stand (from left) British Foreign Secretary Sir Anthony Eden, U.S. Secretary of State Edward R. Stettinius, British Foreign Undersecretary Sir Alexander Cadogan, Soviet Foreign Minister Vyacheslav M. Molotov and W. Averell Harriman, American Ambassador to the Soviet Union.

Lublin government. When it was suggested to Stalin that he contact the Lublin Poles and arrange with them to meet at Yalta with representatives of the Mikolajczyk faction from London, Stalin protested that the "émigré" Poles—as he derisively called them—had collaborated with the Germans. The next day, he said that he had tried to telephone the Lublin Poles but could not reach them. Then he abruptly changed the subject to something that would please his allies: the United Nations charter.

Stalin agreed to drop his demand that each Soviet republic be given a vote in the assembly: Votes for the Soviet Union, the Ukraine and Belorussia would suffice. The Americans disliked giving the Soviet Union two extra votes, but they did not argue. "We were greatly relieved that he reduced his demand from 16 to two additional votes," Harriman recalled.

The Americans were also relieved when Stalin agreed to go to war with Japan within two or three months of the German surrender. The American military feared that without Soviet aid the War might last through 1946, and that a planned invasion of Japan might cost a million American casualties. Stalin's price was high, however. He said that unless the Soviet Union was given the Kurile Islands and the lower half of Sakhalin Island (just north of Japan), along with leases on the ports of Dairen and Port Arthur and permission to run railroads in Manchuria, he would be unable to make the Russian people understand why they were going to war with Japan. In an agreement not made public for one year—nor revealed to the Chinese leader, Chiang Kai-shek—Stalin got most of what he wanted.

To Churchill, the whole Far East matter seemed "remote and secondary." He was more concerned with preventing the Soviet Union from dominating postwar Europe. Stalin wanted to dismember Germany into helpless principalities controlled by the Big Three. Churchill insisted that the French also should have a zone of occupation and participate fully in running postwar Germany. France's cooperation would be vital in the inevitably long Allied occupation, said Churchill. Who knew, he asked, how long the United States would keep its forces in Europe? Britain needed a strong France in order to help bear any future attack by a resurgent Germany.

Roosevelt said that an American presence of two years or

so would suffice. Suddenly, recalled H. Freeman Matthews, the American delegation's specialist on European affairs, "I saw Stalin's eyes light up. Nothing could have pleased him more." Stalin formally gave in on the issue of French participation at a later session.

The occupation of Berlin was discussed only briefly. The conference merely confirmed the decision that had been made the previous November during meetings in London among lower-echelon British, Soviet and American diplomats: The three Allies would occupy Berlin jointly, with the city itself situated in the Soviet zone. The question of access to the city, it was determined, would be left to the military planners.

On the point of German reparations, Stalin was adamant and grim. According to Harry Hopkins, "Stalin rose and gripped the back of his chair with such force that his brown hands went white at the knuckles. He spat out his words as if they burnt his mouth. Great stretches of his country had been laid to waste, he said, and the peasants put to the sword. Reparations should be paid to the countries that had suffered most. While he was speaking, nobody moved."

Stalin mentioned a figure of $20 billion worth of goods, factories and equipment, with half paid to the Soviet Union. Churchill objected that the figure was too high; he feared that the burden would leave Germany unable to feed itself and thus make it a ward of the Allies. A protocol was signed stating that the figure was only "a basis for discussion," though Stalin would later claim that Roosevelt and Churchill had agreed to that amount.

When the matter of Poland came to issue, Soviet Foreign Minister Molotov read a formal proposal that the country's border with Germany be moved westward to the line of the

PURLOINING A DICTATOR'S DOODLE

During the daily battle of wits at the Yalta Conference, Stalin continued his well-known habit of doodling while waiting for interpreters to catch up.

U.S. State Department aide H. Freeman Matthews was tantalized by the doodles. He decided to capture one as a souvenir "at the risk of being shot by those toughs"—Stalin's guards. At the end of a work session, Matthews furtively scooped up a doodle—unnoticed by Stalin or the secret-service guards.

The doodle (far right) was studied by a psychoanalyst unaware of the doodler's identity. He called it the work of a man "flexibly shifting his position but always pressing relentlessly toward his goals."

Oder and western Neisse Rivers—deep in German territory—to make up for territory to be given the Soviet Union in eastern Poland.

"It would be a pity," Churchill said, "to stuff the Polish goose so full of German food that it died of indigestion." Such a shift in the border, he said, would require moving six million Germans from Silesia and East Prussia alone. Stalin dismissed that argument by insisting that most Germans had already fled the territory in question.

Eventually, the Americans and British agreed not to oppose the Soviets' boundary proposals, and to establish "a Polish Provisional Government of National Unity" to embrace all Polish factions. Stalin agreed to free elections, but the final Yalta communiqué established no time frame. When Admiral William D. Leahy, Roosevelt's chief military aide, read the document, he protested: "Mr. President, this is so elastic the Russians can stretch it all the way from Yalta to Washington without even technically breaking it." Roosevelt agreed, but said that the agreement was "the best I can do for Poland at this time."

Less than a month later, Leahy would be proved correct when the Soviets refused to allow the Mikolajczyk government to join the provisional government. The Soviets also would renege on another agreement involving territory the Red Army had "liberated." Rumania was supposed to be controlled by a joint commission composed of Soviet, British and American representatives, but the American and British commissioners found that they served no function except to report to their governments on the tightening of Soviet controls.

Amid a barrage of last-minute amendments and changes in the Yalta documents, the conference ended on February 11 when the three leaders signed the final communiqué over lunch in the Czar's billiard room at the Livadia Palace.

Let Stalin sign first, suggested the President. "He has been such a wonderful host." Churchill jokingly nominated himself to sign first because he was the oldest of the Big Three and his name came first alphabetically. Stalin agreed, saying that if he signed first, everyone would think he had run the conference.

At Yalta early on February 6, Stalin made a radiotelephone call that influenced the end of the War more than anything discussed by the Big Three. The call went to the headquarters of General V. Y. Kolpakchi's Sixty-ninth Army on the Oder near Poznań, and the connection was made while Marshal Zhukov was meeting with the five army commanders of his First Belorussian Front. They were discussing the drive on Berlin.

Zhukov picked up the phone. General Vasily Chuikov, the commander of the Eighth Guards Army, was sitting nearby and overheard Stalin say, "Where are you? What are you doing?"

Zhukov explained that he was in conference, planning the Berlin operation with his army commanders.

"Having heard this report," Chuikov later wrote, "Stalin told the commander of the front, and I understand it came as a surprise to him, to stop planning the Berlin offensive and start working out an operation to deal with the German 'Vistula' group of armies in Pomerania."

Suddenly the drive on Berlin was postponed—for reason or reasons unknown. Undoubtedly Stalin was being cautious; his armies had traveled far and fast and he wanted them to have time to regroup and bring up supplies. Prob-

Matthews stands behind the delegation representing the United States, not far from Stalin (left).

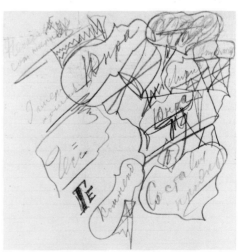

Stalin's doodle features sharp, jagged teeth, bulbous domes, the Russian phrase "I have told the truth" (bottom right) and the repeated English word "commend" (top and bottom left).

187

ably he wanted to capture more territory before the fall of Berlin froze his armies in place. Possibly he wanted more time to exploit his victories on the secret battlefield of Kremlin politics. And conceivably he wanted the Western Allies to bleed a little longer before he delivered the *coup de grâce* to Germany; the Americans and the British had experienced nothing in this war, Stalin frequently said, that could compare with the suffering of the Russians, who had lost more than 20 million people in the fighting—perhaps as many as 30 million.

Certainly Stalin wanted the Germans to suffer more for all they had done to the Russian people. And suffer the Germans did, especially in East Prussia.

Along the roads into East Prussia, posters went up reading, "Red Army Soldier: You are now on German soil; the hour of revenge has struck!"

Back in October, the East Prussians had been given a foretaste of Russian vengeance at the town of Nemmersdorf, just across the Polish border. Said a lieutenant with the Hermann Göring Division: "On the road through Nemmersdorf, I saw a whole column of refugees who had been rolled over by Russian tanks; not only the wagons and teams, but also a good number of civilians, mostly women and children, had been squashed flat by the tanks. At the edge of the road and in the farmyards lay the corpses of civilians who evidently had not all been killed during military operations but had been murdered systematically."

A civilian named Karl Potrek told how the people of Nemmersdorf died: "In a farmyard stood a cart to which four naked women were nailed through their hands in a cruciform position. Beyond stood a barn, and to each of its two doors a naked woman was nailed through the hands in a crucified posture. In the dwellings, we found a total of 72 women, including children, and one old man, all dead . . . holes in their necks. Some babies had their heads bashed in. In one room, we found an old woman sitting on a sofa. Half of her head had been sheared off with an ax or a spade."

By the end of January, Rokossovsky's tanks had reached the Baltic coast at Elbing. General Chernyakhovsky's Third Belorussian Front had pushed deep into East Prussia from the east, the First Baltic Front under General Ivan Bagramyan was bearing in from the north, and East Prussia's long death agony had begun.

Josefine Schleiter, a medical student from Osterode, was one of the hundreds of thousands who fled westward. "The roads were full of refugees, carts and people on foot," she recalled. "Suddenly tanks rolled up, and on all sides there were soldiers in snow shirts. The confusion was so great that one did not know at first whether they were German or Russian soldiers, but then we saw German soldiers with their hands up. They were collected together and led away.

"The tanks rushed through the rows of carts. Carts were hurled into the ditches, where there were entrails of horses, and men, women and children were fighting with death. Wounded people were screaming for help. Next to me a woman was bandaging her husband, who was losing blood from a big wound.

"Behind me, a young girl said to her father, 'Father, shoot me!' 'Yes, Father,' said her brother, who was about 16 years old, 'I have no chance.' The father looked at his children, tears streaming down his cheeks, and he said in a quiet tone, 'Wait a little while longer, children.'"

Josefine Schleiter observed more horrors a few miles outside Osterode, in a cow barn. "There were more than a hundred people there. People were sitting on the stone troughs. Some of the men fetched wood and were making a little fire. If one stood near it, one could warm oneself a little. Terrible hours followed, particularly for the women. From time to time, soldiers came in, also officers, and fetched girls and young women. No shrieking, no begging, nothing helped. With revolvers in their hands, they gripped the women by their wrists and dragged them away. A father who wanted to protect his daughter was taken into the yard and shot. The girl was all the more the prey of these wild creatures. Toward morning she came back, terror in her childlike eyes; she had become years older during the night. We were all overcome by sadness and desperation."

About a million and a quarter East Prussians escaped overland or by boat to the Danzig-Pomerania area. Most crossed the Frisches Haff, a frozen five-mile-wide lagoon, and the adjacent Frische Nehrung, a slender sandspit running from the tip of the Samland Peninsula to the Vistula estuary east of Danzig. The ice on the lagoon was thick enough to bear the weight of people and carts, but not Soviet tanks. The trip was a harrowing one. Soviet planes bombed the ice and the people on it. Those who crossed in February had to contend with the added hazard of a thaw. One refugee remembered:

"The ice was breaking, and at some places we had to drag ourselves through foot-deep water. We continually tried the surface with sticks. Bomb craters compelled us to make detours. We often slipped, and thought we were already lost. With our clothes wet through and through, movement was difficult. But deadly fear drove us on in spite of our shivering bodies.

"I saw women do superhuman things. As leaders of treks they instinctively found the safest way for their carts. Household utensils were lying scattered all over the ice; wounded people crept up to us with imploring gestures, dragged themselves along on sticks, or were pushed forward on little sledges by friends.

"For six hours we passed through this valley of death. Then, exhausted, we reached the Nehrung."

On the Nehrung, an almost solid mass of humanity and animals moved along a single, rutted road at a rate of two or three miles a day, the glittering ice of the Haff on one side, the open sea on the other. Some hanged themselves; demented mothers threw their children into the sea. Dead horses were cut up and eaten. Even worse off were thousands of Russian prisoners, ragged and starving, also being marched across the Nehrung.

At Pillau, Königsberg's open-water port on the Nehrung, and at Kahlberg, to the south, ships took some of the refugees aboard. But the Soviet vengeance did not stop at the water's edge. On January 30, the Soviet submarine *S-13*, under Captain A. I. Marinesko, torpedoed and sank the *Wilhelm Gustloff,* and more than 6,000 of the 7,000 refugees on the ship were drowned. Marinesko's submarine scored again on February 10 when it sank the *Steuben,* with 3,500 refugees aboard.

Once Rokossovsky, Chernyakhovsky and Bagramyan all got on the move, East Prussia was beyond saving. Nevertheless, Hitler had issued orders to hold Königsberg—designated a fortified place—and what was left of East Prussia at all costs. What was left was not much: a 40-mile-deep beachhead embracing the Samland Peninsula north and east of Königsberg and reaching about half the length of the Frisches Haff on the southwest. The Third Panzer Army was on the north, the Fourth Army on the south.

Unlike most of Hitler's fortified places, Königsberg was actually fortified. Despite heavy bombing and repeated assaults, the city managed to hold out for nine weeks, until the 9th of April, and even then four Soviet armies were required to capture it.

By that time, Stalin had won more provinces for the Soviet Union. Since his February 6 postponement of the offensive against Berlin, Stalin's Red Army had captured Pomerania, West Prussia and East Prussia except for the tip of the Samland Peninsula. In the Balkans, Soviet forces were driving west through Czechoslovakia and northwest through Austria and, after a long, hard struggle, were on the verge of taking Vienna.

But the Soviet armies would pay dearly in blood for Stalin's long delay in assaulting Berlin. The hundreds of thousands of German refugees who were streaming in from the East were telling their terrifying stories of Soviet revenge, and the accounts of these atrocities were steeling the surviving Wehrmacht forces. When Stalin finally unleashed his last offensive on April 16, every German soldier and many German civilians would defend Berlin with fear and desperation, fighting not for the Führer's lost cause, but for their very lives.

RETURNING HOME

An 83-year-old patriarch, with his barefooted daughter and granddaughter, reclaims the ruins of his home, destroyed by the retreating Germans in 1943.

REBUILDING CITIES AND SHATTERED LIVES

"Mama!" begins a child's note to a parent lost in the liberation of Voronezh. "Dad and I come here at 10 every morning and wait for you."

"With every hour Kiev becomes more animated," wrote a Soviet correspondent after the Ukrainian capital was liberated on November 6, 1943. "People are returning from nearby towns and settlements where they had fled to escape abduction to Germany. Only a few hours ago the big building on Institutskaya Street was empty, and now we see people carrying trunks, bedding and iron stoves into it."

Kiev and other liberated Russian regions were like the earth after a long winter: New signs of life sprouted everywhere. Hidden stores of arms, fuel, food and seed appeared miraculously as soon as the Wehrmacht retreated. Buried treasures—civic monuments and valuable machinery—were dug up and restored to use. Thousands of wandering children, their parents killed or deported to slave-labor camps, were picked up by Soviet troops and partisans and taken to receiving centers. The partisans themselves, after the long underground struggle against the occupation, now emerged in a new role. "Yesterday's guerrillas," wrote an observer in Rzhev, "now head the city's municipal offices."

Facing up to the epic task of repairing or replacing war damages estimated at 2.6 trillion rubles (208 billion wartime U.S. dollars), the Russian people began at once to rebuild their towns and cities and broken lives. Trade unions and collective farms opened homes for the orphans. Teams of architects, following close behind the Red Army, joined with local workers and returning refugees to put up new buildings utilizing standardized designs and prefabricated parts. The old and the young worked long hours; people did their regular jobs, then planted gardens and cleared the rubble from wrecked factories and mines.

By the summer of 1945, the enormous work of reconstruction was already bearing fruit: In formerly occupied territories, factories and farms were producing from one third to one half of their prewar output. "I sometimes wonder where I find the strength," said 60-year-old Ivan Ilyin, a blacksmith with two sons at the front. "But since we've been freed, it's like a load dropped from your heart—I work and don't feel the least bit tired."

Red Army soldiers help an evacuated family move their possessions back into their house. The shoeless woman in front is carrying her prized icon.

A Stalingrad woman searches the ruins of her home. She had refused evacuation and survived the five-month battle for the city.

A tepee-like shelter constructed of timber serves as a temporary home for a Belorussian family while they rebuild their farmhouse.

MAKING DO WITH NEXT TO NOTHING

"We settled where we could," wrote a youth leader in Stalingrad in 1944. "Some people managed to establish themselves in a wooden dormitory, which had been knocked together slapdash, others in canvas tents. Several girls even settled in a smashed German staff bus." Dugouts and the basements of bombed buildings sufficed for many others.

Everything had to be checked for booby traps. The Germans had attached explosives to coat racks, pianos and drawers—and had even wired houses to blow up when power was restored. Some 100,000 mines were found in the Stalingrad area during the 18 months after liberation.

Despite the danger, people everywhere sifted through the rubble for salvageable items. An electrical worker won fleeting fame by collecting enough scrap wire for 70 miles of electric cable. A wheel from a wrecked train and assorted bits of salvaged machinery were assembled into a primitive sawmill. Nothing was wasted. "Glass was collected literally in pieces," wrote an official. "In settlements and gorges, dumps and attics—little by little, everything was swept up and put to use."

A peasant family in the reconquered region of Orlovsk gathers to share a meal in 1943. Stacks of bricks suggest that the salvage work has just begun.

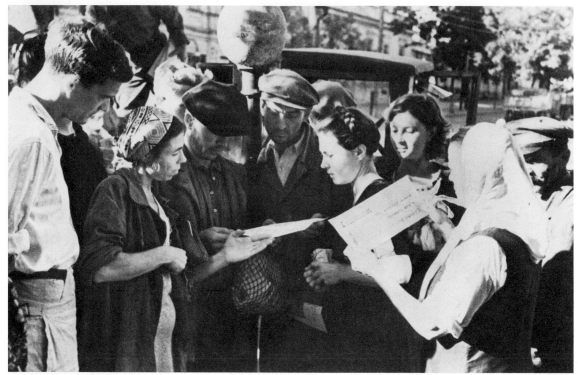

Newly liberated civilians read war news in the first Soviet Information Bureau leaflets distributed in Taganrog.

A Russian bell ringer shares the belfry of his village church with its sprawled former tenant—a dead German soldier.

Confirming her faith, a young child kisses a wooden cross during a postliberation religious service held in a Ukrainian village on the Dnieper River in 1944.

RENEWED DEDICATION TO THE PATRIOTIC WAR

As Soviet forces recaptured each town and village, they were often greeted by local people hungry for information after years of German censorship and propaganda. Crowds questioned soldiers and officials incessantly, making "a solid ring about them," according to a report from Kiev, and "cheering loudly" at their answers.

The Soviet news agencies were quick to reestablish contact. Just a day after the liberation of Kharkov, a radio transmitter was flown in and began spreading the news of Soviet advances—and exhorting redoubled efforts for final victory.

Such appeals were hardly needed. In the first year of liberation, 858 industrial units, including 51 large mines, went back to work in the Donets Basin alone.

Tens of thousands of volunteers from across the Soviet Union hurried west to speed reconstruction. Aircraft workers rebuilt a Stalingrad plant at their own ex-

pense. And when eastern farms returned 600,000 head of livestock that had been evacuated before the German occupation, they added 40,000 as a gift to help rebuild the herds in the west.

"People send us gifts every day," said a Stalino city official. "We've just had a hundred tons of fish from Dagestan and a truckload of medicines from Moscow. Telegrams pour into my office, advising me of the dispatch of machinery, cattle and clothing from friends in Siberia, Kazakhstan and the Urals."

A WORK FORCE OF DETERMINED WOMEN

Russian women, who were already doing the lion's share of the labor on the home front, were further taxed by the mountainous task of helping to rehabilitate the liberated regions.

In Sevastopol, devastated by German bombardment, seamstress Irina Chervyakova organized 18 fellow workers to rebuild their factory—repairing floors and plastering walls. Her seamstress brigade then went on to help rebuild a railroad station, a community center and a road. Alto-

gether, the 19 women gave 7,000 hours of work to the reconstruction effort.

Women who worked on farms volunteered to do factory work when their daily chores were finished. The cleaning women of Rzhev toiled as volunteer bricklayers for a few hours a day starting at 4 a.m. And every woman grasped every spare moment to refurbish her own battered home.

Many of the women had intensely personal motives for their desire to rebuild. "While we were retreating from Rzhev," said a kindergarten director named Malinovskaya, "the fascists bombed us. My two little girls were killed. I am avenging my daughters by my work."

Women students of the Leningrad Mining Institute, some of them recently returned from evacuation, repair the school drawing room.

Young women clear rubble from a street in Stalino in April 1945. Reconstruction work had been going on here since the Ukrainian city was liberated in September of 1943.

Working alongside a Red Army engineer, women in Leningrad resurrect an equestrian statue from its underground cache after the German siege was lifted in January 1944.

Three little girls delightedly skip rope in a cleared street of Leningrad. The girls had survived the 29-month siege in which approximately a million citizens perished of starvation, malnutrition, exposure, disease and German bombardment.

BIBLIOGRAPHY

Alexander, Jean, *Russian Aircraft since 1940*. London: Putnam & Company, 1975.

Angelucci, Enzo, and Paolo Matricardi, *World War II Airplanes*, Vol. 2. Rand McNally, 1977.

Armstrong, John A., ed., *Soviet Partisans in World War II*. The University of Wisconsin Press, 1964.

Bamm, Peter, *The Invisible Flag*. Transl. by Frank Herrmann. London: Faber and Faber, 1956.

The Battle of Kursk. Moscow: Progress Publishers, 1974.

The Battle of Orel: July 1943. London: Hutchinson, 1943.

Bender, Roger James, and Hugh Page Taylor, *Uniforms, Organization and History of the Waffen-SS*, Vol. 2. Roger James Bender and Hugh Page Taylor, 1971.

Bialer, Seweryn, ed., *Stalin and His Generals: Soviet Military Memoirs of World War II*. Pegasus, 1969.

Bór-Komorowski, Tadeuz, *The Secret Army*. London: Victor Gollancz, 1950.

Boyd, Alexander, *The Soviet Air Force since 1918*. Stein and Day, 1977.

Brezhnev, Leonid I., *Malaya Zemlya*. U.S.S.R.: Krasnaya Zvezda Publishing House, 1978.

Bruce, George, *The Warsaw Uprising: 1 August-2 October 1944*. London: Rupert Hart-Davis, 1972.

Burns, James MacGregor, *Roosevelt: The Soldier of Freedom*. Harcourt Brace Jovanovich, 1970.

Byrnes, James F., *Speaking Frankly*. Harper & Brothers, 1947.

Caidin, Martin, *The Tigers Are Burning*. Hawthorn Books, 1974.

Carell, Paul, *Scorched Earth: Hitler's War on Russia*, Vol. 2. Transl. by Ewald Osers. London: George G. Harrap, 1970.

Chant, Christopher, *Kursk*. London: Almark Publishing, 1975.

Chuikov, Vasily I.:
The End of the Third Reich. Moscow: Progress Publishers, 1973.
The Fall of Berlin. Holt, Reinhart and Winston, 1967.

Churchill, Winston S.:
The Second World War: Closing the Ring. Houghton Mifflin, 1951.
The Second World War: Triumph and Tragedy. Bantam Books, 1962.

Clark, Alan, *Barbarossa: The Russian-German Conflict, 1941-1945*. William Morrow, 1965.

Collins, James L., Jr., ed., *The Marshall Cavendish Illustrated Encyclopedia of World War II*. Marshall Cavendish, 1972.

Cooper, Matthew:
The German Army, 1933-1945: Its Political and Military Failure. London: Macdonald and Jane's, 1978.
The Nazi War against Soviet Partisans, 1941-1944. Stein and Day, 1979.

Craven, Wesley Frank, and James Lea Cate, eds., *The Army Air Forces in World War II*, Vol. 3, *Europe: Argument to V-E Day*. The University of Chicago Press, 1951.

Daugherty, William E., *A Psychological Warfare Casebook*, The Johns Hopkins Press, 1958.

Deane, John R., *The Strange Alliance: The Story of Our Efforts at Wartime Cooperation with Russia*. The Viking Press, 1947.

Deborin, Grigory, *Thirty Years of Victory*. Moscow: Progress Publishers, 1975.

De Zayas, Alfred M., *Nemesis at Potsdam: The Anglo-Americans and the Expulsion of the Germans*. London: Routledge & Kegan Paul, 1977.

Drum, Karl, *Airpower and Russian Partisan Warfare*. Arno Press, 1968.

Eden, Anthony, *The Memoirs of Anthony Eden, Earl of Avon: The Reckoning*. Houghton Mifflin, 1965.

Ehrenburg, Ilya, *Men, Years—Life*, Vol. 5, *The War: 1941-1945*. Transl. by Tatiana Shebunia. The World Publishing Company, 1964.

Embassy of the Union of Soviet Socialist Republics Information Bulletin. Washington, D.C.

Feis, Herbert, *Churchill, Roosevelt, Stalin: The War They Waged and the Peace They Sought*. Princeton University Press, 1957.

Fitzgibbon, Louis, *Katyn*. Charles Scribner's Sons, 1971.

Garlinski, Jozef, *Poland, SOE and the Allies*. London: George Allen and Unwin, 1969.

Goerlitz, Walter, *History of the German General Staff: 1657-1945*. Transl. by Brian Battershaw. Frederick A. Praeger, 1953.

Great Patriotic War of the Soviet Union, 1941-1945: A General Outline. Moscow: Progress Publishers, 1974.

Grechko, Andrei A., *Liberation Mission of the Soviet Armed Forces in the Second World War*. Transl. by David Fidlon. Moscow: Progress Publishers, 1975.

Green, William, *Famous Fighters of the Second World War*. Doubleday, 1957.

Grey, Ian, *Stalin: Man of History*. Doubleday, 1979.

Gross, Jan Tomasz, *Polish Society under German Occupation: The General Gouvernement, 1939-1944*. Princeton University Press, 1979.

Grossman, Vasily Semenovich, *Red Army in Poland and Belorussia*. London: Hutchinson, 1945.

Guderian, Heinz, *Panzer Leader*. Transl. by Constantine Fitzgibbon. E. P. Dutton, 1952.

Harriman, W. Averell, and Elie Abel, *Special Envoy to Churchill and Stalin: 1941-1946*. Random House, 1975.

Heilbrunn, Otto, *Partisan Warfare*. Frederick A. Praeger, 1962.

Higham, Robin, and Jacob W. Kipp, eds., *Soviet Aviation and Air Power: A Historical View*. Frederick A. Praeger, 1977.

Howell, Edgar M., "The Soviet Partisan Movement: 1941-1944." United States Department of the Army, Pamphlet No. 20-244, August 1956.

Hull, Cordell, *The Memoirs of Cordell Hull*, Vol. 2. Macmillan, 1948.

Humble, Richard, *Hitler's Generals*. Doubleday, 1973.

Hyde, H. Montgomery, *Stalin: The History of a Dictator*. Farrar, Straus and Giroux, 1971.

Icks, Robert J., *Tanks and Armored Vehicles: 1900-1945*. WE Inc., 1970.

Infield, Glenn B., *The Poltava Affair: A Russian Warning, An American Tragedy*. Macmillan, 1973.

Irving, David, *Hitler's War*. The Viking Press, 1977.

Jones, Robert Huhn, *The Roads to Russia: United States Lend-Lease to the Soviet Union*. University of Oklahoma Press, 1969.

Jukes, Geoffrey, *Kursk: The Clash of Armor*. Ballantine Books, 1968.

Keegan, John, *Waffen-SS: The Asphalt Soldiers*. Ballantine Books, 1970.

Khrushchev, Nikita S., *Khrushchev Remembers*. Ed. and transl. by Strobe Talbott. Little, Brown, 1970.

Konev, Ivan S.:
The Great March of Liberation: Poland Achieves Freedom. Moscow: Progress Publishers, 1972.
Year of Victory. Moscow: Progress Publishers, 1969.

Korbonski, Stefan:
Fighting Warsaw: The Story of the Polish Underground State, 1939-1945. Transl. by F. B. Czarnomski. Minerva Press, 1968.
The Polish Underground State: A Guide to the Underground, 1939-1945. Transl. by Marta Erdman. East European Quarterly, 1978.

Krieger, Evgeny, *From Moscow to the Prussian Frontier*. London: Hutchinson, 1945.

Kulski, Julian Eugeniuz, *Dying, We Live: The Personal Chronicle of a Young Freedom Fighter in Warsaw (1939-1945)*. Holt, Rinehart and Winston, 1979.

Leahy, William D., *I Was There: The Personal Story of the Chief of Staff to Presidents Roosevelt and Truman Based on His Notes and Diaries Made at the Time*. McGraw-Hill, 1950.

Liddell Hart, B. H.:
The German Generals Talk. William Morrow, 1948.
History of the Second World War. G. P. Putnam's Sons, 1970.

Lochner, Louis P., ed. and transl., *The Goebbels Diaries: 1942-1943*. Greenwood Press, 1948.

Mackiewicz, Joseph, *The Katyn Wood Murders*. London: Hollis & Carter, no date.

Macksey, Kenneth:
Guderian: Creator of the Blitzkrieg. Stein and Day, 1975.
The Partisans of Europe in World War II. London: Hart-Davis, MacGibbon, 1975.
Tank Warfare: A History of Tanks in Battle. Stein and Day, 1971.

McNeill, William Hardy, *America, Britain & Russia: Their Cooperation and Conflict, 1941-1946*. Johnson Reprint Corporation, 1970.

Majdalany, Fred, *The Fall of Fortress Europe*. London: Hodder and Stoughton, 1968.

Manstein, Erich von, *Lost Victories*. London: Methuen, 1955.

Matthews, H. Freeman, *Memoirs of a Passing Era*. Unpublished ms.

Mellenthin, Friedrich W. von:
German Generals of World War II: As I Saw Them. University of Oklahoma Press, 1977.
Panzer Battles: A Study of the Employment of Armor in the Second World War. Ed. by L. C. F. Turner. Transl. by H. Betzler. University of Oklahoma Press, 1956.

Meretskov, Kirill A., *Serving the People*. Moscow: Progress Publishers, 1971.

Mikolajczyk, Stanislaw, *The Rape of Poland: Pattern of Soviet Aggression*. McGraw-Hill, 1948.

Moran, Lord, *Churchill: Taken from the Diaries of Lord Moran—The Struggle for Survival, 1940-1965*. Norman S. Berg, 1976.

"Operations of Encircled Forces: German Experiences in Russia." United States Department of the Army, Pamphlet No. 20-234, January 1952.

Orska, Irena, *Silent is the Vistula: The Story of the Warsaw Uprising*. Transl. by Marta Erdman. Longmans, Green, 1946.

Payne, Robert, *The Rise and Fall of Stalin*. Simon and Schuster, 1965.

Rauch, Georg von, *A History of Soviet Russia*. Transl. by Peter and Annette Jacobson. Frederick A. Praeger, 1964.

"Rear Area Security in Russia: The Soviet Second Front behind the German Lines." United States Department of the Army, Pamphlet No. 20-240, July 1951.

Rokossovsky, Konstantin K., *A Soldier's Duty*. Moscow: Progress Publishers, 1970.

Rozek, Edward J., *Wartime Diplomacy: A Pattern in Poland*. John Wiley & Sons, 1958.

Salisbury, Harrison E.:
The 900 Days: The Siege of Leningrad. Harper & Row, 1969.
The Unknown War. Bantam Books, 1978.

Schieder, Theodor, ed., *The Expulsion of the German Population from the Territories East of the Oder-Neisse Line*. Bonn: Federal Ministry for Expellees, Refugees and War Victims, 1957.

Schwabedissen, Walter, *The Russian Air Force in the Eyes of German Commanders*. United States Air Force Historical Division, Research Studies Institute, Air University, 1960.

Seaton, Albert:
The Russo-German War: 1941-1945. Praeger, 1970.
Stalin as Military Commander. Praeger, 1975.

Sherwood, Robert E., *Roosevelt and Hopkins: An Intimate History*. Harper & Brothers, 1948.

Shtemenko, Sergei M.:
The Last Six Months: Russia's Final Battles with Hitler's Armies in World War II. Transl. by Guy Daniels. Doubleday, 1977.
The Soviet General Staff at War: 1941-1945. Moscow: Progress Publishers, 1970.

Snell, John L., ed., *The Meaning of Yalta: Big Three Diplomacy and the New Balance of Power*. Louisiana State University Press, 1956.

Solovyov, Boris, *The Battle of Kursk*. Moscow: Novosti Press Agency Publishing House, 1973.

Speer, Albert, *Inside the Third Reich*. Transl. by Richard and Clara Winston. Avon Books, 1970.

The Staff of *Strategy & Tactics* magazine, *War in the East: The Russo-German Con-*

flict, 1941-1945. Simulations Publications, 1977.

Stalin, Josef:
  The Great Patriotic War of the Soviet Union. Greenwood Press, 1945.
  On the Great Patriotic War of the Soviet Union. London: Hutchinson, 1943.

Stein, George H., *The Waffen-SS: Hitler's Elite Guard at War, 1939-1945.* Cornell University Press, 1966.

Stettinius, Edward R., Jr., *Roosevelt and the Russians: The Yalta Conference.* Greenwood Press, 1949.

Stockwell, Richard E., *Soviet Air Power.* Pageant Press, 1956.

Stroud, John, *The Red Air Force.* London: The Pilot Press, 1943.

Stypulkowski, Zbigniev, *Invitation to Moscow.* Walker and Company, 1950.

Sydnor, Charles W., Jr., *Soldiers of Destruction: The SS Death's-Head Division, 1933-1945.* Princeton University Press, 1977.

Tenenbaum, Joseph, *Race and Reich: The Story of an Epoch.* Twayne Publishers, 1956.

Thorwald, Juergen, *Flight in the Winter.* Ed. and transl. by Fred Wieck. Pantheon Books, 1951.

Trevor-Roper, Hugh R., ed.:
  Blitzkrieg to Defeat: Hitler's War Directives, 1939-1945. Holt, Rinehart and Winston, 1971.
  Final Entries, 1945: The Diaries of Joseph Goebbels. Transl. by Richard Barry. G. P. Putnam's Sons, 1978.
  Hitler's Secret Conversations: 1941-1944. Farrar, Straus and Young, 1953.

Ulam, Adam B., *Stalin: The Man and His Era.* The Viking Press, 1973.

Wagner, Ray, ed., *The Soviet Air Force in World War II.* Transl. by Leland Fetzer. Doubleday, 1973.

Warlimont, Walter, *Inside Hitler's Headquarters: 1939-1945.* Transl. by R. H. Barry. Frederick A. Praeger, 1964.

Werth, Alexander, *Russia at War: 1941-1945.* E. P. Dutton, 1964.

Windrow, Martin, *Waffen-SS.* London: Osprey, 1971.

Wykes, Alan, *The Siege of Leningrad: Epic of Survival.* Ballantine Books, 1968.

Young, Peter, ed., *Atlas of the Second World War.* Berkley Publishing Corporation, 1974.

Zagórski, Waclaw, *Seventy Days.* Transl. by John Welsh. Maidstone, Kent, England: George Mann, 1957.

Zawodny, J. K.:
  Death in the Forest: The Story of the Katyn Forest Massacre. University of Notre Dame Press, 1962.
  Nothing but Honor: The Story of the Warsaw Uprising, 1944. Hoover Institution Press, 1978.

Zhukov, Georgy K.:
  Marshal Zhukov's Greatest Battles. Transl. by Theodore Shabad. London: MacDonald, 1969.
  The Memoirs of Marshal Zhukov. Delacorte Press, 1971.

Ziemke, Earl F., *Stalingrad to Berlin: The German Defeat in the East* (Army Historical series). Office of the Chief of Military History, United States Army, 1968.

ACKNOWLEDGMENTS

For help in the preparation of this book, the editors wish to thank Sadie Alford, Novosti Press Agency, London; Gamer Bautdinov, Novosti, Rome; Hans Becker, ADN-Zentralbild, Berlin, DDR; Dana Bell, U.S. Air Force Still Photo Depository, 1361st Audio-Visual Squadron, Arlington, Virginia; Leroy Bellamy, Prints and Photographs Division, Library of Congress, Washington, D.C.; Carole Boutté, Senior Researcher, U.S. Army Audio-Visual Activity, The Pentagon, Arlington, Virginia; Bureau Soviétique d'Information, Paris; Lou Casey, Chevy Chase, Maryland; Samuel Daniel, Prints and Photographs Division, Library of Congress, Washington, D.C.; V. M. Destefano, Chief of Reference Branch, U.S. Army Audio-Visual Activity, The Pentagon, Arlington, Virginia; K. Dunin-Borkowska, Arlington, Virginia; Deborah Edge, National Archives and Records Service, Audio-Visual Division, Washington, D.C.; Victoria Edwards, Sovfoto, New York City; Fotokhronika-TASS, Moscow; Marylou Gjernes, U.S. Army Center for Military History, Alexandria, Virginia; General Heinz Guderian (Ret.), Bonn; Dr. Emanuel F. Hammer, New York City; Dr. Von Hardesty, National Air and Space Museum, The Smithsonian Institution, Washington, D.C.; Werner Haupt, Bibliothek für Zeitgeschichte, Stuttgart; Dr. J. Hoskins, Library of Congress, Washington, D.C.; Jerry Kearns, Prints and Photographs Division, Library of Congress, Washington, D.C.; Heidi Klein, Bildarchiv Preussischer Kulturbesitz, Berlin (West); Dr. Roland Klemig, Bildarchiv Preussischer Kulturbesitz, Berlin (West); Stefan Korbonski, Washington, D.C.; William H. Leary, National Archives and Records Service, Audio-Visual Division, Washington, D.C.; Donald S. Lopez, Assistant Director for Aeronautics, National Air and Space Museum, The Smithsonian Institution, Washington, D.C.; Ido Martelli, Milan; Alice Masters, Administrative Officer, International Monetary Fund, Washington, D.C.; H. Freeman Matthews, Washington, D.C.; Paul McLoughlin, Franklin D. Roosevelt Library, Hyde Park, New York; Mary Ann McNaughton, U.S. Army Center for Military History, Alexandria, Virginia; Timothy Mulligan, Modern Military Branch, National Archives, Washington, D.C.; Meinhard Nilges, Bundesarchiv, Koblenz, West Germany; Novosti, Moscow; Thomas Oglesby, National Archives and Records Service, Audio-Visual Division, Washington, D.C.; Yves Perret-Gentil, Institut d'Histoire du Temps Présent, Paris; Andrzej Pomian, Washington, D.C.; Teresa M. C. R. Pruden, Alexandria, Virginia; Michel Rauzier, Institut d'Histoire du Temps Présent, Paris; Vladimir Remes, Prague; Dr. Paul Schmidt-Carell, Hamburg; Axel Schulz, Ullstein Bilderdienst, Berlin (West); Arlene Farber Sirkon, Chief, Still Photo Library Division, U.S. Army Audio-Visual Activity, The Pentagon, Arlington, Virginia; Peter Southard, Library, National Air and Space Museum, The Smithsonian Institution, Washington, D.C.; C. G. Sweeting, National Air and Space Museum, The Smithsonian Institution, Washington, D.C.; Ray Teichman, Franklin D. Roosevelt Library, Hyde Park, New York; Marilyn Murphy Terrell, Alexandria, Virginia; Helmut Thöle, Munin Verlag, Osnabrück, West Germany; Douglas Thurman, Office of Presidential Libraries, National Archives, Washington, D.C.; James H. Trimble, Archivist, National Archives, Still Photo Branch, Washington, D.C.; Paul White, National Archives and Records Service, Audio-Visual Division, Washington, D.C.; Marie Yates, U.S. Army Audio-Visual Activity, The Pentagon, Arlington, Virginia; J. K. Zawodny, Avery Professor of International Relations, Claremont Graduate School, Claremont, California.

The index for this book was prepared by Nicholas J. Anthony.

INDEX

Numerals in italics indicate an illustration of the subject mentioned.

A

Aircraft types: B-17 Fortress, 160, *161*, 162-163; C-47 Skytrain, 86; C-54 Skymaster, 182; I-16 fighter, *120*; I-153 fighter, *120*; Ilyushin, 42, *112-113*, *118-119*; Junkers, *35*, 103, 111; LaGG fighter, 120, *121*; La-5 fighter, 120, *121*; Messerschmitt, 120, 122, 124-125; MiG fighter, *122*; P-39 Airacobra, *114*; Pe-2 bomber, *119*; PO-2 utility, *116-117*, 119, 162; Spitfire, *122*; Stuka, *33*; TB-3 bomber, *118*; Yakovlev, *122*, *123*, 132
Akhtyrka, 55-57
Albania, 178
Allmendinger, Karl, 111
Antonescu, Ian, 20, 31
Antonov, Aleksei E., 183-184
Ardennes counteroffensive, 178-181
Atrocities: by German Army, 137; by Red Army, 69, 182, 188-189
Austria, 189
Azerbaijan, 59
Azov, Sea of, 61

B

Bach-Zelewski, Erich von dem, 157-160, 163, *176*
Bagramyan, Ivan K., 127, 129, 188-189
Bagration, Operation. *See* Belorussia campaign
Bäke, Franz, 38-39, 101-102
Balaklava, 111
Balkans, 127, 137, 189
Baltic Sea region, 126-127, 179-180
Baranów, 179-181
Batov, P. I., 132-134
Beasley, Tom, *70*
Belgorod, 24, *map 25*, 26, 38, *42*, 54-55, *map 56*
Belorussia campaign, 111, 126-128, *map 129*, 130-137, 140, 154
Berezina River, 131, 134-135, 137
Berezino, 135
Berggoltz, Olga, 99
Berlin: occupation of and access to, 186; Soviet drive on, 23, 179-180, 182, 187, 189
Berling, Zygmunt, 162, 181
Black Sea region, *map 22*, 106, 108, 110-111, *150-161*
Bobrik, 35
Bobruisk, 127, 129, 131-135, 137
Bór, General (Tadeusz Komorowski), 156-157, 159-160, 162-163, *176*
Braun, Eva, 21
Breslau, 180-182
Brest-Litovsk, 137
Brezhnev, Leonid I., *29*
Brindisi, Italy, 159
British Broadcasting Corporation, 166
Bryansk, 86
Bryansk Forest, 158
Budapest, 179, 181
Bug River, 25, 100, 106-107, 137, *148-149*, 154
Bukrin Bend, 64-66
Bulgaria, 126, 137
Busch, Ernst, 126, 129-131, 135
Butovo, 32
Butyrki, 35

C

Cadogan, Alexander, *184-185*
Cairo, 71
Carpathian Mountains, *88-89*, 99, 106, 108, 140, 178-180
Chelm, 154
Cherkassy, 67, 99-101, *map 102*, 103, *104-105*, 106, *146*
Chernyakhovsky, Ivan D.: in Belorussia campaign, 127, 129-131, 135, 137; Lithuania, drive on, 137; in Soviet 1945 offensive, 181, 188-189
Chervyakova, Irina, 198
Chiang Kai-shek, 186
Chistyakov, I. M., 34, 36
Chortkov, 107
Chruściel, Antoni. *See* Monter, Colonel
Chuikov, Vasily, 154, 187
Churchill, Winston: and Ardennes counteroffensive, 179-180; and Germany, occupation of, 186; and Germany, reparations by, 186; and Poland border shifts, 187; and Poland, future of, 71; and Sword of Stalingrad, 70; at Teheran conference, 67-69, 71; and Warsaw Uprising, 159-160, 163; at Yalta conference, 183, *184-185*, 186-187
Citadel, Operation. *See* Kursk campaign
Constanta, *110*, 111
Courland, 178
Cracow, 181
Crimea campaign, 60-61, 96, 108-111, *118-119*, *123*, *150-151*
Czechoslovakia, 189

D

Dagestan, 197
Dairen, 186
Danube River valley, 126
Danzig, 180, 189
Degrelle, Leon, 105
Desna River, 61, 64-66
Dirlewanger, Oscar, 157-159
Dnepropetrovsk, 24
Dnieper River, 23-24, 54-55, *map 56*, 60-63, 64, 65-67, 74, *75*, 76, 82, *83*, 96, 99, 101-102, 106, 110, 126, 131
Dniester River, 106-108, *146-147*
Donets River and Basin, 23-24, 38-39, 54, 74, 197
Dresden, 180
Dubrovka, 36
Dudergof, 98
Dzurzhentsy, *map 102*, 103-105

E

East Prussia, 127, 179-180, 187-189
East Wall, 63, 97
Eastern Front, *map 22*
Eden, Anthony, 69, 183, *184-185*
Ehrenburg, Ilya, 131
Elbe River, 180
Elbing, 188

F

Fastov, 67
Fermello, Bruno, 34
Finland, Gulf of, 97
Fortified places, 106-107, 129, 135, 154-155, 182, 189
France, 187
Frederick the Great, 179
Frische Nehrung, 189
Frisches Haff, 189

G

Germany: aircraft production, 62; armed forces strength, 20-21; austerity program, 20-21; civilian casualties, 189; dismemberment planned, 186; evacuees and refugees, 181, 188-189; Jews, extermination program, *157*; and Katyn Forest massacre, *68*, 69; occupation, plans for, 186; oil stocks, 179; propaganda campaigns, 63; recruiting expanded, 21; reparations by, plans for, 186, 188; tank production, 25, 30, 62; war matériel production, 21, 179. *See also* Hitler, Adolf
Germany, Air Force of. *See* Luftwaffe
Germany, Army of: antiaircraft defenses, 162; antitank measures and weapons, 6-7, 9, *14*, 39, 57; artillery fire support, 15, 33, *44-45*; artillery losses, 36, 131; artillery strength, 21, 42, 44-45, 55, 62, 97, 180; atrocities by, 137; booby traps, use of, 195; camouflage, use of, *33*; casualties, 8, 36, 39, 57, 60, 63, 103, *104-105*, 110, 135, 137, 163; civilians, removal by, 63, 74, *75*, 102, 176; demolitions operations, 63, *72-73*, 74, *76-79*, *82-83*, 99, 137, *147*, 156, 162-163, 168, *191*; equipment losses, *104-105*; executions by, 67; explosive gas, use of, 163; fortifications by, 97; General Staff reorganization, 61; intelligence estimates and reports, 35, 97, 126, 179; manpower shortages, 21, 179; medical services, 103; mine clearance by, 32, 34; mining operations, 180, 195; morale status, 67, 105; panic in, 137; prisoners lost by, 90, 101, 105, 111, 130-131, 135, *136*, 137, 144, 151; river crossings by, 33, 105, 108; rocket assaults by, *11*, 15; ruses by, 38-39; supplies seized by, 63-64, *74*, 76, 102; supply systems and operations, 97, 102, 108, 110; tank operations and losses, 6-17, 23-26, 32-39, *40-53*, 56-57, 60, 90, 101-103, 108, 135, 155; tank strength, 21, 25, 42, 55, 60, 62, 97, 101-102; training programs, 30; troop-unit strength, 21-22, 32, 34, 42, 55, 60, 62, 97, 103, 111, 129, 180, 184. *See also* Hitler, Adolf
Gneisenau Line, 110
Gnilets, 35
Gniloi Tikich River, *map 102*, 103-105
Goebbels, Joseph, 20-21
Golikov, F. I., 23-24, 28
Gollwitzer, Friedrich, 130
Gorbatov, Aleksandr, 132-134
Gorbunov, Vladimir, 120
Gorky, 59
Gorky, Maxim, *18-19*
Govorov, L. A., 97-98
Graivoron, 57
Grechko, Andrei A., 66
Greece, 178
Greznoye, 37
Grossman, Vasily, 132
Guderian, Heinz: and Ardennes counteroffensive, 178-179, 181; and Eastern Front campaign, 20; and Kharkov campaign, *31*; and Kursk campaign, 30; and Soviet 1945 offensive, 178-179, 181; and tank production, 30
Gudkov, Mikhail, 120
Guerrilla forces and operations, 31, 63-64, *84-95*, 106, 129, *134*, 158, 192
Gurevich, Mikhail, 122

H

Halder, Franz, 23
Harriman, W. Averell, 160, *184-185*, 186
Hartmann, Erich, 120
Haupt, Peter, 182
Hausser, Paul: in Kharkov campaign, *8*, 10, 12, 15-16, 18, 24; in Kursk campaign, 37-38
Hill 239, *map 102*, 103-105
Himmler, Heinrich, 8; executions ordered by, 157-158; and Kharkov campaign, *18*, 23; and Soviet 1945 offensive, 178, 182;

and Warsaw Uprising, 157-158, 163
Hitler, Adolf: and Ardennes counteroffensive, 178-179, 181; and austerity program, 21; and Belorussia campaign, 126, 129-131, 135; and Crimea campaign, 110-111; and defeatism, punishment for, 21, 106; and Dnieper campaign, 54, 60, 61, 62-63; and East Wall construction, 63, 97; and Eastern campaign, 20-21; and fortified places policy, 106-107, 129, 135, 154-155, 182, 189; and General Staff reorganization, 61; and Kharkov campaign, 8, 15, 18, 56-57, 60; and Kursk campaign, 25-26, 28-31, 33, 39; and Leningrad campaign, 97, 99; and Normandy campaign, 96; optimism of, 179; and Orel campaign, 55; and Poland campaign, 154-155; *Schutzstaffel*, loyalty to, 8-9; and *Scorched Earth* operation, 63, 74, 76, 82, *190-191*; and Sicily campaign, 39, 56; and Soviet 1945 offensive, 178-179, 181-182, 189; and Stalingrad campaign, 23; and tank production, 25, 30; and Ukraine campaign, 100-102, 105-108; and Warsaw Uprising, 158, 163
Hitter, A. (German general), 130-131
Hollidt, Karl, 60-61
Hopkins, Harry, 183, 186
Horthy, Miklos, 20
Hoth, Hermann: in Dnieper campaign, 67; in Kharkov campaign, 10, 16, 24; in Kursk campaign, 23-24, 28, 32-34, 36-39
Hube, Hans, 101, 108
Hull, Cordell, 69
Hungary, 126, 137, 149

I

Ilmen, Lake, *map 98*, 99
Ilyin, Ivan, 192
Ilyushin, Sergei V., 114, 119
Italy, 61, 179, 184
Izyum, *72-73*

J

Jaenecke, Erwin, 110-111
Jankowski, Jan S., 156
Japan, 186
Jassy, *148*
Jews, German extermination of, *157*
Jodl, Alfred, 30
Jordan, Hans, 131, 135

K

Kahlberg, 189
Kalinin, Mikhail I., 96
Kaminski, Mieczyslaw, 158-159
Kanev, 64, 101
Kattenau, 181
Katukov, Mikhail Y., 31-32, 34, 36-37
Katyn Forest massacre, *68*, 69
Kazakhstan, 197
Kazan, 59
Keitel, Wilhelm, 30
Kempf, Werner, 33, 36, 38
Kerch Strait, 109, *117*
Kessler, Alfred A., *161*
Kharkov campaign, *6-19*, 23-24, 55, *map 56*, 57, 60, 197
Khersones, Cape, 111
Khilki, 102-104
Khrushchev, Nikita S., 32, 36-37, 66
Kiev, 23, 61, 65-67, 100-101, 192, 197
Kirov, 55
Kirovograd, 100-101
Klaipeda, *142-143*
Kleist, Ewald von, 23, 106-107, 110
Kluge, Günther von: in Dnieper campaign, 61, 63; and General Staff reorganization, 60-61; in Kursk campaign, 21, 24, 30, 39, 60

Köhne (German lieutenant), 57
Kolpakchi, V. Y., 187
Komarovka, 102-104
Komorowski, Tadeusz. *See Bór, General*
Konev, Ivan S.: in Belgorod campaign, 55; in Kharkov campaign, 54-55; in Kursk campaign, 29, 39; in Poland campaign, 155, 181-182; Rumania, drive on, 106-107; in Soviet 1945 offensive, 180, 182; in Ukraine campaign, 100-101, 106-107
Königsberg, 180, 189
Kościuszko, Tadeusz, 155
Kovel, 106-107, 154
Krasnoye Selo, 98-99
Kravchenko, A. G., 65-66
Kreiger, Evgeny, 137
Krivoshein, S., 33, 36
Küchler, Georg von, 97-99
Kurile Islands, 186
Kursk campaign, 18-24, *map 25*, 26-39, *40-53*, 54, *map 56*, *84-85*
Kutuzov, Operation. *See Orel*

L

Latvia, Soviet drive on, *143*
Lavochkin, Semyon, 120
Leahy, William D., 187
Leathers, Frederick J., *184-185*
Leipzig, 179
Lend-Lease shipments, 62, 114, 127
Leningrad, 20, *map 22*, *23*, 96-97, *map 98*, 99, *138-139*, *199*, *200-201*
Leningrad Mining Institute, *199-201*
Lieb, Theobald, 103-105
Lindemann, Georg, 97-99
Lithuania, 137, *142-143*
Livny, 35
Lublin, 154-155
Lublin Committee. *See Polish Committee of National Liberation*
Luchki I and II, 37
Lucy. *See Rössler, Rudolf*
Luftwaffe: aircraft losses, 111; aircraft strength, 21, 42, 55, 97, 129; bombing strikes by, *161*; oil stocks, 179; photographic reconnaissance by, 30; supply operations by, 108; tactical air support by, 10, 32-33, 37-38
Lützow (Soviet cruiser), 98
Lvov, 107-108
Lysyanka, 102-105, 140
Lyutezh, 64-67

M

Mackensen, Eberhard von, *82*
Magnuszew, 179-181
Majdanek, *157*
Malaya Zemlya, 29
Malenkov, Georgy M., 128
Malinovsky, Rodion Y., 61, 106
Maloarkhangelsk, 35
Malta, 182
Manchuria, 186
Manstein, Erich von: and civilians, removal of, 74; and decimation proposal, 57; and Dnieper campaign, 54, 60, 61, 62-63, 67; and General Staff reorganization, 60-61; and Hitler faith in *Schutzstaffel*, 8; in Kharkov campaign, 57, 60; in Kursk campaign, 21, 23-24, 30-32, 39, 55-56; and *Scorched Earth* operation, 74; in Ukraine campaign, 100-101, 103, 105-107
Marina Gorka, 137
Marinesko, A. I., 189
Marshall, George C., 184
Martinek (German general), 131
Maslennikov, I. I., 98
Masurian Lakes, 180
Matthews, H. Freeman, 186, *187*

Mellenthin, Friedrich von, 30, 62-63
Meretskov, Kirill A., 97-99
Mikolajczyk, Stanislaw, 154, 156, 159, 163, 186-187
Mikoyan, Artyom I., 122
Milosna, 156
Minsk, *94*, 127, 129, 135, 137, 144, 154
Mius River, 23, 60-61
Model, Walter: in Belorussia campaign, 135; in Kursk campaign, 24, 28-30, 32, 34-36, 39, 54; in Leningrad campaign, 99; in Orel campaign, 55; and tank production, 30; in Ukraine campaign, 107-108
Modlin, 179
Mogilev, 129, 131
Mokotów, 158, 160, 163
Molotov, Vyacheslav M.: and Belorussia campaign, 128; at Moscow and Teheran conferences, 67, 69, 71; and Poland border, 186-187; and Warsaw Uprising, 155, 160; at Yalta conference, *184-185*
Molotychi, 35
Monter, Colonel (Antoni Chruściel), 156
Moran, Lord, 182-183
Moscow: conference at, 67-69; German drive on, 21, 126; relief for refugees by, 197; victory celebrations in, 56, 66, 107
Murmansk, 118
Mussolini, Benito, 20, 56

N

Nagykanizsa, 179
Narew River, 179-180
Nefedov, P. P., 65
Neisse River, 187
Nemmersdorf, 188
Nida River, 181
Normandy campaign, 71, 96
North Africa campaign, 20
Novgorod, *map 98*, 99
Novorossiisk, 20

O

Oboyan, 33-34, 36-37
Ochota, 159
Oder River, 71, 154, 179, 181-182, *183*, 184, 186
Odessa, 151
Okop, 61
Okuniew, 156
Olkhovatka, 35
Oppeln, 181
Oranienbaum, 97, *map 98*
Orel, 24, *map 25*, 26, 34, 36, 42, 54-55, *map 56*, *79*
Orlovsk, *194-195*
Orsha, 129, 131
Osipovichi, 80, *144*
Osóbka-Morawski, Edward, 155
Osterode, 188
Overlord, Operation. *See Normandy campaign*

P

Panther Position, 97, *map 98*, 99
Partisan forces. *See Guerrilla forces and operations*
Paulus, Friedrich, 20
Pena River, 31, 36
Perekop Isthmus, 109-110
Pervomaisk, 100, 106
Petrov, Ivan Y., 109
Piat antitank weapon, 159
Pillau, 189
Pokryshkin, Aleksandr, *114*
Poland: borders, Soviet shifts of, 155, 186-187; campaign in, *1*, 126-127, 137, 154-155, 157, 163, 181-182; children in uprising, *170-171*; civilian casualties, 159-160, 163,

173; government, Soviet plans for, 68, 71, 154, 184, 187; guerrilla forces, *134;* Home Army strength, 156; independence discussed, 69; uprising in, 154-163, *164-177;* women in uprising, *167, 177*
Polish Committee of National Liberation, 154-155, 184
Poltava, *161*
Pomerania, 187, 189
Ponyri, 35-36
Popel, Nikolai K., 34
Popov, Markian M., 54
Porsche, Ferdinand, 25
Port Arthur, 186
Potrek, Karl, 188
Poznań, 180, 182, 187
Praga, 155-158, *159,* 162, 180
Pravda, 59
Pregel River, 180
Pripyat Marshes, 66, *87,* 106, 111, 127
Prokhorovka, 33-34, 36-39
Proskurov, 106
Prut River, 106-107
Psyol River, 33, 37
Pulawy, 179-181
Pulkovo Heights, 98
Pushkin, 98, *141*

Q
Quincy, U.S.S., 182

R
Radio Kościuszko, 155
Radość, 156
Radzymin, 156
Raus, Erhard, 57, 60
Red Air Force: aircraft armament, 119, 122-123; aircraft development and production, 62, 114-122; aircraft losses, *47,* 114; aircraft strength, 21, 55, 97, 114, 122, 127; personnel strength, 114; photographic reconnaissance by, 131; sorties, number flown, 46, 98, 115, 134; surprise strikes by, 117; tactical air support by, 35, 37-38, 42, *46,* 98, 110-111, 114, *118-119,* 130-135, *144,* 154; women in, *115,* 117
Red Army: airborne operations, 64-65, *118* amphibious operations, *109;* antitank measures and weapons, 12, 26, 32, 42, *43, 49,* 62; artillery fire support by, 32-34, *44,* 98, 104, 130-131, 140, *142-144, 148-149,* 154, 180-181, *183;* artillery strength, 21, 55, 62, 66-67, 97, 127, 154, 180-181; atrocities by, 69, 182, 188-189; bridge construction and repair, *180;* camouflage, use of, *43-44;* casualties, 10, 39, 65; cavalry, use of, 101, 132, 140, *151;* collaborators, treatment of, 91, *92-93;* commanders, relations with Stalin, 28, 34, 55, 64, 98, 127-129; demolitions operations, 31, 42, 86, *90,* 129; flamethrowers, use by, 35; fortifications by, 35; guerrilla forces against, 106; guerrilla forces supporting, 31, 63-64, *84-95,* 129, 134, 158, 192; intelligence estimates and reports, 26, 29; manpower, prodigal use of, 62, 101, 140; medical service, *116-117,* 127; mine clearance by, 131, 180; mining operations, 21, 32, 35, 42; mortar assaults, 104, 132; naval gunfire in support of, 98, 131, 134; patrol operations, 34; prisoners lost, 10; river crossings by, *1,* 23, *64,* 65-66, 83, 134, *146-147,* 162, *180;* rocket assaults by, 33, 104; ruses by, 66; security measures, 66; smoke screens, use of, 132; sniper operations, *15;* soldier, stoicism of, 62; supply system and operations, 23, 31, 59, 97, 127, 155, 162; tank operations and losses, 10-12, 23, 32, 35-39, 57, 65-67, 98-108,

132-135, 140, *144, 148-149,* 154-155, 181-182, 188; tank strength, 21, 50, 55, 60, 62, 97, 110, 127, 180, 184; training programs, *88;* troop-unit strength, 21-22, 28, 32, 55, 60, 62, 97, 110, 127, 129, 180; women as guerrillas, *94. See also* Stalin, Josef
Red Cross, International, 69
Red Navy, 131
Reilly, Mike, 183
Reinefarth, Heinz, 158-159
Reinhardt, Georg-Hans, 129-131, 179
Rhine River, Allied drive on, 23, 184
Riga, *143*
Rokossovsky, Konstantin K.: in Belorussia campaign, 127-129, *130,* 131, 135, 137, 140; in Dnieper campaign, 61, 67; in Kursk campaign, 28, 34-35; in Orel campaign, 54; in Poland campaign, 154-155, 163; in Soviet 1945 offensive, 180-181, 188-189
Roosevelt, Franklin D.: and Germany, occupation of, 186; and Manila capture, 183; and Normandy campaign, 71; physical deterioration, 182-183; and Poland, future of, 71; and Poland, government of, 187; and Sword of Stalingrad, 70; at Teheran conference, 67-69, 71; and Warsaw Uprising, 160; at Yalta conference, 182, *184-185,* 186-187
Rössler, Rudolf (Lucy), 26, 28, 29, 32-33
Rostov, 23
Rotmistrov, Pavel A., *37, 38, 39,* 57
Rowecki, Stefan, 157
Royal Air Force, 159, 175
Rozan, 179-181
Rudel, Hans-Ulrich, *35*
Ruhr region, 179
Rumania, Soviet drive on, 89, 126, 137, *140, 148,* 178
Russian Army. *See* Red Army
Rzhava, 31
Rzhavets, 35 39
Rzhev, 192, 198

S
S-13 (Soviet submarine), 189
Sacred Cow (aircraft), 182
Sakhalin Island, 186
Saki airfield, 182
Samland Peninsula, 189
Schleiter, Josefine, 188
Schlossberg, 181
Schmidt, Gustav, 56-57
Schörner, Ferdinand, 107-108, 110, 181
Schutzstaffel (SS): atrocities by, 159; Hitler, loyalty to, 8-9; in Kharkov campaign, *11-17,* 18, 24, 56-57; in Kursk campaign, *23-24,* 32-34, 36-39, *42;* master-race concept, 8, *9;* in Ukraine campaign, 101-105, 107-108; in Warsaw Uprising, 157-158, 163
Scorched Earth, Operation, 63, *72-83, 190-191*
Seim River, 33
Semyonov, I. D., 64
Seret River, 108
Serock, 179-181
Sevastopol, 23, 110-111, *152-153,* 198
Seydlitz-Kurzbach, Walther von, 103
Shaulyai-Telshai railway, *143*
Shtemenko, Sergei M., 55, 109, 111
Siberia, 197
Sicily, 39, 56
Silesia region, 154, 181, 187
Simferopol, 110
Sivash region, *109,* 110
Smolensk, 23, 68-69, *77*
Snow, operations in, *10-11*
Sokolovsky, Vasily D., 54
Soldatskoye, 32
Soviet Army. *See* Red Army

Soviet Union: bridges, construction and repair, 31; civilian casualties, *80-81,* 137, 200-201; civilians, defense by, 31, *43;* evacuees and refugees, *190-197;* forced-labor deportations from, 63; and Katyn Forest massacre, 68-69; Lend-Lease shipments to, 62, 114, 127; news reports by, *196;* and Polish government-in-exile, 69; Polish uprising, incitement to, 155-156, 162; propaganda campaigns, 94, 103, 155, 181-182; railroad construction, 31; reconstruction program, *58-59,* 192, *194-195, 198-199;* road construction and repair, 31; Rumania, control of, 187; second front, pressure for, 69; tank production, 25, 62; war damages, estimated, 192. *See also* Red Air Force; Red Army; Red Navy; Stalin, Josef
Speer, Albert, 21, 30, 62, 192
Stahel, Reiner, 157
Stalin, Josef: and air bases, Allied use of, 71, 160, 162-163; and Ardennes counter-offensive, 180; and Balkans, drive on, 127, 137; and Belorussia campaign, 127-139; and Berlin, drive on, 187, 189; and Bulgaria, drive on, 137; commanders, relations with, 34, 55, 64, 98, 127-129; and Crimea campaign, 96, 109-110; decorations and awards policy, 64; and Dnieper campaign, 54-55, 64-67, 96; doodling by, 186, *187;* and Germany, dismemberment of, 186; and Germany, reparations by, 186, 188; and Hungary, drive on, 137; and Japan, war against, 186; and Katyn Forest massacre, *68,* 69; and Kharkov campaign, 23, 56; and Kursk campaign, 28; and Leningrad campaign, 96-97; and Lithuania, drive on, 137; and manpower, prodigal use of, 62; and Orel campaign, 55; and Poland campaign, 137, 154; and Poland government, 68, 71, 154, 184, 187; and Rumania, drive on, 137; and Soviet 1945 offensive, 160, 183-184, 187; and Sword of Stalingrad, *70;* and tactical air support, 114; at Teheran conference, 67-69, 71, 127, 160; territorial demands by, 186; and Ukraine campaign, 101; and United Nations Organization, 186; and victory celebrations, 56; and Warsaw Uprising, 159-160, 162-163; at Yalta conference, 23, 183, *184-185,* 186, 187; and Yugoslavia, drive on, 137
Stalingrad, 8, 16, 20-21, 23, *58-59, 194, 195,* 197
Stalino, 197, *198-199*
Stary Oskol, 31
Steinkeller, von (German general), 131
Stemmermann, Wilhelm, 102-104
Stettinius, Edward R., *184-185*
Steuben, S.S., 189
Street fighting: in Dzurzhentsy, 103; in Jassy, *148;* in Kharkov, *14,* 15; in Warsaw, 154-163, *164-177*
Sumy, 57
Sword of Stalingrad, *70*

T
Taganrog, *80-81,* 196
Taman Peninsula, 60-61
Tank types: Ferdinand, 25, *26-27,* 34-35, *52-53;* Goliath, 35, 160; KV1, 25; Mark III, 25, 49; Mark IV, *6-7, 13,* 25, 30, 32-33, 38, *50;* Panther, 25, 30, 32-33, 36, 38, *42,* 57, 101-102; Stalin, *132-133;* T-34, 12, *24,* 25, 36-39, *40-41, 50-51,* 57, 65-66, 100, 103, 105, *145;* Tiger, 24, 25, *31,* 32-33, 36-38, 48-49, 57, 86, 101-102
Tarasov, Soviet captain, 124-125
Teheran conference, 54, 67, 69, *70,* 71, 127, 160
Ternopol, 106

Terrain, effect on operations, 30-31, 111
Teryomov, P. A., 134-135
Tetervino, *37*
Tikhonov, Nikolai, 97
Tippelskirch, Kurt von, 131, 135, 137
Tiraspol, 107
Tito, Marshal, 154
Tolbukhin, F. I., 60, 109-111
Torun, 182
Tyoploye, 36

U

Ukraine: air bases, Allied use of, 71, 160, *161*, 162-163; campaign in, 99-108, 140, *146-147, 150-153*; separatist movement in, 106
Ultra decoding system, 28
Uman, 103
United Nations Organization, 69, 186
United States Army Air Forces, 160, *161*, 162, 175
Urals region, relief by to refugees, 197

V

Vasilevsky, Aleksandr W.: in Belorussia campaign, 127; in Crimea campaign, 110-111; in Kursk campaign, 28
Vatutin, Nikolai F., *86;* death of, *86*, 106; in Dnieper campaign, 61, 64-67; in Kharkov campaign, 55-57; in Kursk campaign, 23-24, 28, 32, 37-38, 54; in Ukraine campaign, 100-101
Vershinin, K. A., 131

Vienna, 189
Vilna, *134*
Vinnitsa, 60, 100, 106
Vistula River, *1*, 23, 154-158, 163, 179, *180*, 189
Vitebsk, 129-131
Volchansk, 32
Volga River, 21
Volkhov River, 99
Volkssturm, 179
Vormann, Nikolaus von, 101, 135
Voroshilov, Kliment E., 70, 109-110
Vyazma, 29

W

Waffen-SS. *See Schutzstaffel*
Walsh, Robert, 161
Warsaw, 23, 154, 180; Soviet occupation of, 181; uprising in, 154-163, *164-177*
Weather, effect on operations, 24, 64, 66, 98-103, 106, *107*, 108, 180-182
Werth, Alexander, 91
West Prussia, 189
West Wall, Allied drive on, 23
Wilhelm Gustloff, S.S., 189
Wilkinson Sword Company, 70
Wisch, Theodor, *13*
Wöhler, Otto, 101-102
Wola, 158-159
Wolomin, 156
Women: in guerrilla forces, *94, 167;* in Red Air Force, *115*, 117

Y

Yaila Mountains, 183
Yakovlev, Aleksandr S., 122
Yalta conference, 182-183, *184-187*
Yeremenko, Andrei I., 109-110
Yugoslavia, 137, 178

Z

Zagórski, Waclaw, 156, 162
Zakharov, Matvei V., 127, 131, 137
Zaporozhye, 23-24, 61, 82
Zaporozhye Dam, 82
Zapun Heights, 111
Zawodny, J. K., 166
Zbruch River, 108
Zeitzler, Kurt: and Belorussia campaign, 129-130; and Crimea campaign, 110; and Dnieper campaign, 61; and Kursk campaign, 23-26, 28, 30; and Ukraine campaign, 106-107
Zhitomir, 67
Zhukov, Georgy K.: in Belorussia campaign, 127, 129; and Berlin, drive on, 182, 187; and Dnieper campaign, 65; in Kursk campaign, 28, 34; in Poland campaign, 137; and Rumania, drive on, 106; in Soviet 1945 offensive, 180-182; in Ukraine campaign, 101, 106-108
Ziemski, Karol, 163
Zitadelle, Operation. *See* Kursk campaign
Zoliborz, 158, 160, 162-163
Zumpel (German lieutenant), 39

Printed in U.S.A.